1990

CAMBRIDGE GREEK AND LATIN CLASSICS

HORACE

EPISTLES

BOOK II

AND

EPISTLE TO THE PISONES

('ARS POETICA')

EDITED BY

NIALL RUDD

Professor of Latin, University of Bristol

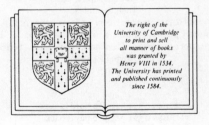

The right of the
University of Cambridge
to print and sell
all manner of books
was granted by
Henry VIII in 1534.
The University has printed
and published continuously
since 1584.

CAMBRIDGE UNIVERSITY PRESS

CAMBRIDGE

NEW YORK   PORT CHESTER   MELBOURNE   SYDNEY

Published by the Press Syndicate of the University of Cambridge
The Pitt Building, Trumpington Street, Cambridge CB2 1RP
40 West 20th Street, New York, NY 10011, USA
10 Stamford Road, Oakleigh, Melbourne 3166, Australia

First published 1989

Printed in Great Britain at The Bath Press, Avon

British Library cataloguing in publication data

Horace
Epistles, Book II. and Epistle to the
Pisones (Ars poetica) – (Cambridge Greek and
Latin classics)
1. Poetry in Latin, to ca 500 – Texts with
commentaries
I. Title   II. Rudd, Niall
871'.01

Library of Congress cataloguing in publication data

Horace.
[Epistulae. Liber 2]
Epistles, book II and Epistle to the Pisones (Ars poetica) /
Horace; edited by Niall Rudd.
p.   cm. – (Cambridge Greek and Latin classics)
Latin text; introd. in English.
Bibliography.
Includes index.
ISBN 0 521 32178 6. – ISBN 0 521 31292 2 (pbk.)
1. Epistolary poetry, Latin.   2. Poetics – Poetry.   I. Horace.
Ars poetica. 1989.   II. Rudd, Niall.   III. Series.
PA6393.E4 1989
871'.01 – dc20   89-7129
                                              CIP

ISBN 0 521 32178 6 hard covers
ISBN 0 521 31292 2 paperback

CONTENTS

871.01
R915

135,309

PREFACE

Over a century has passed since the appearance of A. S. Wilkins's admirable edition of Horace's *Epistles* and *Ars Poetica* (1885); and the useful, though less detailed, commentaries by E. C. Wickham, J. C. Rolfe, and E. P. Morris are all over eighty years old. So a new work, designed for that same readership, has been long overdue. The chances of producing it were greatly improved by the publication of the third and final volume of C. O. Brink's *Horace on Poetry* in 1982. The virtues of that massive and meticulous work are well known. It remains, and will long remain, the standard study of Horace's literary epistles. But those same virtues entail certain drawbacks. In price the volumes are now beyond the means not only of students but also of teachers; much of the information supplied is needed only by specialists; and some readers (including the present editor) occasionally find the sophistication and subtlety of Brink's exposition rather daunting.

So there is room, I hope, for something shorter and simpler. In attempting to provide it I have, with his kind permission, reproduced Professsor Brink's text, except at a few points listed on pp. 38–9. In matters of dispute I mention the more important variants and conjectures, and suggest reasons for preferring one reading to another. No *apparatus criticus*, however, is provided; for this, the reader is referred to Brink or to the Teubner text by Shackleton Bailey. Nor is there any account of the complex process of transmission; information on that subject can be found in Brink II 1–54 and III 1–10, and in Tarrant's section on Horace in *Texts and transmission*.

On questions of interpretation I have not gone back beyond Bentley, except to consult the ancient scholiasts. Apart from Brink, my chief sources have been Orelli, Kiessling–Heinze, and Wilkins, and I owe those scholars a heavy debt. It did not seem necessary, however, to attribute every convincing view to its first exponent; still less to refute and admonish by name those with whom I disagreed. Just occasionally, those consulted did not happen to provide quite what I wanted to say; and often they disagreed with one another; so I had to choose which line to follow. On any given point my choice may, of course, be wrong; but I have tried to write in a way which will ensure that my mistakes are visible. Some readers may find the illustrations rather meagre. But to save space it seemed sufficient to cite, and sometimes quote, just one or two passages, and then refer to the relevant section of the *Oxford Latin dictionary*; other parallels can usually be found in Brink.

The essays in the Introduction are no more than they claim to be – i.e. introductory essays; and the notes do not offer a great deal in the way of literary appreciation. Fuller discussions, however, are not hard to find; a few (like those of Fraenkel, Kilpatrick, and McGann) are listed in the Bibliography. What is true of literary appreciation also applies to other areas, like Roman religion, Latin lexicography, Hellenistic literary theory, and the origins of Greek drama. Such large and complex subjects are better dealt with in books and articles. To have discussed them here (even if I had possessed the necessary erudition) would have distracted attention from the author. It would also have changed the purpose of the book, which is to provide the basic kinds of background information, to explain points of syntax and thought-sequence, and in general to elucidate the poet's meaning in its most fundamental sense. Such procedures, in their turn, serve the further aim of making available to students these very attractive and influential epistles – poems which, in their way, are just as original and unique as the *Odes*.

It remains to thank my old friend, Professor Kenney, for the trouble he has taken over this edition. He has persuaded me to clarify and amplify many notes, and has saved me from numerous errors (those remaining are, of course, my own). He also pointed out at an early stage that, to conform to the convention of the series, the first personal pronoun should be confined to the Preface – a wise principle. Accordingly, I now step back, and invite the reader to think about Horace.

Bristol, 1988   N.R.

ABBREVIATIONS

H.	Horace
AP	*Ars Poetica*
C.	*Carmina*
CS	*Carmen Saeculare*
E.	*Epistulae*
I.	*Iambi (Epodes)*
S.	*Saturae*

A.A.M.	*Abhandlungen der Akademie . . . in Mainz*
A.J.P.	*American Journal of Philology*
A.P.	*Anthologia Palatina*
B.	Brink
Ben.	Bentley
B.I.C.S.	*Bulletin of the Institute of Classical Studies*
CAH	*Cambridge Ancient History*
CHCL	*Cambridge History of Classical Literature*
CIL	*Corpus Inscriptionum Latinarum*
C.J.	*Classical Journal*
CPG	*Corpus Paroemiographorum Graecorum*
C.Q.	*Classical Quarterly*
C.R.	*Classical Review*
FPL	*Fragmenta Poetarum Latinorum*, ed. W. Morel
G–L	Gildersleeve and Lodge (references are to paragraphs)
H.S.C.P.	*Harvard Studies in Classical Philology*
ILLRP	*Inscriptiones Latinae Liberae Reipublicae*, ed. A. Degrassi
ILS	*Inscriptiones Latinae Selectae*, ed. H. Dessau
J.H.S.	*Journal of Hellenic Studies*
J.R.S.	*Journal of Roman Studies*
K–H	Kiessling–Heinze
M.H.	*Museum Helveticum*
O.	Orelli
OCD	*Oxford Classical Dictionary*
OLD	*Oxford Latin Dictionary*
P.B.S.R.	*Papers of the British School at Rome*

P-C	Pickard-Cambridge
Phil.	*Philologus*
Porph.	Porphyrio
ps.-Acr.	pseudo-Acro
RE	*Realencyclopädie der Klassischen Altertumswissenschaft*
Rh.M.	*Rheinisches Museum*
ROL	*Remains of Old Latin*, ed. E. H. Warmington
SB	D. R. Shackleton Bailey, *Q. Horati Flacci opera* (Stuttgart 1985)
T.A.P.A.	*Transactions of the American Philological Association*
TLL	*Thesaurus Linguae Latinae*
W.	Wilkins
Wk.	Wickham
Wo.	Woodcock

Fuller details are given in the Bibliography.

INTRODUCTION

1. THE EPISTLE TO AUGUSTUS
(*EPISTLES* 2.1)

One day Horace received a letter from the Emperor which contained
the following reproach: *irasci me tibi scito, quod non in plerisque eius modi
scriptis mecum potissimum loquaris; an uereris ne apud posteros infame tibi sit
quod uidearis familiaris nobis esse?* 'I want you to know I'm cross with
you for not talking to me rather than others in your numerous
writings of that kind; are you afraid that if you are seen to be a friend
of mine it will blight your reputation with posterity?' Suetonius, who
presumably found a copy of the letter in the palace archives, introduces the quotation by saying *post sermones uero quosdam lectos nullam sui
mentionem habitam ita sit questus* (*Life of Horace*, Loeb edn II 486–8),
'After reading some of the *sermones* he complained that he had not
been mentioned.' No weight need be attached to Suetonius' *mentionem*;
it was address that Augustus wanted, not just mention. The phrase
quosdam sermones is vague. It could refer to any of the *Epistles* (though
probably not the *Ars Poetica*); it might even include some of the *Satires*,
since none of those, either, had been addressed to Augustus. *post . . .
lectos* would refer most naturally to a first reading; but that is not necessary, and other factors tell against it. Augustus could easily have
read *E.* 1 and *E.* 2.2 before the end of 19 B.C. But to judge from the
sequence in Suetonius' chapter, the complaint came later than the *CS*
and *C.* 4. So if we take the usual view that *C.* 4 was finished in the
summer of 13 B.C. after Augustus' return from Gaul, we may suppose
as a working hypothesis that the Emperor's complaint came in the
early autumn. Perhaps after congratulating the poet on *C.* 4, the letter
said something like 'When are we to have the pleasure of seeing more
of your *sermones*? I was reading some of them last week and realised
that it's six years since you gave us your last collection. And, talking of
your *sermones*, I want you to know I'm cross with you, etc.' Leaving
a reasonable interval for laziness and creativity, we might then date
Horace's reply, viz. *E.* 2.1, to the early part of 12 B.C. Such a date
would take account of the altars set up in 12 B.C. for the new cult of

1

the *Lares* and the *Genius Augusti* at the *compita* (16);[1] of Horace's resumption of lyric writing in *C.* 4 (112–13); and of the Alpine victories of Tiberius and Drusus in 15 B.C. (252–3). For the general chronological sweep of the epistle see below p. 10.

In considering the different things, favourable and otherwise, which were said about Augustus, one has to bear in mind the speaker's background. A member of the old senatorial order could point to Augustus' complicity in the murder of Cicero, his savage vengeance on Perusia, and, later, his harsh treatment of the two Julias and his relegation of Ovid; beyond such details lay the undoubted fact that Caesar's heir had finally destroyed the old republic. A member of the equestrian order, however, might dwell on Augustus' refusal to carry out another purge after his return from Egypt in 29 B.C., his ability to inspire loyalty in two such different men as Maecenas and Agrippa, and his wise promotion of new administrative and artistic talent; beyond all that lay the equally undoubted fact that after seventy-odd years of intermittent civil war the Princeps had brought peace and order, and had fostered the recovery of civilised life. Such contradictory views were inevitable in the case of a man who wielded such vast power for over half a century. At this remove in time, however, it is surely evident that for all his ruthlessness and lack of charm he was the only man who could, in Syme's words, have 'saved and regenerated the Roman people'.[2]

As for Horace, he had been born in 65 B.C., just two years before Octavian (the future Augustus); he had fought against him at Philippi in 42 B.C.; returned to Rome under an amnesty; obtained a secretaryship in the treasury; and with the help of Virgil and Varius had attracted the attention of Maecenas. By accepting Maecenas' offer of patronage in early 37 B.C., Horace took the first step towards association with Octavian's party. Yet he did not attack Antony and his followers, nor did he pay any attention (deferential or otherwise) to

---

[1] See Taylor 185, 191.

[2] These are the closing words of Syme's *The Roman revolution*, a seminal work which is far from complimentary to Augustus. Jones supplies a compact and judicious survey. In addition to some good photographs there is much of value in Earl. A fascinating account of Augustus' influence on English literature is given by Erskine-Hill. For a very different view of the question see the lively and learned study by Weinbrot.

Octavian until the time of Actium, when he mentioned him in *I*. 1 and 9 and in *S*. 2.1, 5 and 6. Those poems were published in 30 B.C. In the next seven years Augustus came to occupy a more significant place in Horace's poetry. He is mentioned in nearly one in five of the odes in Books 1–3, and plays a prominent part in 1.2, 1.12, 1.37, 3.4, and 3.25. But before talking too readily of adulation we must remember what Augustus had achieved, and what he meant to the vast majority of Roman citizens who did not belong to senatorial families. Again, Horace himself had been treated with consideration during his period of political disenchantment, and by now he had come to believe that any hope of recovery rested with Augustus. Finally, those laudatory passages in the *Odes* have to be assessed in terms of ancient panegyric. When compared with the *Panegyricus Messallae* or the *Laus Pisonis*,[3] or with later effusions like Statius' poem on the equestrian statue of Domitian (*Silu*. 1.1), Horace's tributes seem quite restrained.

As well as profiting from Horace's skill as a *uates*, Augustus would have liked to employ him on a more personal basis, perhaps because of his experience in the civil service. In a letter to Maecenas (about 25 B.C.?) he said 'As I am over-worked and unwell I would like to deprive you of our friend Horace. So he will give up sponging at your table and come here to my royal table to help me with my correspondence' (Suet. *Life of Horace*). It was a unique opportunity for power and enrichment which most people would have seized with alacrity. But not Horace. He remembered that his health was very uncertain, and politely declined. To his credit, Augustus, who was not used to being turned down, acquiesced. He even wrote inviting Horace to use the official residence as his own – 'if his health permitted'. This does not mean, of course, that Horace enjoyed or sought a position of social equality. One cannot imagine him replying in kind when the Emperor called him 'an unsullied cock' or 'a delightful mannikin' (Suet. *Life of Horace*). Nor did he venture to address him in any of his *Epistles*. As we have seen, Augustus was slightly piqued at this and made the protest discussed above. That could not be ignored, and so the *Epistle to Augustus* was duly written.

The main problem was one of tone. The recipient of a Horatian

---

[3] For the *Panegyricus Messallae* see Tibullus, Loeb edn, 306–22; for the *Laus Pisonis* see *Minor Latin poets*, Loeb edn, 294–314.

epistle was not usually accorded any superior status; he was expected
to listen politely to what the poet had to say; and sometimes he was
chided for his moral shortcomings. That would hardly do for Augustus. Yet a protracted eulogy would be equally out of place. What
Horace did was to write a general essay of some 200 lines on the one
subject which bound them together, viz. poetry and its role in the
state. To this he added a formal preface (1–17) and a longer, more
relaxed, conclusion (214–70), in both of which he addressed the Emperor directly.

The essay begins with a complaint about the conservatism of contemporary taste. This may cause surprise, for there is a tendency to
think that as a 'classical poet' Horace was at ease in his environment
and happily in tune with the reading public. That is a misconception.
In his day Horace was a modern poet and had in large part to create
his own audience. In satire he found himself at odds with the admirers
of Lucilius (S. 1.10), and his highly original Odes never had a popular
appeal. Even among the educated, who might have been expected to
appreciate what he had done, his recognition was delayed by class
prejudice – he was a freedman's son (S. 1.6.6, 45, 46; E. 1.20.20). This
lack of rapport with many of the middle-aged and elderly helps to explain his address uirginibus puerisque in C. 3.1.4 and his delight at being
acknowledged by young people (C. 4.3.13–16).

The style of this protest (18–92) is continuously lively. Greeks and
Romans are weighed in a balance; allegedly corresponding literary
periods are contrasted like olives and nuts; an imagined contest in
painting, music, and wrestling takes place between the Romans and
'the oily Achaeans'; do poems, we are asked, improve with age like
wine? Then there are several lines of Socratic debate, ending in the
collapse of the critic who 'relies on the calendar, using age as a
measure of quality and spurning whatever has not been hallowed by
Our Lady of Funerals'. The arguments are sharp and cogent: too
schematic a parallel with Greece leads to absurdities; just because Ennius is the father of Latin poetry that does not mean he is comparable
to Homer. (Actually Homer was not, strictly speaking, the first Greek
poet; he came at the end of a long oral tradition. But the Romans
knew little about that.) How can one distinguish between 'old and
admirable' and 'new and detestable'? In what year or month should
the line be drawn? The truth is that older people condemn what they
themselves don't like; they're ashamed to heed their juniors or admit

that what they were taught as youngsters ought to be done away with. Finally, a quite unanswerable argument: if the Greeks had been so hostile to novelty, what would now be old?

Though satirical, the tone remains reasonable: sometimes the public is right, sometimes wrong (63–4); I'm not *attacking* the work of Livius Andronicus or campaigning for its abolition; I'm only asking for some critical discrimination (69–70). Once or twice, it is true, the exaggeration draws close to fantasy. To claim, for instance, that some people regarded as canonical the treaties made by the Roman kings with Gabii or the Sabines is like contending that in the opinion of some people today no historian has managed to improve on the Domesday Book. It is also going too far to pretend that Naevius was still in wide circulation and was thought of as 'almost recent'. Nevertheless, allowing for some amusing hyperbole, Horace's picture was basically true. The writers to whom he refers (Ennius, Pacuvius, and Accius; Plautus and Terence) were cited again and again by Cicero in the previous generation; the aged and influential Varro, to whom such authors were not 'archaic', was only fifteen years dead; no doubt in conservative circles they were still admired.

The epistle then continues with two brief but not unfriendly caricatures. After the Persian wars the Greeks delighted in novelty to the point of childishness (93–102). Here we are still in touch with Greek novelty as described at the end of the last section, but the emphasis has shifted to frivolity, which provides a contrast to early Roman earnestness: nothing mattered in those days except law and business (103–7). But now all that has changed; the Romans have taken to composing verse as a dinner-time amusement (108–17). Such an activity, however amateur, is not all bad: writing keeps a man out of mischief. Also (and now the tone becomes more serious and some of Horace's own interests come to the fore) the poet educates children; he promotes moral awareness by praising good deeds; he comforts the unfortunate and supplies the words for public prayers (as in the *CS*). The poet has therefore a unique and valuable place in the life of the community (118–38). It is worth remembering here that the Romans had an oral educational system. They recited poetry and composed speeches instead of writing essays. At present 'rote learning' is much despised; but the Roman practice does not sound strange to those who learned Macaulay's *Horatius* before they were in their teens.

The sturdy Italian farmers of old had their ceremonies (a link with the prayers in the last paragraph). But their jesting became crude and aggressive and had to be restrained by law.[4] Art came with the conquest of Greece; for epic, the hexameter superseded the old Italian Saturnian used by Naevius, and Roman writers began to imitate Greek tragedy, though with insufficient attention to polish (139–67). This takes us back to the stage, but the emphasis now is on clumsiness of composition. Comedy, we are told, is stylistically exacting – a fact ignored by Plautus, who cared only about his fee (168–76). Here Plautus the playwright is cleverly described in terms of Plautus the actor: he goes charging slipshod across the stage and doesn't care if the play falls flat on its face. Another factor discouraging style is the playwright's heavy dependence on the goodwill of the audience (177–207). In the middle of a performance the groundlings may call for a boxing match, as they did in the days of Terence. Even the better sort are entirely engrossed with vulgar pageants. This is another exaggeration, for we were informed earlier on that the *palliata* (i.e. Roman comedies in Greek costume and setting) regularly filled the theatre (60–1). But consistency is of little importance compared with the vividness of Horace's description:

> The curtain is up for four-hour periods, if not longer,
> as squadrons of cavalry and hordes of infantry hurtle past;
> fallen kings are dragged across with their hands pinioned;
> chariots, carriages, wagons, and ships rumble along,
> carrying works of bronze and ivory taken from Corinth.

Later the much-bejewelled performer makes his entrance:

> He walks on stage and at once is greeted with frenzied applause.
> 'Has he said something already?'
>   'No.'
>   'Then why are they clapping?'
> 'It's his woollen coat, dyed in Tarentum to rival a violet.'

The pop artist and his audience go back a long way. Then, in words which recall the end of the previous section (166–7), Horace makes it clear that his scorn is not directed at the legitimate theatre: the great tragedian who plays on his emotions, carrying him away to Thebes or

---

[4] This passage is included in the discussion of drama in the essay on the *AP*.

Athens, is like a magician (208–13). Those lines, which are seldom noticed, are interesting for two reasons: first, they show Horace as a sympathetic theatre-goer willingly suspending disbelief; and secondly they prove once again that tragedies were still performed. Horace is not talking as a reader, for the *lector* comes in by way of contrast in the following line.

Beginning the final section (214ff.), and addressing Augustus directly, Horace says 'Spare a thought for the poet who relies on the reader rather than on the spectator.' This returns us once more to non-dramatic poetry, poetry written in the high style suitable for honouring the Emperor.

Looking back over the literary discourse one notices that when it speaks of specific genres it mentions tragedy, comedy, epic, and choral lyric, but not love elegy. One view, advanced in recent years by Syme,[5] is that by omitting love elegy Horace is issuing a sort of covert manifesto against the whole genre represented by Gallus, Propertius, Tibullus, and Ovid. That may well oversimplify the matter. More than one sort of modern writing could find shelter under the umbrella extended in the first 100 lines or so of *E*. 2.1. Catullus, for instance, would not have quarrelled with the stylistic complaints about Naevius and Ennius. When Horace says

> indignor quicquam reprehendi, non quia crasse
> compositum illepideue putetur sed quia nuper (76–7)

> It makes me annoyed that a thing should be faulted, not for being crudely or clumsily made but simply for being recent,

he is using terms which would have been quite acceptable to anyone writing in the Alexandrian tradition. And when he goes on to make fun of amateur, dinner-table, poets (109–10) he is certainly not directing his wit at the highly professional love elegists. Another point to bear in mind is that when specific genres are mentioned nothing is said of the informal, personal type of lyric associated with Horace himself. So the explanation of these omissions should be sought mainly in the area of decorum. It may be true that, although there are elegiac

---

[5] Syme (3) 177ff. and (5) 359. The case is rather different with the *AP*, which is not addressed to Augustus. See below, p. 33.

themes in the *Epodes* and *Odes*, Horace on the whole found the ethos of love elegy, with its rather narrow obsessions, unappealing. (One may think of his silence regarding Gallus and Propertius, and of the two occasions on which he urged Tibullus (*C.* 1.33) and Valgius (*C.* 2.9) not to give way to self-pity.) But even if he had been more enthusiastic he could hardly have discoursed on the poetry of love and wine, whether lyric or elegiac, to one who was now *circa lustra decem* and who a few years before had made it clear that his regime sternly disapproved of self-indulgence (18 B.C., cf. *moribus ornes* in line 2). The *Epistle to Augustus* was a public poem. Only the major public genres, then, were appropriate to the occasion.

We turn now to what might be termed the courtly framework of the epistle. The opening lines are characteristically beguiling: as Caesar is busy governing Italy, it would be unpatriotic for Horace to detain him with a long discourse (*longo sermone*). We almost forget that Augustus had asked for it (a point which is tactfully ignored), and that in fact *E.* 2.1 is longer than any other epistle except the *Ars Poetica*. It is less easy to come to terms with the next section (5–17), which, after comparing Augustus (to his advantage) to the great culture-heroes of Greece and Rome, reaches a climax of deferential enthusiasm:

> praesenti tibi maturos largimur honores,
> iurandasque tuum per numen ponimus aras,
> nil oriturum alias, nil ortum tale fatentes (15–17)

> But *you* are honoured in good time while still among us.
> We build altars on which to swear by your divinity,
> declaring your like has never been and never will be.

Readers raised in Judaeo-Christian monotheism may find this odd or even shocking; but such honours were regularly paid to Hellenistic monarchs on the grounds that a person of superhuman power must necessarily be divine. Since the apotheosis of Julius Caesar, Octavian had been *diui filius*, and it was accepted that he would become a deity himself after his death. In the mean time, while he used the phenomenon of ruler worship very astutely to enhance his power, Augustus tried to impose certain distinctions. In Egypt he was worshipped as a god; in Asia and Bithynia temples were built to him but only in conjunction with *Roma*; in Rome itself Augustus resisted full divine honours, remembering how Julius Caesar had outraged the nobility by accepting them. Over the years, however, he had sanctioned various other types of tribute, and he had recently agreed that an image of his *genius*, or guardian spirit, should be set up among the *Lares Augusti* (the ancestors of his own house) and worshipped at the revived crossroads ceremonies connected with the dead.[6] The *genius* is what Horace means here by *numen* (16; cf. *C.* 4.5.34–5).

Though for convenience we are treating lines 1–17 separately as an introductory address, they are carefully woven into the fabric of the poem. Not only are Greek and early Roman figures brought in for comparison, as they are later on, but the flattery of Augustus turns out to be connected with the subsequent critique of the public's taste. Although Horace's way of putting it is altogether more tactful, the essence of his contention is 'since the superiority of your political genius is acknowledged today, in your lifetime, the same should be true of our poetic genius'. If we are right about this, the Emperor is not just being flattered or educated; he is being used.

The closing part of the courtly framework is much longer (214–70). It grows out of the previous section, for as playwrights depend on an audience (177–81), poets are dependent on their readers. Such poets merit Augustus' attention. Why? Because if he neglects them his great library in the temple of Palatine Apollo will remain unfilled. Thus the Emperor is being reminded of a standard which he himself has set. Moreover, that earlier act of munificence is not complete; it represents a continuing obligation.

The climax which lies ahead is a more emphatic assertion of the value of poets to what we would call the imperial propaganda. But Horace prepares for that climax by first diminishing himself and his fellow-writers for non-poetic reasons: they are tactless, thin-skinned, easily depressed, and over-optimistic. Then, in another Greek/Roman comparison, he adds some amusing lines on Alexander the Great, praising his artistic, but not his poetic, taste (he paid good money to the wretched Choerilus).[7] Augustus' literary taste has been vindicated by the praises of Virgil and Varius. Horace's own tribute, already

[6] See Taylor, chapters 6 and 7.

[7] Horace here is manipulating the story. Because Alexander gave Choerilus a gold coin for every good line, Horace alleges that he had no taste in poetry. But ps.-Acro says Choerilus received only seven coins in all.

paid in the *Odes* (especially *C.* 4.5 and 15), is ignored. Instead, he wishes he could rise to an epic

> Rather than writing talks
> that creep on the ground, I'd sooner celebrate mighty deeds,
> describing the lie of the land, the course of rivers, the setting
> of forts on mountain summits, barbarous kingdoms, and then
> the ending of strife throughout the world by your command,
> Janus guardian of peace locked behind his bars,
> and the Parthian overawed by your imperial might –
> if only my powers matched my yearning.

There, with a hint of irony (for such grandeur is not for him), Horace respectfully imitates the style which he is declining. The lines reinforce the framework of the poem in two ways. First, *sermones*, 'talks', glances back to *sermone* (4). Secondly, the list of the Emperor's achievements recalls those mentioned in 1–3. Taken together, the lists range over many years, summarising the blessings of the *pax Augusta*. Thus, leaving aside the slightly earlier reference to Palatine Apollo which was dedicated in 28 B.C. (216), we have the closure of the temple of Janus in 29 and 25 or 24 (255),[8] the recapture of the standards from Parthia in 20 (256), the *leges Iuliae* of 18 (2–3), the victories of Tiberius and Drusus in 15 (252–3), and the revival of the *Compitalia* in 12 (16).

The lines quoted above represent the higher end of the *sermo*'s stylistic register; but it was not Horace's practice to finish at that level. So after the climax comes a diminuendo, satirising by contrast the work of *incompetent* eulogists. To avoid embarrassing Augustus, Horace imagines himself as the unfortunate recipient of such a poem – a poem

---

[8] For the dating of these closures see Syme (3) 25. He puts the third closure in 8 or 7 B.C. Horace gives a similar list of events, with a similar purpose, in *C.* 4.15.4–16. Neither that list nor the list in *E.* 2.1.251–6 attempts to preserve chronological order; so it is going too far to say that the closure of Janus is brought into relation with the submission of Parthia – a connection which is condemned by Syme as 'totally illicit' (5) 89. Nor is any close link indicated by the syntax – *rettulit . . . et . . . restituit . . . et clausit . . . et iniecit emouitque . . . et reuocauit* in *C.* 4.15; cf. *-que et* in *E.* 2.1.255–6, where each unit illustrates the peace described in 254.

so bad that, instead of immortalising him, it ensures his extinction. Our last glimpse is of the poem, containing the 'corpses' of both its subject and its writer, being carried down to the unsavoury Subura for use as wrapping paper.

The *Epistle to Augustus* was placed first in Book 2 because of its distinguished addressee; it was not the first to be written. Before we consider the earlier *Epistle to Florus*, it may be useful to glance back and remind ourselves of where Horace found the idea of the verse epistle and how he developed it. The earliest examples known are the epistles in amusing verses, *uersiculis facetis* (or *factis*?), which Sp. Mummius sent to his friends from Corinth in 146 B.C. (Cic. *Att.* 13.6.4). There must have been many such pieces in the decades which followed; for Lucilius, writing between 130 and 100 B.C., used the *epistula non magna* as an instance of a *poiema* (a short poem or a section of a long one) as distinct from a *poiesis* (a long work seen as a whole) (*ROL* III 404–6). Lucilius probably included several epistles in his *saturae*; fragments of one have survived in which he remonstrates with a friend for not coming to visit him when he was sick (*ROL* III 186–93). Horace did not follow this practice. Instead, he distinguished the two sub-forms, excluding epistles from his two books of satires, and writing only epistles when he returned to hexameter poetry after 23 B.C. According to the scholiasts in their introductions to *S.* 1, he entitled the satires *Sermones* ('Talks') and the epistles *Epistulae*.[9] This points to the distinction noted by ps.-Acro in his introductory note to *E.* 1.1, namely that in the *Epistles* the addressees are thought of as being absent instead of present. Other changes too are observable. The moral emphasis moves from censure to affirmation; while there are still passages of ridicule, Horace offers more discussion and advice; names are much less frequent. Again, since the *Epistles* contain little dialogue, Horace is less concerned to reproduce the effect of fluid debate. So the thought ends more often at the end of a line; elisions are less num-

---

[9] Horace also used *sermo* (i) in the sense of style (e.g. *S.* 1.10.11), (ii) to refer to what was actually an epistle (*E.* 2.1.4); sometimes, too, *sermones* covers his hexameter poetry as a whole (*E.* 1.4.1, 2.1.250). To avoid confusion, therefore, the satires are here referred to as *Satires* and the epistles as *Epistles*; the term *sermones* is reserved for the hexameters in general.

erous; and the diction is more restrained, with fewer plebeian words, fewer metaphors, and no obscenities.[10]

This rather more formal approach recalls the opinions of the Greek critic Demetrius, who included some remarks on prose letters in his essay *On Style*, a work much indebted to Aristotle. According to Demetrius, a letter should be somewhat more studied than a dialogue 'since the latter represents spontaneous utterance, whereas the former is written out and is sent, so to speak, as a gift' (224). A letter to a friend should be written in a simple, direct style, avoiding abstruse subject-matter (229, 231), and revealing the sender's personality (227). Long, stilted missives are not letters at all, but rather disquisitions with the heading 'Dear So-and-So' (228). It is not certain that Horace could have known Demetrius' work,[11] but clearly *E.* 1 is written from a rather similar point of view. This is less true of *E.* 2, with its two long compositions; and it hardly applies to the *AP*. Unlike a personal letter, the *AP* is concerned with the literary interests of the Pisones mainly as a point of departure; similarly, in *E.* 2.2, Florus as a man is less important than he was in *E.* 1.3; in fact his only function is to complain, and so induce Horace to set down his reasons for not returning to lyric poetry. This does not mean that Florus' complaint should be taken as fiction. Those who make that assumption would have assured us that Augustus' complaint too was a fiction, had that complaint been mentioned by Horace and not by Suetonius.

2. THE EPISTLE TO FLORUS (*EPISTLES* 2.2)

In late 21 or early 20 B.C. Augustus, then on the island of Samos, ordered Tiberius Claudius Nero, the future emperor, to lead an army overland through Macedonia to Armenia, where he was to place Tigranes II on the throne. This task was accomplished in the following May.[12] In the mean time Augustus proceeded east to accept from

[10] For studies of *E.* 1 see Kilpatrick (1), McGann (2), and McLeod.

[11] Demetrius has been dated variously from the 3rd cent. B.C. to the 1st cent. A.D.; see Grube (2) 120–1 and Schenkeveld 135–45. For further comment on Demetrius' work see Grube (1), and Schenkeveld. A compact survey of ancient letter-writing is provided by Ussher (2).

[12] See *CAH* x 260–65.

Phraates of Parthia the standards captured from Crassus at Carrhae in 53 B.C. and from Antony in 40 and 36. Returning to Rome in October 19 B.C., Augustus awarded the *ornamenta praetoria* to Tiberius, who to judge from Dio's phrasing (54.10.4) had returned with him. The present poem therefore falls between the completion of *E.* 1 (late 20 or early 19 B.C.) and the autumn of 19.

On the staff of Tiberius, who was only 23 in 19 B.C., was the young Julius Florus, who was also the recipient of *E.* 1.3. In the earlier poem he is addressed not only as a barrister (23) and legal expert (23–4) but also as a poet. According to Porphyrio on *E.* 1.3.1, Florus wrote satires derived from Ennius, Lucilius, and Varro. To judge from *E.* 1.3.21 (*quae circumuolitas agilis thyma?*) and 24 (*seu condis amabile carmen*) he also wrote pieces in a gentler vein – probably lyrics (cf. *C* 4.2. 27–32). This would lend point to the testimony in *E* 2.2.24–5 that Florus had badgered Horace into promising some odes; and that promise in turn would indicate that after refusing Maecenas' request to resume lyric composition (*E.* 1.1.1–12) Horace was already beginning to relent before Augustus commissioned the *CS.*

In his *Epistles* Horace often reveals at once why he is writing. But not here. Florus, and the reader, have to wait. In the mean time they are asked to imagine a commercial deal. 'Suppose someone offered you a slave, and after commending his virtues added that he had once been caught slacking. In view of the man's candour you wouldn't try to sue him, would you?' Horace cleverly suggests the seller's way of talking: e.g. *extrudere merces*, 'to palm off the goods'; *res urget me nulla*, 'I'm under no pressure to sell'; *meo sum pauper in aere*, 'I'm poor, but not in the red'; *nemo hoc mangonum faceret tibi*, 'none of the dealers would do this for you'; *non temere a me quiuis ferret idem*, 'I wouldn't offer this bargain to everyone'. Then the style takes on a legal flavour; in fact there are a dozen legal phrases between 16 and 25, and the notions of law and property recur throughout the poem (see below).

Finally at 20 Horace comes to the point: 'I told you I was a wretched correspondent, yet you still complain that I haven't written and that I haven't sent you the lyrics which you were expecting.' The tactics are ingenious. Horace presents Florus with a kind of parable (rather like that given by Nathan to David in 2 Samuel 12). As a result, by the time he has reached 25 the aggrieved Florus has been put in the wrong. Nevertheless, although Horace speaks firmly to his young friend, offering him neither a letter nor a set of lyrics, he does provide something of both, viz. a verse epistle.

Before leaving this section it is worth remarking that when the parable is worked out Horace is seen to correspond to both the seller and the slave. Like the seller, he warned Florus about possible snags in the transaction; but being a singer with a smattering of Greek literature, prone to evade his responsibilities, he also represents the defective merchandise.

In 26 Horace sets off on one of his stories: a soldier in Lucullus' army was robbed of his savings. In anger he led a charge on an enemy position and was handsomely rewarded. Shortly after, the general called on him to lead another attack 'Go, my man, go where your courage summons you.' But the soldier answered 'If you want someone to go . . . go, find a man who has lost his wallet.' Once again, the relevance only gradually becomes apparent. After losing everything at Philippi Horace was aggressive and energetic; now that he has plenty of money he would be mad to write poetry instead of getting a good night's sleep. In this famous passage of autobiography serious and at times tragic recollections are summoned up in a throwaway, almost flippant, style. As schoolboy, student, and soldier Horace seems to have cut an unimpressive figure. Possibly he did, but it is more likely that the middle-aged poet is being rather unfair to his own former self. The humorous self-depreciation is designed to mollify Florus.

It is plain by now that the structure of the epistle is a series of excuses. The third is very brief 'I'm getting old; what would you have me do?' – *quid faciam uis*? (55–7). The desired answer is 'nothing'. Then, taking up *quid faciam uis* in a different sense ('What do you want me to compose?') Horace moves on to another excuse 'I can't satisfy everyone; each friend wants something different' (58–64). The poet sounds like a host trying to cater for a number of demanding guests. The idea of competing demands leads on to the next excuse 'Again, how can I write in Rome, where I'm subjected to so much physical and mental strain (65–86)?' This gives Horace a splendid opportunity for a satirical attack on city life – an attack which clearly appealed to Juvenal. (Compare the chaotic scene in 72–5 with Juv. *Sat.* 3.236–56.)

Another feature of city life (*Romae* in 87 provides the link) is the mutual congratulation that goes on in poetic cliques. If you write poetry and want your work to be admired you have to attend the recitations of others – a great disincentive, and a further excuse.

This section includes a mock battle in which Horace and an elegist exchange compliments. He calls Horace 'Alcaeus' and in return is dubbed 'Callimachus' or, if that is not thought to be extravagant enough, 'Mimnermus'. Can the elegist be identified? On the one hand, any elegist worth his salt would have treasured comparison with either of the poets mentioned, and no parody of any particular figure can be discerned in the style. On the other hand, Propertius does salute Callimachus in 2.1, 3.1, 3, and 9 (4.1.64, where he actually calls himself 'the Roman Callimachus', is later than the epistle), and elsewhere he claims that in the matter of love a line of Mimnermus is better than the whole of Homer (1.9.11). So if we are asking about Horace's intention, no confident answer can be given; at the same time it would be strange if no Roman readers thought of Propertius. The tone of the exchange (in which Horace, of course, is a participant) is amusingly satirical rather than hostile; but it should be added that the elegist (whoever is meant) can hardly be excluded from the *genus irritabile uatum* (102) – a phrase which Pope sharpened and expanded in characteristic style: 'this jealous, waspish, wronghead, rhiming Race' (*Imitation* of *E.* 2.2, 148).

The next excuse runs as follows. 'Incompetent poets are pleased with what they write; but to produce a genuine poem is a painful business involving severe self-criticism' (106–40). In an excellent piece of classical theory Horace uses the metaphor of a censor to describe the effort of composing a *legitimum poema*. The censor/poet will remove whatever words are 'insufficiently illustrious', 'lacking in solidity', and 'unworthy of their place of honour', phrases which are all applicable to figures who have disgraced themselves in public life. The censor, however, when revising the rolls, could also admit new names; so the poet too 'will admit new words which have been begotten by father Need'.

Horace continues with the image of a great river, powerful and pure, enriching the soil of Latium. Callimachus had deprecated the use of the great river as a metaphor of true poetry because it carried so much rubbish in its water (*Hymn to Apollo* 108–9). With that in mind Horace himself had compared Lucilius to a muddy river (*S.* 1.4.11).

But now Horace has gone beyond that position and is talking of Latin epic in full knowledge of the *Aeneid*. Sadly Virgil, who was travelling home with Augustus and was therefore probably in the company of Tiberius and Florus, was to die on reaching Italy in September, 19 B.C.

The idea of fertility leads to a third metaphor, drawn this time from the tending of vines or olives: 'the poet will check excessive growth, smooth what is too rough, and take out what is feeble' (122–3).[13] The final metaphor is that of a dancer who can represent the agile and the ponderous with equal ease; but that ease is deceptive, for it has been acquired by painful effort (124–5).

All the metaphors are illuminating, whether political, economic, or artistic. But the most suggestive is that of the horticulturalist; for it brings out most clearly Horace's view that poetry is a raw force of nature which has to be disciplined by art. In all the literary epistles art gives rise to fascinating discussion. Nature does not, but it is regularly acknowledged; and those who think they can dispense with it are invariably ridiculed.

After talking of the demands of art Horace adds 'Rather than go through all the effort again I'd sooner be a crazy scribbler delighted at his own work.' This kind of delusion is illustrated by the story of the mad theatre-goer at Argos who applauded non-existent plays and was justifiably annoyed when his friends had him cured.

'Anyhow, I ought to be concentrating on philosophy instead of wasting my time on frivolities' (141–216). This is the final, and most fully elaborated, excuse; and it represents Horace putting his intentions into practice. The section begins with *sapere*, which appears at first to carry on the idea of sanity, but then turns out to have an ethical meaning. The *ludus* to be abandoned (142) is that of writing lyric; and the *modi* to be mastered are those of morality rather than poetry. The precepts start with a medical analogy: dropsy isn't cured by drinking, nor greed by making money (145–57). Then, passing to law, Horace dwells on the futility of purchasing property: '*usus* (in the legal sense) gives a kind of ownership as distinct from purchase. And

---

[13] Cf. Cato, *De agr.* 44 (olives) 'make the stems smooth'; Columella, *RR* 4.10.2 (vines) 'the vine should be trimmed ... the smooth, straight vine without a scar is the best'.

use (in the ordinary sense) is just as good as purchase. Even purchase itself is never more than temporary; so what good are large estates? Everything in the end is reaped by Death, who cannot be bribed by gold' (158–79). The terms of the argument are taken from Roman law: *proprium, mancipare, usus* etc.; but Horace as a layman avoids the manner of a technical expert ('if one is to believe the lawyers' in 159). Also, instead of speaking of litigation in city courts, he takes us into the countryside. We hear of corn, grapes, and chickens; a kettle boiling on a log fire in the chilly evening; a line of poplar trees. As in Gray's *Elegy*, the antiquity of the scene leads us back over earlier generations; and from that we move easily to thoughts of transience.

'People differ in temperament. One man spends his days energetically making money, while his brother is a pleasure-loving idler. I myself aim at the mean' (180–204). The transition is smoothed over by ending the previous section with 'gold' and beginning this one with 'jewels, marble, ivory etc.'. Horace's claim to moderation is then taken up in the final section (205–16). 'You say you aren't a miser; well, have you got rid of other vices too – ambition, superstition, intolerance? If you can't live properly make way for those who can.' The person addressed here is certainly not young Florus. In a sense it is the reader, for all Horace's epistles have a general application. But the words take on a special sharpness when they are seen as Horace's address to himself (*mecum loquor* in 145). There was, after all, perhaps a hint of complacency in his claim to moderation; and one of Horace's attractions as a moralist is his self-awareness. The closing injunction (*lusisti satis* etc.) has the right ironic flavour for an ageing hedonist.

We have noted how the poem is organised as a series of pleas. This is a characteristically Roman feature. One recalls how Catullus aroused sympathy for Ariadne by allowing her to make an effective case against her lover, as though an unseen jury were sitting on the beach of Naxos. Dido's speeches are no less rhetorical in conception. The present instance is by contrast light-hearted, but the legalistic framework is still apparent. And the forensic ambience does not stop there. For throughout the poem runs a preoccupation with law and property. Thus we have the sale of a slave and its legal implications (1–25); theft and one man's reaction to it (26–40); loss of property and Horace's reaction to it (50–4); the thefts perpetrated by the years (55–7); the Roman jurist and his admirer (87–9); the *legitimum poema* and the censor (109–19); the theft of illusions (139–40); property and conveyancing (158–79); opposite attitudes to property (180–9); inheritance (191–2); extreme and unwise uses of property (192–9). It is no accident that the most gravely impressive lines in the poem – lines with an unmistakably Lucretian resonance – comment on the transience of ownership (171–9).

Though not a 'literary epistle' in the same central sense as *E.* 2.1 and the *AP*, the *Epistle to Florus* is a delightful piece of work. One can understand why the Emperor felt a certain pique at not receiving anything similar; and it is not surprising that its wit and wisdom should have stimulated Pope (1688–1744) to produce one of his most successful and inventive *Imitations*.[14] The times were propitious. The social structure of the late seventeenth and early eighteenth century; the relation of the capital to the countryside; the desire for country houses; the respect for order and clarity in literature, religion, and social behaviour; the confidence that contemporary standards were superior to anything that had gone before – these and many other factors combined to produce an English 'Augustan age'.[15]

In the middle of that period a poet emerged who, unlike Horace, knew little of school, university, or court life, and nothing of war (for he was cruelly disabled). Nevertheless, the common pattern of attentive father, classical education, civil war, defeat, eviction, poverty, and eventual literary success gave Pope a natural sense of affinity with his Roman predecessor, to such an extent that he turned his house at Twickenham (then a village outside London) into an English equivalent of the Sabine farm.

In writing *The Second Epistle of the Second Book of Horace*, Pope had not only to follow the situation and argument of the original but also to achieve a comparable range of tone. This could only be done by listening carefully to the text. But he did not feel confined to the text. He was willing to use the Latin as a point of departure, drawing by free association on lines from the *Satires*, *Odes*, and *Ars Poetica*, moving backwards to Lucretius and forwards to Juvenal, incorporating ideas from Bentley's text or the Delphin's paraphrase. At the same time

[14] For a comparative analysis see Rudd.
[15] See, e.g., *The Pelican guide to English literature* IV, pts. 1 and 2, and also the bibliography.

he had to build a new artefact, capable of standing on its own feet: an English, eighteenth-century, Christian poem, inhabited by real people. The result was simultaneously an independent creation and an extended literary allusion, advertising its debt not only by its title but also by having the Latin text printed *en face*. As Pope's *Imitations of Horace* appeared, it became clear that he had raised creative imitation to a new height – a height to be equalled only by Johnson's 'London' and 'The Vanity of Human Wishes'. Today his imitation of *Epistles* 2.2 continues to offer a highly illuminating critique of the *Epistle to Florus*.

3. THE EPISTLE TO THE PISONES
(*'ARS POETICA'*)

Title

Originally the work may have been called *Epistula ad Pisones*; certainly its status as an epistle is implied by the grammarian Charisius (fourth century A.D.) who cites the work by the phrase *Horatius in Epistularum*.[16] But Quintilian (first century A.D.) referred to it as the *ars poetica* (Pref. to Trypho, 2) and as the *liber de arte poetica* (8.3.60), and the first of these two titles has stuck. In the manuscript tradition the *Ars Poetica* does not follow *E.* 2.1 and 2.2, but appears second after the *Odes*, or fourth after the *Odes*, *Epodes*, and *Carmen Saeculare*. So it seems never to have formed part of the second book of *Epistles*; we cannot even be sure that it was published by Horace himself.

Date

This is controversial. The most likely hypothesis is that Horace addressed the *Ars Poetica* to Lucius Calpurnius Piso (the Pontifex) and his sons in about 10 B.C., not long after the father had returned from his campaigns in Thrace.[17] This is in line with what Porphyrio says in his note on the opening lines: *hunc librum, qui inscribitur de arte poetica, ad*

---

[16] Charisius, ed. K. Barwick (Teubner), p. 263.9; 265.1.
[17] The best exposition of this view is by Dilke.

Lucium Pisonem, qui postea urbis custos fuit, eiusque liberos misit; nam et ipse Piso poeta fuit, et studiorum liberalium antistes. The phrase *urbis custos* refers to the fact that Piso was made *Praefectus Vrbi* by Tiberius in A.D. 13. Piso's father, L. Calpurnius Piso Caesoninus (cos. 58 B.C.), was the patron of the Greek Epicurean and epigrammatist Philodemus;[18] and Piso himself was the patron of Antipater of Thessalonica.[19] So this squares with what Porphyrio says about Piso's literary interests.

The Pontifex was born in 48 B.C., held the consulship in 15 B.C., and after a long and distinguished career died in A.D. 32.[20] No sons have been positively identified. Of the possibilities discussed by Syme[21] the most promising is the Gaius Piso whose first shave is commemorated in an epigram of Apollonides;[22] the boy is addressed there as the son of a Lucius Piso. But even if no sons of the Pontifex can be located in our records, that does not prove that no sons of his reached adolescence. As Syme remarks, 'deaths have to be allowed for among young *nobiles*, verifiable for some within reach of their consular year'.[23] It is true that our hypothesis requires an early marriage. As Lucius Piso was born in 48, to have had sons of, say, 15 and 14 in 10 B.C. he must have been married by 26 B.C. But this is not hard to imagine. Moreover, his daughter Calpurnia, who married L. Nonius Asprenas (cos. A.D. 6), was probably born before 19; so in any case one should assume a marriage at least in the late 20s B.C.

If this theory is right, it affects the interpretation of other points in the poem. Virgil (53–5), who died in 19 B.C., cannot have been alive. (We have no information about Varius, who is mentioned in the same passage.) Aulus Cascellius (371), who was born in 104 B.C. or earlier, must have been at least 94 if he was still living. Easier, then, to assume he was dead, and to supply *sciebat* rather than *scit*. As for Tarpa (386–7), the use of *et . . . et*, which links him with Piso senior and Horace, suggests he was still alive. If we assume he was 35 when he judged plays for Pompey in 55 B.C. (Cic. *Fam.* 7.1.1), he was now 80.

---

[18] For Philodemus see Grube (2), chap. 12, and Nisbet (1), Appendix III.
[19] See Gow and Page II, index under Antipater and Piso.
[20] See Syme (5), chap. 24.
[21] Syme (4) and (5) 378–81.
[22] *A.P.* 10.19; Gow and Page II 163.
[23] Syme (4) 340.

Other scholars, believing Porphyrio mistaken, have dated the *Ars Poetica* ten years or so earlier, connecting it with another Piso, viz. Cn. Calpurnius Piso, who was probably born in the 70s, was consul in 23, and certainly had two sons.[24] These men, however, do not sound like the sort who would have been friendly with Horace or keen on poetry. The elder son, according to Tacitus (*Ann.* 2.43), was *ingenio uiolentus* and had inherited his father's *ferocia*. Seneca records, as an example of *furor* and *iracundia*, an appalling incident in which he had three soldiers under his command put to death (*De ira* 1.18.3–6). The younger son, known as the Augur, also kept up the family tradition of *ferocia*. He is called *nobilis ac ferox uir* by Tacitus (*Ann.* 4.21). There is also a stronger and more specific objection. The elder of Cn. Piso's sons was born in 44 or 43 B.C., was quaestor probably in 19 or 18, and eventually consul in 7. The elder son in the *Ars Poetica*, however, was being 'moulded in the right way by his father's voice' (366–7). That suits a boy in his teens, not a young man entering the quaestorship.

So, although the theory cannot be proved, it is preferable to assume that the *Ars Poetica* was Horace's last work, and that when he said he was not writing himself (*nil scribens ipse* in 306) he meant that, after completing his fourth book of *Odes*, he was no longer composing lyrics.

Structure

The text of this edition has been divided according to the scheme which follows. Other suggestions are mentioned below.

I	1–152	*A poem's composition: general precepts*
	1–37	harmony and the difficulty of achieving it.
	38–41	transition (the desirability of choosing material within one's powers could be seen as rounding off the section on harmony; but it is also used to introduce the remarks on *facundia*, 'fluent and appropriate diction', and *ordo*, 'arrangement' or, more generally, 'organisation').
	42–5	arrangement – a matter of saying the right thing at the right time and place.

[24] The case is well argued by Nettleship and by W. 330–3. This theory eases the problems about Virgil, Cascellius, and Tarpa, but aggravates the problem of the Pisones.

46–8   diction as affected by arrangement (*serendis* and *iunctura*
            supply a link with the last point; *nouum* and *notum* anti-
            cipate what follows).

48–72   diction as affected by the age of words.

73–98   diction as affected by genre, which involves not only
            metre but also tone and stylistic level. (The mention of
            Telephus and Peleus in 96 looks forward to the next sec-
            tion, where the same names recur in 104.)

99–118   diction as affected by emotion and character. (That
            Horace is still thinking of diction can be seen by identify-
            ing words of 'saying' in 104, 106, 107, 111, 112, and
            114.)

119–52   the choice and presentation of material. (In 119–27 the
            particular kind of material mentioned is character; so
            once more a smooth join is contrived with the preceding
            section.) The choice of material should be, preferably,
            traditional (128–30); the treatment should be fresh and
            individual (131–5). In 136ff. Horace talks about how to
            begin, drawing his illustrations this time from epic. The
            choice of *when* to begin (146ff.), as of what to omit (149–
            150), is a matter of organisation, which reminds us of
            what has been said about *ordo* (42–8). And the need to
            relate the beginning to the body of the poem (136–45),
            like the need to blend fact and fiction (151), reaffirms the
            principle of harmony (1–37).[25]

The return to the idea of harmony suggests some sort of break after
152. This is supported by the new address (*tu*) in 153 and by the introduction of a new (though related) subject.

II 153–294 *Drama: precepts and history*
    153–78   credibility of characters.
    179–88   propriety of stage presentations.

---

[25] An interesting parallel to this section, with its subdivisions, may be found
in Dionysius, *Letter to Pompeius* 3, a work close in time to the *AP*: the task of a
historian is (*a*) to choose a suitable subject, (*b*) to decide where to begin and
how far to proceed, (*c*) to consider what to include and what to leave out, (*d*) to
arrange everything harmoniously.

Neoptolemus

Having seen, at least in outline, what the *AP* is about, we can now take account of a rather tantalising remark of Porphyrio's, *in quem librum congessit praecepta Neoptolemi* τοῦ Παριανοῦ *de arte poetica, non quidem omnia, sed eminentissima*, 'He incorporated in this book the pre-

cepts of Neoptolemus of Parium [in Bithynia] about the art of poetry
– not indeed all of them, but the most conspicuous.' Neoptolemus was
a poet, scholar, and critic, probably writing in the third century B.C.[26]
For long we possessed only a few fragments of his work, and nothing
from his (presumably prose) dissertation on the art of poetry. So little
could be made of Porphyrio's remark. In 1918, however, Jensen published his study of a papyrus containing fragments of the fifth book of
Philodemus' work 'On Poems'. There Philodemus, using an intermediate source (a certain Philomelus), criticised a number of earlier
authorities, one of whose names ended in -τόλεμος. By accepting the
restoration 'Neoptolemos', scholars were now able, if only indirectly,
to recover some of the views of Horace's putative source. These views
will be mentioned presently.

First, however, we must ask whether the organisation of the *AP*
owed anything to Neoptolemus. Here, too, Philodemus' papyrus
opened up a larger discussion. In 1905 Norden had distinguished two
sections: *ars* (1–294) and *artifex* (295–476).[27] Then Jensen discovered
that, according to Philodemus, Neoptolemus had 'set [the poet] as an
element of the art alongside *poiema* and *poiesis*' – εἶδος παρίστησι τῆς
τέχνης μετὰ τοῦ ποήματος καὶ τῆς ποήσεως.[28] Then, assuming that
Neoptolemus' treatise was arranged under those three headings,
Jensen applied the same threefold division to the *AP*. Since that time
there has been much disagreement. In 1946 L. P. Wilkinson still preferred to see the poem as an undivided list of precepts.[29] In 1939
Steidle based his work on Norden's division, while Dahlmann (1953)
contended that *poiema*, *poiesis*, and *poietes* did not represent divisions of Neoptolemus' work at all, but were simply three terms defined
in the introduction – a position supported by Greenberg.[30] Becker has
taken yet another line, distinguishing 1–40 as introduction, 40–250 as
the Greek systematic section, and 251–476 as Horace's own contribution.[31] Those who have followed Jensen have agreed that the final sec-

[26] B. I 43–78.
[27] Norden 507.
[28] This and other Greek quotations from Philodemus/Neoptolemus are
taken from B. I 55.
[29] Wilkinson 97–8.
[30] Dahlmann 104–11; Greenberg 265–7.
[31] Becker 64–112.

tion of the *AP* (295–476) concerns the poet; but there has been some dispute about the precise interpretation of *poiema* and *poiesis* and how lines 1–294 should be divided between them. Immisch thought *poiesis* came first;[32] Brink argues strongly for 1–40 introduction, 41–118 *poiema* (style), 119–294 *poiesis* (content).[33]

The approach adopted here has been to propose a scheme for the *AP* without any reference to Neoptolemus. What happens, then, when Neoptolemus' terms are applied to it? The third term, *poietes* (*poeta*), suits 295–476 very well. The first term, *poiema*, is less satisfactory. As it meant a verse, a short poem, or a part of a long poem, it does not fit the opening lines on organic unity. Even if, with Brink, we set aside those lines and regard them as an introduction, we still have a problem. For although diction or style could be seen as a feature, 'belonging to a *poiema*' (ποιήματος μόνον τὴν σύνθεσιν τῆς λέξεως μετέχειν), the organisation or arrangement of subject-matter (τάξις or *ordo*) could not easily be brought under the same heading. Finally, the second term, *poiesis*, when distinguished from *poiema*, meant a major poetic work with a plot or story, e.g. a tragedy or an epic. The papyrus says 'only the plot belongs to the *poiesis*' – τῆς ποιήσεως εἶναι τὴν ὑπόθεσιν μόνον. Hence *poiesis* can hardly be accepted as a category for the various things which Horace includes in his remarks about drama, e.g. the historical survey of music, the section on satyr-plays, and the lines on the iambic metre.

Our failure to discern a threefold division in the *AP* corresponding to that which Jensen attributed to Neoptolemus need not cause undue dismay. For even if we are wrong, and Horace *did* adopt a *poiema, poiesis, poeta* scheme from Neoptolemus, he cannot have regarded it as of major importance. If he had, he would have taken more trouble to make it clear.

Sources

We start from Porphyrio's note, referred to above. The fragmentary evidence does indeed suggest that at least a few of Horace's *praecepta* were contained in Neoptolemus' treatise. In his note on 1 Porphyrio

[32] Immisch 33–119.
[33] B. 14–14.

135, 309

says *primum praeceptum est* Περὶ τῆς ἀκολουθίας 'the first precept is about consistency' – an idea handled in the opening section of the *AP*. More specifically, Neoptolemus is said to have maintained that the good poet would 'bestow harmony (ἁρμονία) or coherence (συνέχεια?) even on large poems'. This view is implied in what Horace says of Homeric epic, e.g. *primo ne medium, medio ne discrepet imum* (152). Another phrase attributed to Neoptolemus describes the poet as 'the man who has art and power', τὸν τὴν τέχνην καὶ τὴν δύναμιν ἔχοντα. This foreshadows Horace's combination of *ars* and *ingenium* in *AP* 408–11. Yet another of Neoptolemus' tenets was that, as well as employing attractiveness (ψυχαγωγία), the complete poet must benefit his listeners (ὠφελεῖν) and teach them lessons (χρησιμολογεῖν). One thinks of

> non satis est pulchra esse poemata; dulcia sunto,
> et quocumque uolent animum auditoris agunto (99–100);
> aut prodesse uolunt aut delectare poetae
> aut simul et iucunda et idonea dicere uitae (333–4);
> omne tulit punctum qui miscuit utile dulci,
> lectorem delectando pariterque monendo (343–4).

It is unlikely, however, that Neoptolemus' work showed much originality. Certainly the ideas preserved in Philodemus' papyrus can be found in earlier writers. Thus the need for organic unity, which we associate with Aristotle's *Poetics*, chapters 7 and 8, had already been asserted by Plato. 'Every discourse must be organised like a living creature, having a body of its own, not being without head or foot, having a trunk and extremities, in proportion to one another and designed as a whole' (*Phaedr.* 264c). Again, while Neoptolemus may have invented the verb χρησιμολογεῖν, the blending of attractiveness with utility had been adumbrated by Plato, who imagined the champions of poetry pleading that it was οὐ μόνον ἡδεῖα ἀλλὰ καὶ ὠφελίμη (*Rep.* 10.607D and E); the idea was probably developed by Theophrastus, Heracleides, and other followers of Aristotle.[34] Other ideas which occur in the *AP*, and are *not* attested in the fragments of Neoptolemus, can also be found in previous sources, especially in Aristotle. The need to adjust diction to emotion (*AP* 99–113) was noted in Aristotle's *Rhetoric* 3.7.3–5; diction as an expression of character (*AP*

---

[34] Barwick 56; for the Peripatetics see Podlecki.

114–18) appeared in *Rhetoric* 3.7.6–7; and Horace's famous passage on the ages of man (156–78) turns out to be a version of *Rhetoric* 2.12–14.

Finally, we should bear in mind that before Horace's time Roman writers like Lucilius, Cicero, and Varro had already introduced Greek ideas to Italy. The obligations owed to friends, parents, and country (*AP* 312–13), which had been studied by the Greek Stoic Panaetius in his περὶ τοῦ καθήκοντος ('On Appropriateness'), were referred to by Lucilius in his lines on *uirtus* (*ROL* III 1196–1208) and by Cicero in his *De officiis* 1.53–8. Although Aristotle had maintained that 'given equal natural talent, those dramatists who are themselves emotionally affected are the most convincing' (*Poet.* 17.1455a30–2), Horace may not have known that passage.[35] When he wrote the famous lines *si uis me flere, dolendum est primum ipsi tibi* (*AP* 102–3), he could easily have been drawing on Cicero's discussion in *De orat.* 2.188–97. Likewise, when Horace was warning the prospective poet that, in order to develop his *ingenium* and perfect his *ars*, he would have to practise hard over many years (*AP* 408–15), he might have recalled that after talking of *ingenium* and *ars* in *De orat.* 1.113ff. Cicero had gone on to say *et exercitatio quaedam suscipienda uobis est* (147ff.). It was not necessary to go back to the Greeks, though Horace could have found the same idea in several writers, including Plato: εἰ μέν σοι ὑπάρχει φύσει ῥητορικῶι εἶναι, ἔσει ῥήτωρ ἐλλόγιμος προσλαβὼν ἐπιστήμην τε καὶ μελέτην (*Phaedr.* 269D), 'if you have natural rhetorical ability, you will become a notable orator provided you build on it by acquiring knowledge and practice'.[36]

In this complex Graeco-Roman tradition, then, we should not assume that Horace had always a specific source in mind. As, in the *Odes*, he took over and adapted a range of themes from Pindar, Alcaeus, Callimachus, Meleager, and others, so in the *AP* he presented literary and rhetorical theories drawn from many quarters. The poem is most lively and memorable when the material, whether Greek or Roman, has been 'processed' in a characteristically Hora-

[35] Several important topics in the *Poetics* do not appear in the *AP*; see p. 34 below.

[36] For illustrations from Protagoras, Isocrates, Simulus, and others, see Shorey.

tian way. Before pointing to passages where this has occurred, we must note briefly what Horace says about drama and then raise the controversial question 'Are the sections on drama relevant to Horace's Rome?'

Drama

By examining together Virgil, *Georg.* 2.380–96, Livy 7.2, Horace, *E.* 2.1.139–55, *AP* 220–4, 275–84, Tibullus 2.1.51–8, and a number of later passages, scholars have inferred a theory of drama which derived tragedy, comedy, and satyr-play from a common origin, viz. the performances which took place at rustic festivals of Bacchus.[37] The theory has been traced back to Hellenistic critics, in particular Eratosthenes (*c.* 275–194 B.C.), who apparently advanced it in his work *On Old Comedy* and in his poem *Erigone.* The important intermediary between Greece and Rome was the learned Varro (116–27 B.C.), who in his *De scaenicis originibus* and elsewhere presented the theory in a way which suggested (i) an evolutionary process whereby A developed into B and B into C, (ii) a broad parallel between the origins of Greek and Roman drama (see on *E.* 2.1.139–55), and (iii) comparability between Greek and Roman writers (see on *E.* 2.1.57–8).

After Varro different aspects of the theory were selected, and variations occurred. Livy exemplified feature (i) by suggesting that Roman drama developed by a continuous process in which Etruscan dancers were parodied by young men exchanging raillery in verse; these exchanges became more professional in the medleys known as *saturae*; then Livius Andronicus *ab saturis* ('on the basis of the medleys'?)[38] first introduced a play with a plot, i.e. put on an adaptation of a Greek play. While each of these phases is probably authentic (though some disbelieve in the *saturae*), the suggestion that one arose in some sense from the other is quite spurious. (ii) is exemplified by Virgil, who pointed to the parallel between early Greek and early Italian celebrations in honour of Bacchus

---

[37] See C. O. Brink, 'Horace and Varro' in *Entretiens Hardt* 9 (1962) 189–91, and his references to Meuli and Waszink.

[38] Some think Livius actually wrote *saturae*, but that seems very unlikely.

> praemiaque ingeniis pagos et compita circum
> Thesidae posuere, . . .
> nec non Ausonii, Troia gens missa, coloni
> uersibus incomptis ludunt . . . (*Georg.* 2.382–6)

The fullest example of (iii) is found much later in Quintilian's remarks about elegy, history and oratory (*IO* 10.93, 101, 105–13).

Horace handles the theory with considerable independence. When he talks of Greek Old Comedy in *AP* 281–4, he first says (correctly) that it became an official institution later than tragedy;[39] then he adds that after winning much praise it caused offence by going too far and had to be restrained by law. The Greek evidence for such a law is late and unsatisfactory, and it is used simplistically to explain the decline of the chorus in middle and new comedy.[40] How the idea arose is uncertain, but it probably went back at least as far as the second century B.C. and was taken over by Varro in the first. In *E.* 2.1.139–55 we are told that in Italy at harvest festivals there developed a custom of exchanging raillery in rough verse. In time this 'Fescennine licence' caused offence by going too far and had to be restrained by law.[41] Here there is a parallel of sorts between Greek and Italian, but the correspondence is very inexact. No serious attempt is made to present the Fescennine verses as the counterpart of Old Comedy or as the ancestor (however indirect) of the *palliata*. (If there *was* a parallel, it was rather with early iambics of the kind mentioned by Aristotle, *Poet.* 4.1448b30–1449a5.) Finally, in regard to (iii) Horace differs from Varro in his assessment of early Roman comic writers. To Varro, Plautine comedy represented a classic achievement, whereas in Horace's view Plautus was a slovenly craftsman (*E.* 2.1.170–76), and the habit of comparing Plautus to Epicharmus, and Afranius to Menander, was a chauvinistic cliché (57–8). Even in the more favourable

---

[39] Cf. Aristotle, *Poet.* 5.1449b1.

[40] See Maidment and Halliwell.

[41] Horace (or his source) was probably thinking of the law in the Twelve Tables which forbade anyone to chant hostile words or to compose a *carmen* so as to bring ill repute or disgrace on another (*ROL* iii, Table 8, la). There is no reason, however, to connect the enactment of the law with the excesses of Fescennine verse.

judgement given in *AP* 285-91 Roman drama is criticised for its lack of finish.

As for tragedy, Thespis is said to have invented the form; Aeschylus then brought in mask, robe, and buskin; introduced a lofty style; and had his plays acted on a low stage (*AP* 275-80). No corresponding process could be found in Italy; but a parallel could be drawn between the Greeks, whose tragedy developed in the period of peace 'after the [Persian] wars had been laid aside' (*E.* 2.1.93-4, 102) and the Romans, who began to *imitate* Thespis, Aeschylus, and Sophocles 'after the Punic wars' (*E.* 2.1.161-3). Neither phrase was strictly accurate; accuracy would have spoilt the pattern.

So far there is no serious problem of relevance. The tragedies of Pacuvius and Accius, the *palliatae* of Plautus, Caecilius, and Terence, and the *togatae* of Afranius and Atta were still being performed to appreciative audiences in Horace's day (*E.* 2.1.55-62, 79-81). As for contemporary work, we hear of Fundanius' comedies and the tragedies of Pollio and Varius;[42] Horace speaks of tear-jerking plays by a certain Pupius (*E.* 1.1.67); perhaps one should include Propertius' much-disputed friend Lynceus (2.34.41), the Turranius mentioned by Ovid (*Pont.* 4.16.29), and Ovid's own *Medea* (Quint. *IO* 10.1.98), though probably none of these was staged. There is no reason to assume that the list is complete. But even if it is true (as it may be) that little new work was being done, that would not prove the *AP* irrelevant; for various people, including Horace and the Pisones, might well have hoped for a revival.

The position of satyr-plays is much less clear.[43] The tragic poet who competed for the prize of a goat, says Horace, subsequently brought on woodland satyrs (*AP* 220-2). While it is true that in a day's performance the Greek trilogy was followed by a satyr-play, that is not what Horace has in mind. He is talking of a historical development, one commonly ascribed to Pratinas of Phlius (sixth-fifth century

---

[42] Fundanius, *S.* 1.10.40-2; Pollio, *S.* 1.10.42-3, *C.* 2.1.9-12; Varius, Quintilian *IO* 10.1.98, Tacitus, *Dial.* 12.26-7.

[43] For this genre see the introductions to the editions of Euripides' *Cyclops* by Ussher (1) and Seaford. The evidence for satyrs in Rome has been freshly assessed by Wiseman.

B.C.), who wrote both tragedies and satyr-plays.[44] Aristotle had said that tragedy emerged 'from satyric' (ἐκ σατυρικοῦ, *Poetics* 4.1449a20). If 'satyric' means 'the satyr-play', then Pratinas' achievement has to be explained as a revival (reasserting the importance of Dionysus), not as an innovation. This can hardly be reconciled with Horace's *temptauit* and *nouitate* (222–3). Aristotle's 'satyric' could refer, not to the fully-fledged satyr-play, but to an earlier, more primitive, kind of performance with dancing satyrs. That would be compatible with Horace, but it raises other questions about the *Poetics* which cannot be pursued here.[45] At any rate satyr-plays became a feature of Athenian dramatic festivals; they were given a fresh boost by Sositheos' *Lityerses* and Lycophron's *Menedemus* in Alexandria;[46] and they continued to be produced in the Greek world until the second century A.D.[47]

When we come to Rome, ignorance closes in. There was a sizeable Greek population in the capital, and many Romans understood the Greek language. So it is no surprise to learn that Greek stage performances were held there from time to time;[48] actors were available from towns like Neapolis (Naples) and Puteoli, where the Greek theatre flourished. We do not know that satyr-plays were included in these shows, but it would be unwise to rule them out.[49] Our ignorance of satyr-plays in Latin is scarcely less complete. Satyrs were, of course, familiar in poetry, wall-painting, and sculpture;[50] and Horace and Virgil speak of satyrs dancing (*E.* 2.2.125, *Ecl.* 5.73). According to Nicolaus (Athenaeus 6, 261c) Sulla wrote *satyricas comoedias*, but these

[44] P-C (1) 65–8.

[45] In particular, can ἐκ σατυρικοῦ be reconciled with ἀπὸ τῶν ἐξαρχόντων τὸν διθύραμβον (*Poet.* 4.1449a11), as Webster thinks (P-C (1) 34, 96)?

[46] Seaford 20.

[47] Sifakis 126.

[48] Plut. *Marius* 2.2; Cic. *Fam.* 7.1.3; *ILLRP* 803; Nicolaus of Damascus, *Life of Aug.* 9.19; Suet. *Iul.* 39.1; Cic. *Att.* 16.5.1; Suet. *Aug.* 43.1; *ILS* 5050, 157–61.

[49] Even Old Comedy should not be ruled out. Talking of Augustus' interest in *Graecae disciplinae*, Suetonius says *delectabatur etiam comoedia ueteri et saepe eam exhibuit spectaculis publicis* (*Aug.* 89.1). Those who cannot accept this may argue that Suetonius was wrong, but not that he meant something else.

[50] There is abundant evidence in Webster; but nothing that clearly illustrates a satyr-play in Latin.

may have been Atellan farces. Porphyrio on *AP* 221 says Pomponius wrote satyric plays entitled Atalante, Sisyphos, and Ariadne. Were these, too, just mythological burlesques, or were they satyr-plays in the strict sense? Horace himself says that Roman poets left no Greek form untouched – *nil intemptatum nostri liquere poetae* (*AP* 285). Perhaps that was just a rhetorical exaggeration. Again, there is no suggestion in the *AP* that if one of the Pisones were to write a satyr-play he would be doing anything new or daring. That, of course, is an argument from silence; but given Horace's interest in pioneering work it should not be rejected too lightly. Finally, Vitruvius, writing in Horace's day, says that Roman theatres have three types of scenery: tragic, comic, and satyric, the last being painted with trees, caves, mountains, and other rural features (5.6.9; cf. 7.5.2). It is not easy to understand what is meant if satyr-plays were unknown. None of these points comes near to proof, but taken together they are enough to discourage dogmatism.

A word should be added about music. In *AP* 202–19 Horace says that formerly the pipe (*tibia*) was not, as it is now, bound with brass and a rival of the trumpet. It was slender, had few holes, and was ancillary to the chorus. The audience was small and well behaved. After the victorious nation expanded, rhythms and tunes became undisciplined – naturally enough, in view of the mixed audience. The piper flaunted himself. The lyre also became more elaborate, and the thought affected an oracular obscurity.

Parallels to most of these points can be found in Aristotle, *Pol.* 8.6.1341a29ff. and 8.7.1341b15, and before that in Plato, *Laws* 3.700c–e. (See also the notes on 203–4 and 216.) So the terms of the description are taken from Greek sources (though Horace's tone is less polemical and didactic). That does not mean that a Roman reader would have found the passage bogus. Such an idea is *a priori* unlikely. Also, pipes with silver sleeves occluding the apertures have been found at Pompeii,[51] and Livy confirms that theatre-performances in general *had* become more elaborate at that time (7.2.13). What Horace has done again, is to take advantage of certain very broad similarities between Greek and Roman experiences; but this time, instead of saying 'as, in Greece, music declined into vulgarity, so the

[51] Howard 7; for the Greek *aulos* see Barker 14–16.

same thing happened in Rome', he has drawn a composite Graeco-Roman sketch, borrowing from Plato and Aristotle but supplying Roman as well as Greek details – *Genius* (210) as well as *Delphis* (219) – and at one point being deliberately ambiguous (*uictor* in 208).[52] A rather similar mixture of Greek musical criticism, Roman tradition, and contemporary experience had been presented by Cicero; audiences who once were filled with the pleasant sternness of the music of Livius Andronicus and Naevius now jumped up and down, twisting their necks and eyes in time with the undulations of the tunes. Sparta was right in obliging Timotheus to reduce his strings to seven (*De leg.* 2.39).

The questions touched on above are all legitimate and, at different levels, important. But with so famous a work as the *AP* there is a danger that one's perception and enjoyment may be stifled by various kinds of scholarly comment. A new reader should not worry too much about Horace's debt to Varro, or Neoptolemus, or Aristotle. The *AP* is not a quasi-philosophical treatise. It is less inclusive, less of a critical credo, than we are sometimes led to believe.

As in *E.* 2.1, there is a good deal of comment on poetic values in general, but in specific genres the range of interest is very limited. We hear almost nothing of iambic (79–80) or the personal lyric of love and wine (85),[53] in spite of Horace's own achievement in those areas; scarcely more attention is paid to didactic poetry (391-9) and official lyric (83–4, 404–5). This neglect may well mirror both the bias of the Greek critical tradition and the literary interest of the Pisones and others. But in the case of elegy a further factor seems to be at work. Certain kinds of elegiac verse *are* mentioned, however briefly, viz. those associated with lamentation (75), votive offerings (76), and warfare (401–3). But love-elegy is ignored, although there was a substantial body of work in the genre, both in Greek and Latin. We cannot point by way of explanation to the official status of the recipient, as in *E.* 2.1. So it does look as if we are dealing with an element of personal prejudice. Mere indifference hardly explains the omission.

---

[52] Williams (2) also sees the section as a blend of Greek and Roman, but he believes that the elements are fused 'in a totally imaginary world' (353).

[53] See the Appendix, pp. 230ff.

Again, whoever called the poem *ars poetica* correctly observed its focus. It concentrates on those aspects of poetry which are amenable to rational discussion. *ingenium* (inborn talent) is either taken for granted (408–11) or derided as a kind of madness (295–301, 453–76). Yet the man who wrote *Descende caelo* (*C.* 3.4), *Quo me, Bacche, rapis* (*C.* 3.25), and *Quem tu, Melpomene, semel* (*C.* 4.3) knew something about inspiration and did not underrate it.

The intellectual level of the *AP* is not uniform. Not only are there elements missing which we find in Aristotle's *Poetics* (nothing, e.g., about recognition, reversal, error, or catharsis), but some of the recommendations which *are* made come across as perfunctory. Thus the so-called 'five-act law', the restriction of the *deus ex machina*, and the ban on the fourth speaking part (189–92) sound like mechanical repetitions of received wisdom. Occasionally, too, when he is in danger of stepping into deeper water, Horace draws back. After affirming the distinction between the comic and the tragic styles, he adds that sometimes comic characters rise above the emotional level of conversation and sometimes tragic characters do not (89–98).[54] Where does that leave the law of the genres? To say that the law is flexible is not informative.

The *AP*, then, is not a systematic handbook of literary theory; nor, in spite of the respect accorded to it in later centuries, was it ever meant to be. It is a lively, entertaining, verse-epistle, written by a well-read man for his friends, who shared his love of poetry and whose company we are invited to join. Such a formulation may sound reductive, but, in the *sermones* at least, that was Horace's way. The *Satires* prepared us for *prima dicte mihi* (*E.* 1.1), and in reading that piece we were not invited to admire the fact that a book of verse-epistles was something new and exciting. Similarly, after *E.* 2.1 we move easily into the *AP*, without noticing that a poem on poetics was a highly original achievement – and a characteristically Horatian one; no ancient manual ever opened with the description of a monstrosity.

Although unmistakably Horatian in tone, the *AP*, unlike *S.* 1.10, *E.* 1.19, and *E.* 2.1, is not the product of controversy; the poet is less involved personally in his subject – a fact which could be seen as further

---

[54] Cf. the opinion cited in *S.* 1.4.45–56.

evidence for a late date. Nevertheless, the Roman flavour still comes through.

The initial impressions are of artistic life – the activities of painters, poets, and potters. Then the background of the city is touched in – first the sculptor near Aemilius' gladiatorial school, then the audience in the theatre, the schoolchildren doing arithmetic, the auctioneer crying his wares. That is the setting for this quasi-informal, quasi-didactic, epistle. But the material is not confined to the present day; literary figures from Rome's recent past, and from much earlier times, are brought in to confirm what is being said. Just as often, Horace calls on the Greeks. Thus at 156–7 he moves aside from argument to illustration; Aristotle's passage on the ages of man (*Rhet.* 2.12–14) is sharpened and compressed, and a few lines are added on the young boy (Horace had a soft spot for schoolboys); then in 176–8 he moves back into his argument. The point about this and other Greek passages is not that they were written centuries earlier in a foreign language, but that they were available now as living *exempla*. We are dealing with a Graeco-Roman culture, just as with Pope's *Imitation* of *E*. 2.2 we are dealing with an 'Augustan' culture.

The features of Horace's didactic style are now familiar – the role played by his friends (Virgil and Varius, the Pisones, Quintilius), the allusions to episodes and characters from literature and mythology, the neat adaptations of traditional sayings (the painter's cypress in 19, the mountain delivered of a mouse in 139), the concise formulation of general truths (*professus grandia turget* in 27, *omne tulit punctum qui miscuit utile dulci* in 343). But as the *AP* is in places more technical than the other epistles, one may notice clever touches like the iambus pictured as a throwing spear (79), the comic 'sock' clothing the metrical foot (80), Tragedy embarrassed like a great lady dancing in public (232), and the adoption of the spondee into the iambus's family (256).

As always, the didactic style is varied. One thinks of the sombre lyrical resonance of the lines on the mortality of words and the transience of human structures (60–72). More often the variation is satirical – the incompetent harpist (355–6), the rich poetic dabbler looking for praise (419–30), the lunatic bard (453–76). Horace passes easily from topic to topic, and through the whole work runs the thread of *decorum*, unobtrusive because of its changing applications (parts should be in proportion to the whole, one's task should be commensurate with one's powers, linguistic innovations should be used with discretion, style should be in keeping with genre, speech should suit character and reflect emotion etc.). This principle more than anything else accounts for the prevailing impression of good sense, the conviction that we are listening to a wise, but not a pompous, man speaking within a civilised society.

After reading the *AP* and trying to appreciate its qualities we can do one other thing – we can question it. For example, why should an artist not produce grotesques? Granted, Vitruvius disliked them (7.5.3–4), but medieval stone-masons and illuminators thought otherwise. Must art imitate nature? Not according to the painters of Byzantium, nor to Matisse and Picasso. 'Know your limitations.' Why? Is not this a depressingly safe counsel? ('Ah, but a man's reach should exceed his grasp, | Or what's a heaven for?' – Browning.) Why the curb on neologisms? Joyce had no such inhibitions. What is wrong with bawdy jokes if 'the buyer of roasted nuts and chick-peas' enjoys them? Why, in other words, should the stage be censored by a social élite? Is the whole business of decorum perhaps simply a device to perpetuate the supremacy of a class? Does not too great an obsession with rules destroy creative spontaneity? (Wordsworth spoke of 'the spontaneous overflow of powerful feelings'.) And why should inborn genius be ridiculed? Coleridge offered a less simple picture, 'And all should cry, Beware! Beware! | His flashing eyes, his floating hair! | Weave a circle round him thrice, | And close your eyes with holy dread, | For he on honey-dew hath fed, | and drunk the milk of Paradise' (*Kubla Khan*).

The counter-examples are seen to be medieval or romantic or modern; which brings out the fact that the *AP*'s ideas are those of classical humanism. As such, they appealed to those later periods in which the dominant taste was similar; it was no accident that after enjoying high esteem for 300 years the poem should have lost its position after the eighteenth century. What we make of it is, of course, up to us. Romanticism died in the First World War; and after nearly a century of modernism some of the *AP*'s views may seem quite attractive.

The *AP*, then, is not a theoretical defence of Horace's own tastes and achievement. It is less than that – and also much more. Because of its

distinctive qualities (and in spite of its shortcomings) it is a classic presentation of the classical outlook. As such, it leads into larger questions of cultural history. With the possible exception of the *Poetics*, no
ancient work of literary criticism is so fertile in suggestion.[55]

4. CHRONOLOGICAL TABLE

B.C.

65	Birth of Quintus Horatius Flaccus in Venusia
63	Birth of Gaius Octavius, the grandson of one of Julius Caesar's sisters. He took the name Gaius Julius Caesar Octavianus after being adopted into the Julian house
44	Assassination of Julius Caesar
42	Battle of Philippi; defeat of Brutus and Cassius
37	Horace joins the circle of Maecenas
35	Publication of *S.* 1
34	Maecenas presents Horace with the Sabine farm
31	Battle of Actium; defeat of Antony and Cleopatra
30	Publication of *S.* 2 and *I.*
27	Octavian accepts the title Augustus
23	Publication of *C.* 1–3
20	Restoration of Crassus' standards by the Parthians
20 or early 19	Publication of *E.* 1
19	The *Epistle to Florus* (*E.* 2.2)
17	Performance of *CS*
13	Publication of *C.* 4
12?	The *Epistle to Augustus* (*E.* 2.1)
10?	The *Epistle to the Pisones* ('*Ars Poetica*')
8	Death of Maecenas; Death of Horace

[55] Scholars like Herrick and Weinberg (I, pt 1, 111–55) have shown how
Aristotelian and Horatian criticism fused before the end of the sixteenth century. But, when they were written, the comments of 'this jaunty epistle' (Wilkinson) differed in nature and purpose from the brilliantly original, but dry and
impersonal, insights of the great natural scientist who had turned his attention
to literature. No one ever smiled at the *Poetics*.

5. DEPARTURES FROM BRINK'S TEXT

Brink's text		*This text*

The Epistle to Augustus

51	leuiter	†leuiter†
73	decorum, [et]	decorum,
115	†medicorum† est	medicorum est
116	†medici†	medici
123	secundo.	secundo;
124	urbi est,	urbi,
145	inuecta	inuenta
168	*no break*	*new paragraph*
246	tulerunt	tulerunt,

The Epistle to Florus

6	eriles	eriles,
15	in scalis, latuit,	in scalis latuit,
77	*new paragraph*	*no break*
78	umbra	umbra;
87	†frater erat Romae†	fautor erat Romae
98	lento, Samnites, ad	lento Samnites ad
198	raptim.	raptim
199	†pauperies immunda domus procul absit†:	(pauperies immunda domus procul absit).

The Epistle to the Pisones

2	uelit, et . . . plumas	uelit et . . . plumas,
3	membris, ut	membris ut
32	unus	imus
44	omittat.	omittat;
45	*printed after 46*	*printed after 44*
60	†pronos† mutantur	priuos mutantur
61a	prima cadunt (*lacuna*)	*ut noua succrescunt nouus et decor enitet illis,*

61b	(*lacuna*) ita uerborum	prima cadunt, ita uerborum
65	†regis† opus,	regium opus,
	†diu palus†	palus prius
131	*new paragraph*	*no break*
170	uti	uti,
172	†spe longus†,	spe lentus,
	⟨p⟩auidusque	pauidusque
177	uiriles:	uiriles,
178	morabimur	moraberis
184	praesens:	praesens;
190	reposci.	reponi.
299	poeta[e],	poetae,
323	*no break*	*new paragraph*
338	ueris:	ueris,
339	uolet (*as actually intended:*	uelit
	see Brink III 592)	
355	caret, et (*but see note ad loc.*)	caret; ut
358	miror, et idem	miror; et idem
361	erit, quae	erit quae
406	finis: ne	finis; ne

EPISTLES BOOK II
EPISTLE TO THE PISONES
('ARS POETICA')

Q. HORATI FLACCI EPISTVLARVM
LIBER SECVNDVS

THE EPISTLE TO AUGUSTUS
(*EPISTLES* 2.1)

Opening address

Cvm tot sustineas et tanta negotia solus,
res Italas armis tuteris, moribus ornes,
legibus emendes, in publica commoda peccem,
si longo sermone morer tua tempora, Caesar.
Romulus et Liber pater et cum Castore Pollux,   5
post ingentia facta deorum in templa recepti,
dum terras hominumque colunt genus, aspera bella
componunt, agros assignant, oppida condunt,
plorauere suis non respondere fauorem
speratum meritis. diram qui contudit hydram   10
notaque fatali portenta labore subegit,
comperit inuidiam supremo fine domari.
urit enim fulgore suo qui praegrauat artes
infra se positas, exstinctus amabitur idem.
praesenti tibi maturos largimur honores,   15
iurandasque tuum per numen ponimus aras,
nil oriturum alias, nil ortum tale fatentes.

Conservative prejudice

sed tuus hic populus, sapiens et iustus in uno
te nostris ducibus, te Grais anteferendo,
cetera nequaquam simili ratione modoque   20
aestimat et, nisi quae terris semota suisque
temporibus defuncta uidet, fastidit et odit;

43

sic fautor ueterum, ut tabulas peccare uetantes
quas bis quinque uiri sanxerunt, foedera regum
uel Gabiis uel cum rigidis aequata Sabinis,   25
pontificum libros, annosa uolumina uatum
dictitet Albano Musas in monte locutas.

   si, quia Graiorum sunt antiquissima quaeque
scripta uel optima, Romani pensantur eadem
scriptores trutina, non est quod multa loquamur;   30
nil intra est olea, nil extra est in nuce duri;
uenimus ad summum fortunae: pingimus atque
psallimus et luctamur Achiuis doctius unctis.

   si meliora dies ut uina poemata reddit,
scire uelim, chartis pretium quotus arroget annus.   35
scriptor abhinc annos centum qui decidit, inter
perfectos ueteresque referri debet, an inter
uiles atque nouos? excludat iurgia finis.
'est uetus atque probus centum qui perficit annos.'
quid? qui deperiit minor uno mense uel anno,   40
inter quos referendus erit: ueteresne poetas,
an quos et praesens et postera respuat aetas?
'iste quidem ueteres inter ponetur honeste,
qui uel mense breui uel toto est iunior anno.'
utor permisso, caudaeque pilos ut equinae   45
paulatim uello et demo unum, demo et item unum,
dum cadat elusus ratione ruentis acerui
qui redit ad fastos et uirtutem aestimat annis,
miraturque nihil nisi quod Libitina sacrauit.

   Ennius et sapiens et fortis et alter Homerus,   50
ut critici dicunt, †leuiter† curare uidetur
quo promissa cadant et somnia Pythagorea.
Naeuius in manibus non est et mentibus haeret
paene recens? adeo sanctum est uetus omne poema.
ambigitur quotiens, uter utro sit prior, aufert   55
Pacuuius docti famam senis, Accius alti,
dicitur Afrani toga conuenisse Menandro,

Plautus ad exemplar Siculi properare Epicharmi,
uincere Caecilius grauitate, Terentius arte.
hos ediscit et hos arto stipata theatro   60
spectat Roma potens; habet hos numeratque poetas
ad nostrum tempus Liui scriptoris ab aeuo.
　　interdum uulgus rectum uidet, est ubi peccat.
si ueteres ita miratur laudatque poetas
ut nihil anteferat, nihil illis comparet, errat;   65
si quaedam nimis antique, si pleraque dure
dicere credit eos, ignaue multa fatetur,
et sapit et mecum facit et Ioue iudicat aequo.
non equidem insector delendaque carmina Liui
esse reor, memini quae plagosum mihi paruo   70
Orbilium dictare; sed emendata uideri
pulchraque et exactis minimum distantia miror;
inter quae uerbum emicuit si forte decorum,
si uersus paulo concinnior unus et alter,
iniuste totum ducit uenditque poema.   75
　　indignor quicquam reprehendi, non quia crasse
compositum illepideue putetur sed quia nuper,
nec ueniam antiquis sed honorem et praemia posci.
recte necne crocum floresque perambulet Attae
fabula si dubitem, clament periisse pudorem   80
cuncti paene patres, ea cum reprehendere coner
quae grauis Aesopus, quae doctus Roscius egit,
uel quia nil rectum nisi quod placuit sibi ducunt,
uel quia turpe putant parere minoribus, et quae
imberbes didicere senes perdenda fateri.   85
iam Saliare Numae carmen qui laudat et illud
quod mecum ignorat solus uult scire uideri,
ingeniis non ille fauet plauditque sepultis,
nostra sed impugnat, nos nostraque liuidus odit.
　　quod si tam Graecis nouitas inuisa fuisset   90
quam nobis, quid nunc esset uetus, aut quid haberet
quod legeret tereretque uiritim publicus usus?

Caricatures of Greece and Rome

ut primum positis nugari Graecia bellis
coepit et in uitium fortuna labier aequa,
nunc athletarum studiis, nunc arsit equorum,   95
marmoris aut eboris fabros aut aeris amauit,
suspendit picta uultum mentemque tabella,
nunc tibicinibus, nunc est gauisa tragoedis;
sub nutrice puella uelut si luderet infans,
quod cupide petiit mature plena reliquit.   100
[quid placet aut odio est quod non mutabile credas?]
hoc paces habuere bonae uentique secundi.
  Romae dulce diu fuit et sollemne reclusa
mane domo uigilare, clienti promere iura,
cautos nominibus rectis expendere nummos,   105
maiores audire, minori dicere, per quae
crescere res posset, minui damnosa libido.
mutauit mentem populus leuis et calet uno
scribendi studio; pueri patresque seueri
fronde comas uincti cenant et carmina dictant.   110
ipse ego, qui nullos me adfirmo scribere uersus
inuenior Parthis mendacior, et prius orto
sole uigil calamum et chartas et scrinia posco.
nauem agere ignarus nauis timet; habrotonum aegro
non audet nisi qui didicit dare; quod medicorum est   115
promittunt medici; tractant fabrilia fabri:
scribimus indocti doctique poemata passim.

The poet's value to the community

hic error tamen et leuis haec insania quantas
uirtutes habeat sic collige: uatis auarus
non temere est animus; uersus amat, hoc studet unum;   120
detrimenta, fugas seruorum, incendia ridet;
non fraudem socio pueroue incogitat ullam

pupillo; uiuit siliquis et pane secundo;
militiae quamquam piger et malus, utilis urbi,
si das hoc, paruis quoque rebus magna iuuari.   125
os tenerum pueri balbumque poeta figurat,
torquet ab obscenis iam nunc sermonibus aurem,
mox etiam pectus praeceptis format amicis,
asperitatis et inuidiae corrector et irae;
recte facta refert, orientia tempora notis   130
instruit exemplis, inopem solatur et aegrum.
castis cum pueris ignara puella mariti
disceret unde preces, uatem ni Musa dedisset?
poscit opem chorus et praesentia numina sentit;
caelestes implorat aquas, docta prece blandus,   135
auertit morbos, metuenda pericula pellit,
impetrat et pacem et locupletem frugibus annum.
carmine di superi placantur, carmine Manes.

Early Roman libertas

agricolae prisci, fortes paruoque beati,
condita post frumenta leuantes tempore festo   140
corpus et ipsum animum spe finis dura ferentem,
cum sociis operum pueris et coniuge fida,
Tellurem porco, Siluanum lacte piabant,
floribus et uino Genium memorem breuis aeui.
Fescennina per hunc inuenta licentia morem   145
uersibus alternis opprobria rustica fudit.
libertasque recurrentes accepta per annos
lusit amabiliter, donec iam saeuus apertam
in rabiem coepit uerti iocus et per honestas
ire domos impune minax. doluere cruento   150
dente lacessiti; fuit intactis quoque cura
condicione super communi; quin etiam lex
poenaque lata, malo quae nollet carmine quemquam
describi; uertere modum formidine fustis

ad bene dicendum delectandumque redacti. 155

Greek influence

Graecia capta ferum uictorem cepit et artes
intulit agresti Latio. sic horridus ille
defluxit numerus Saturnius, et graue uirus
munditiae pepulere; sed in longum tamen aeuum
manserunt hodieque manent uestigia ruris. 160
serus enim Graecis admouit acumina chartis,
et post Punica bella quietus quaerere coepit,
quid Sophocles et Thespis et Aeschylus utile ferrent.
temptauit quoque rem, si digne uertere posset,
et placuit sibi, natura sublimis et acer; 165
nam spirat tragicum satis et feliciter audet,
sed turpem putat inscite metuitque lituram.

creditur, ex medio quia res arcessit, habere
sudoris minimum, sed habet comoedia tanto
plus oneris, quanto ueniae minus. aspice, Plautus 170
quo pacto partes tutetur amantis ephebi,
ut patris attenti, lenonis ut insidiosi,
quantus sit Dossennus edacibus in parasitis,
quam non astricto percurrat pulpita socco;
gestit enim nummum in loculos demittere, post hoc 175
securus cadat an recto stet fabula talo.

Playwright and audience

quem tulit ad scaenam uentoso Gloria curru,
exanimat lentus spectator, sedulus inflat;
sic leue, sic paruum est, animum quod laudis auarum
subruit aut reficit. ualeat res ludicra si me 180
palma negata macrum, donata reducit opimum.

saepe etiam audacem fugat hoc terretque poetam,
quod numero plures, uirtute et honore minores,

indocti stolidique, et depugnare parati
si discordet eques, media inter carmina poscunt   185
aut ursum aut pugiles; his nam plebecula gaudet.
uerum equitis quoque iam migrauit ab aure uoluptas
omnis ad incertos oculos et gaudia uana.
quattuor aut plures aulaea premuntur in horas,
dum fugiunt equitum turmae peditumque cateruae;   190
mox trahitur manibus regum fortuna retortis,
esseda festinant, pilenta, petorrita, naues,
captiuum portatur ebur, captiua Corinthus.

   si foret in terris, rideret Democritus, seu
diuersum confusa genus panthera camelo   195
siue elephans albus uulgi conuerteret ora;
spectaret populum ludis attentius ipsis,
ut sibi praebentem nimio spectacula plura;
scriptores autem narrare putaret asello
fabellam surdo. nam quae peruincere uoces   200
eualuere sonum referunt quem nostra theatra?
Garganum mugire putes nemus aut mare Tuscum,
tanto cum strepitu ludi spectantur et artes,
diuitiaeque peregrinae; quibus oblitus actor
cum stetit in scaena, concurrit dextera laeuae.   205
dixit adhuc aliquid? nil sane. quid placet ergo?
laena Tarentino uiolas imitata ueneno.

   ac ne forte putes me, quae facere ipse recusem,
cum recte tractent alii, laudare maligne,
ille per extentum funem mihi posse uidetur   210
ire poeta, meum qui pectus inaniter angit,
irritat, mulcet, falsis terroribus implet,
ut magus, et modo me Thebis, modo ponit Athenis.

The poet's value to the ruler

uerum age et his, qui se lectori credere malunt
quam spectatoris fastidia ferre superbi,   215

curam redde breuem, si munus Apolline dignum
uis complere libris et uatibus addere calcar,
ut studio maiore petant Helicona uirentem.

   multa quidem nobis facimus mala saepe poetae
(ut uineta egomet caedam mea), cum tibi librum   220
sollicito damus aut fesso; cum laedimur, unum
si quis amicorum est ausus reprehendere uersum;
cum loca iam recitata reuoluimus irreuocati;
cum lamentamur non apparere labores
nostros et tenui deducta poemata filo;   225
cum speramus eo rem uenturam ut, simul atque
carmina rescieris nos fingere, commodus ultro
arcessas, et egere uetes, et scribere cogas.

   sed tamen est operae pretium cognoscere, quales
aedituos habeat belli spectata domique   230
uirtus, indigno non committenda poetae.
gratus Alexandro, regi magno, fuit ille
Choerilus, incultis qui uersibus et male natis
rettulit acceptos, regale nomisma, Philippos.
sed, ueluti tractata notam labemque remittunt   235
atramenta, fere scriptores carmine foedo
splendida facta linunt. idem rex ille poema
qui tam ridiculum tam care prodigus emit,
edicto uetuit ne quis se praeter Apellen
pingeret, aut alius Lysippo duceret aera   240
fortis Alexandri uultum simulantia. quod si
iudicium subtile uidendis artibus illud
ad libros et ad haec Musarum dona uocares,
Boeotum in crasso iurares aere natum.

   at neque dedecorant tua de se iudicia atque   245
munera, quae multa dantis cum laude tulerunt,
dilecti tibi Vergilius Variusque poetae;
nec magis expressi uultus per aenea signa,
quam per uatis opus mores animique uirorum
clarorum apparent. nec sermones ego mallem   250

repentes per humum quam res componere gestas,
terrarumque situs et flumina dicere, et arces
montibus impositas, et barbara regna, tuisque
auspiciis totum confecta duella per orbem,
claustraque custodem pacis cohibentia Ianum,   255
et formidatam Parthis te principe Romam,
si quantum cuperem possem quoque. sed neque paruum
carmen maiestas recipit tua, nec meus audet
rem temptare pudor quam uires ferre recusent.
sedulitas autem stulte, quem diligit, urget,   260
praecipue cum se numeris commendat et arte.
discit enim citius meminitque libentius illud
quod quis deridet, quam quod probat et ueneratur.
nil moror officium quod me grauat, ac neque ficto
in peius uultu proponi cereus usquam,   265
nec praue factis decorari uersibus opto,
ne rubeam pingui donatus munere, et una
cum scriptore meo, capsa porrectus operta,
deferar in uicum uendentem tus et odores
et piper et quidquid chartis amicitur ineptis.   270

THE EPISTLE TO FLORUS (*EPISTLES* 2.2)

'You knew I was a bad correspondent'

FLORE, bono claroque fidelis amice Neroni,
si quis forte uelit puerum tibi uendere natum
Tibure uel Gabiis, et tecum sic agat: 'hic et
candidus et talos a uertice pulcher ad imos
fiet eritque tuus nummorum milibus octo,   5
uerna ministeriis ad nutus aptus eriles,
litterulis Graecis imbutus, idoneus arti
cuilibet; argilla quiduis imitaberis uda;
quin etiam canet indoctum sed dulce bibenti;
multa fidem promissa leuant, ubi plenius aequo   10

laudat uenales qui uult extrudere merces;
res urget me nulla, meo sum pauper in aere;
nemo hoc mangonum faceret tibi; non temere a me
quiuis ferret idem; semel hic cessauit et, ut fit,
in scalis latuit, metuens pendentis habenae;   15
des nummos, excepta nihil te si fuga laedit':
ille ferat pretium poenae securus, opinor.
prudens emisti uitiosum, dicta tibi est lex;
insequeris tamen hunc et lite moraris iniqua?
  dixi me pigrum proficiscenti tibi, dixi   20
talibus officiis prope mancum, ne mea saeuus
iurgares ad te quod epistula nulla rediret.
quid tum profeci, mecum facientia iura
si tamen attemptas? quereris super hoc etiam, quod
exspectata tibi non mittam carmina mendax.   25

'I no longer need the money'

Luculli miles collecta uiatica multis
aerumnis, lassus dum noctu stertit, ad assem
perdiderat: post hoc, uehemens lupus, et sibi et hosti
iratus pariter, ieiunis dentibus acer,
praesidium regale loco deiecit, ut aiunt,   30
summe munito et multarum diuite rerum.
clarus ob id factum donis ornatur honestis,
accipit et bis dena super sestertia nummum.
forte sub hoc tempus castellum euertere praetor
nescio quod cupiens hortari coepit eundem   35
uerbis quae timido quoque possent addere mentem,
'i, bone, quo uirtus tua te uocat, i pede fausto,
grandia laturus meritorum praemia. quid stas?'
post haec ille catus, quantumuis rusticus, 'ibit,
ibit eo quo uis qui zonam perdidit', inquit.   40
  Romae nutriri mihi contigit, atque doceri
iratus Grais quantum nocuisset Achilles.

adiecere bonae paulo plus artis Athenae,
scilicet ut uellem curuo dinoscere rectum,
atque inter siluas Academi quaerere uerum. 45
dura sed emouere loco me tempora grato,
ciuilisque, rudem belli, tulit aestus in arma
Caesaris Augusti non responsura lacertis.
unde simul primum me dimisere Philippi,
decisis humilem pennis inopemque paterni 50
et laris et fundi, paupertas impulit audax
ut uersus facerem: sed quod non desit habentem
quae poterunt umquam satis expurgare cicutae,
ni melius dormire putem quam scribere uersus?

'I am no longer young'

singula de nobis anni praedantur euntes; 55
eripuere iocos, uenerem, conuiuia, ludum;
tendunt extorquere poemata; quid faciam uis?

'I cannot please everybody'

denique non omnes eadem mirantur amantque.
carmine tu gaudes, hic delectatur iambis,
ille Bioneis sermonibus et sale nigro. 60
tres mihi conuiuae prope dissentire uidentur,
poscentes uario multum diuersa palato.
quid dem? quid non dem? renuis tu quod iubet alter;
quod petis, id sane est inuisum acidumque duobus.

'Rome is no place for a poet'

praeter cetera me Romaene poemata censes 65
scribere posse inter tot curas totque labores?
hic sponsum uocat, hic auditum scripta relictis
omnibus officiis; cubat hic in colle Quirini,

hic extremo in Auentino, uisendus uterque;
interualla uides haud sane commoda. 'uerum   70
purae sunt plateae, nihil ut meditantibus obstet.'
festinat calidus mulis gerulisque redemptor,
torquet nunc lapidem, nunc ingens machina tignum,
tristia robustis luctantur funera plaustris.
hac rabiosa fugit canis, hac lutulenta ruit sus.   75
i nunc et uersus tecum meditare canoros.
scriptorum chorus omnis amat nemus et fugit urbem,
rite cliens Bacchi somno gaudentis et umbra;
tu me inter strepitus nocturnos atque diurnos
uis canere et contracta sequi uestigia uatum?   80
ingenium sibi quod uacuas desumpsit Athenas,
et studiis annos septem dedit insenuitque
libris et curis, statua taciturnius exit
plerumque et risu populum quatit; hic ego rerum
fluctibus in mediis et tempestatibus urbis   85
uerba lyrae motura sonum conectere digner?

'Listening to fellow poets is a tedious business'

fautor erat Romae consulti rhetor, ut alter
alterius sermone meros audiret honores,
Gracchus ut hic illi, foret huic ut Mucius ille.
qui minus argutos uexat furor iste poetas?   90
carmina compono, hic elegos. mirabile uisu
caelatumque nouem Musis opus. aspice primum,
quanto cum fastu, quanto molimine circum-
spectemus uacuam Romanis uatibus aedem.
mox etiam, si forte uacas, sequere et procul audi,   95
quid ferat et qua re sibi nectat uterque coronam.
caedimur et totidem plagis consumimus hostem
lento Samnites ad lumina prima duello.
discedo Alcaeus puncto illius; ille meo quis?
quis nisi Callimachus? si plus apposcere uisus,   100

fit Mimnermus et optiuo cognomine crescit.
multa fero, ut placem genus irritabile uatum,
cum scribo et supplex populi suffragia capto;
idem, finitis studiis et mente recepta,
obturem patulas impune legentibus aures.   105

*'Genuine poetry calls for self-criticism; it does not allow
comfortable illusions'*

ridentur mala qui componunt carmina; uerum
gaudent scribentes et se uenerantur et ultro,
si taceas, laudant quidquid scripsere beati.
at qui legitimum cupiet fecisse poema,
cum tabulis animum censoris sumet honesti;   110
audebit, quaecumque parum splendoris habebunt
et sine pondere erunt et honore indigna fruentur,
uerba mouere loco, quamuis inuita recedant
et uersentur adhuc inter penetralia Vestae.
obscurata diu populo bonus eruet atque   115
proferet in lucem speciosa uocabula rerum,
quae priscis memorata Catonibus atque Cethegis
nunc situs informis premit et deserta uetustas.
asciscet noua, quae genitor produxerit usus.
uemens et liquidus puroque simillimus amni   120
fundet opes Latiumque beabit diuite lingua.
luxuriantia compescet, nimis aspera sano
leuabit cultu, uirtute carentia tollet.
ludentis speciem dabit et torquebitur, ut qui
nunc Satyrum, nunc agrestem Cyclopa mouetur.   125
  praetulerim scriptor delirus inersque uideri,
dum mea delectent mala me uel denique fallant,
quam sapere et ringi. fuit haud ignobilis Argis,
qui se credebat miros audire tragoedos,
in uacuo laetus sessor plausorque theatro;   130
cetera qui uitae seruaret munia recto

more, bonus sane uicinus, amabilis hospes,
comis in uxorem, posset qui ignoscere seruis
et signo laeso non insanire lagoenae,
posset qui rupem et puteum uitare patentem.   135
hic ubi cognatorum opibus curisque refectus
expulit elleboro morbum bilemque meraco,
et redit ad sese, 'pol me occidistis, amici,
non seruastis' ait, 'cui sic extorta uoluptas
et demptus per uim mentis gratissimus error.'   140

'I should be devoting myself to the pursuit of wisdom'

nimirum sapere est abiectis utile nugis,
et tempestiuum pueris concedere ludum,
ac non uerba sequi fidibus modulanda Latinis,
sed uerae numerosque modosque ediscere uitae.
quocirca mecum loquor haec tacitusque recordor.   145
si tibi nulla sitim finiret copia lymphae,
narrares medicis; quod quanto plura parasti
tanto plura cupis, nulline faterier audes?
si uulnus tibi monstrata radice uel herba
non fieret leuius, fugeres radice uel herba   150
proficiente nihil curarier. audieras, cui
rem di donarent, illi decedere prauam
stultitiam; et cum sis nihilo sapientior ex quo
plenior es, tamen uteris monitoribus isdem?
at si diuitiae prudentem reddere possent,   155
si cupidum timidumque minus te, nempe ruberes,
uiueret in terris te si quis auarior uno.

  si proprium est quod quis libra mercatus et aere est,
quaedam, si credis consultis, mancipat usus;
qui te pascit ager tuus est, et uilicus Orbi,   160
cum segetes occat tibi mox frumenta daturas,
te dominum sentit. das nummos, accipis uuam,
pullos, oua, cadum temeti; nempe modo isto

paulatim mercaris agrum, fortasse trecentis
aut etiam supra nummorum milibus emptum.   165
quid refert, uiuas numerato nuper an olim?
emptor Aricini quondam Veientis et arui
emptum cenat holus, quamuis aliter putat, emptis
sub noctem gelidam lignis calefactat aënum.
sed uocat usque suum, qua populus assita certis   170
limitibus uicina refringit iurgia; tamquam
sit proprium quicquam, puncto quod mobilis horae
nunc prece, nunc pretio, nunc ui, nunc morte suprema
permutet dominos et cedat in altera iura.
sic quia perpetuus nulli datur usus, et heres   175
heredem alternis uelut unda superuenit undam,
quid uici prosunt aut horrea? quidue Calabris
saltibus adiecti Lucani, si metit Orcus
grandia cum paruis, non exorabilis auro?
gemmas, marmor, ebur, Tyrrhena sigilla, tabellas,   180
argentum, uestes Gaetulo murice tinctas,
sunt qui non habeant, est qui non curat habere.
cur alter fratrum cessare et ludere et ungui
praeferat Herodis palmetis pinguibus, alter
diues et importunus ad umbram lucis ab ortu   185
siluestrem flammis et ferro mitiget agrum,
scit Genius, natale comes qui temperat astrum,
naturae deus humanae, mortalis in unum
quodque caput, uultu mutabilis, albus et ater.
utar, et ex modico quantum res poscet aceruo   190
tollam, nec metuam quid de me iudicet heres,
quod non plura datis inuenerit: et tamen idem
scire uolam, quantum simplex hilarisque nepoti
discrepet et quantum discordet parcus auaro.
distat enim spargas tua prodigus an neque sumptum   195
inuitus facias neque plura parare labores,
ac potius, puer ut festis Quinquatribus olim,
exiguo gratoque fruaris tempore raptim

(pauperies immunda domus procul absit). ego, utrum
naue ferar magna an parua, ferar unus et idem.   200
non agimur tumidis uelis aquilone secundo,
non tamen aduersis aetatem ducimus austris,
uiribus, ingenio, specie, uirtute, loco, re,
extremi primorum, extremis usque priores.

      non es auarus; abi. quid? cetera iam simul isto   205
cum uitio fugere? caret tibi pectus inani
ambitione? caret mortis formidine et ira?
somnia, terrores magicos, miracula, sagas,
nocturnos lemures portentaque Thessala rides?
natales grate numeras? ignoscis amicis?   210
lenior et melior fis accedente senecta?
quid te exempta leuat spinis de pluribus una?
uiuere si recte nescis, decede peritis.
lusisti satis, edisti satis atque bibisti:
tempus abire tibi est, ne potum largius aequo   215
rideat et pulset lasciua decentius aetas.

THE EPISTLE TO THE PISONES
(*'ARS POETICA'*)

I   A POEM'S COMPOSITION: GENERAL PRECEPTS

Harmony and the difficulty of achieving it

HVMANO capiti ceruicem pictor equinam
iungere si uelit et uarias inducere plumas,
undique collatis membris ut turpiter atrum
desinat in piscem mulier formosa superne,
spectatum admissi risum teneatis, amici?   5
credite, Pisones, isti tabulae fore librum
persimilem cuius, uelut aegri somnia, uanae
fingentur species, ut nec pes nec caput uni
reddatur formae. 'pictoribus atque poetis

quidlibet audendi semper fuit aequa potestas.'   10
scimus, et hanc ueniam petimusque damusque uicissim;
sed non ut placidis coeant immitia, non ut
serpentes auibus geminentur, tigribus agni.

    inceptis grauibus plerumque et magna professis
purpureus, late qui splendeat, unus et alter   15
adsuitur pannus, cum lucus et ara Dianae
et properantis aquae per amoenos ambitus agros,
aut flumen Rhenum aut pluuius describitur arcus.
sed nunc non erat his locus. et fortasse cupressum
scis simulare. quid hoc, si fractis enatat exspes   20
nauibus aere dato qui pingitur? amphora coepit
institui; currente rota cur urceus exit?
denique sit quiduis, simplex dumtaxat et unum.

    maxima pars uatum, pater et iuuenes patre digni,
decipimur specie recti. breuis esse laboro,   25
obscurus fio; sectantem leuia nerui
deficiunt animique; professus grandia turget;
serpit humi tutus nimium timidusque procellae;
qui uariare cupit rem prodigialiter unam,
delphinum siluis appingit, fluctibus aprum: 30
in uitium ducit culpae fuga, si caret arte.

    Aemilium circa ludum faber imus et ungues
exprimet et molles imitabitur aere capillos,
infelix operis summa, quia ponere totum
nesciet. hunc ego me, si quid componere curem,   35
non magis esse uelim quam naso uiuere prauo,
spectandum nigris oculis nigroque capillo.

Transition

sumite materiam uestris, qui scribitis, aequam
uiribus, et uersate diu, quid ferre recusent,
quid ualeant umeri. cui lecta potenter erit res,   40
nec facundia deseret hunc nec lucidus ordo.

Arrangement

ordinis haec uirtus erit et uenus, aut ego fallor,
ut iam nunc dicat iam nunc debentia dici,
pleraque differat et praesens in tempus omittat;
hoc amet, hoc spernat promissi carminis auctor.   45

Diction as affected by arrangement (46–8), by the age of words (48–72), by genre (73–98), by emotion and character (99–118)

in uerbis etiam tenuis cautusque serendis   46
dixeris egregie notum si callida uerbum
reddiderit iunctura nouum. si forte necesse est
indiciis monstrare recentibus abdita rerum,
fingere cinctutis non exaudita Cethegis   50
continget, dabiturque licentia sumpta pudenter;
et noua fictaque nuper habebunt uerba fidem, si
Graeco fonte cadent parce detorta. quid autem
Caecilio Plautoque dabit Romanus ademptum
Vergilio Varioque? ego cur, acquirere pauca   55
si possum, inuideor, cum lingua Catonis et Enni
sermonem patrium ditauerit et noua rerum
nomina protulerit? licuit semperque licebit
signatum praesente nota producere nomen.

  ut siluae foliis priuos mutantur in annos,   60
ut noua succrescunt nouus et decor enitet illis,   61a
prima cadunt, ita uerborum uetus interit aetas,   61b
et iuuenum ritu florent modo nata uigentque.
debemur morti nos nostraque; siue receptus
terra Neptunus classes aquilonibus arcet,
regium opus, sterilisue palus prius aptaque remis   65
uicinas urbes alit et graue sentit aratrum,
seu cursum mutauit iniquum frugibus amnis
doctus iter melius, mortalia facta peribunt,
nedum sermonum stet honos et gratia uiuax.

multa renascentur quae iam cecidere, cadentque   70
quae nunc sunt in honore uocabula, si uolet usus,
quem penes arbitrium est et ius et norma loquendi.

   res gestae regumque ducumque et tristia bella
quo scribi possent numero, monstrauit Homerus.
uersibus impariter iunctis querimonia primum,   75
post etiam inclusa est uoti sententia compos;
quis tamen exiguos elegos emiserit auctor,
grammatici certant et adhuc sub iudice lis est.
Archilochum proprio rabies armauit iambo;
hunc socci cepere pedem grandesque coturni   80
alternis aptum sermonibus et populares
uincentem strepitus et natum rebus agendis.
Musa dedit fidibus diuos puerosque deorum
et pugilem uictorem et equum certamine primum
et iuuenum curas et libera uina referre.   85
descriptas seruare uices operumque colores
cur ego si nequeo ignoroque poeta salutor?
cur nescire pudens praue quam discere malo?

   uersibus exponi tragicis res comica non uult;
indignatur item priuatis ac prope socco   90
dignis carminibus narrari cena Thyestae.
singula quaeque locum teneant sortita decentem.
interdum tamen et uocem comoedia tollit,
iratusque Chremes tumido delitigat ore
et tragicus plerumque dolet sermone pedestri,   95
Telephus et Peleus cum, pauper et exsul, uterque
proicit ampullas et sesquipedalia uerba,
si curat cor spectantis tetigisse querella.

   non satis est pulchra esse poemata; dulcia sunto,
et quocumque uolent animum auditoris agunto.   100
ut ridentibus arrident, ita flentibus adflent
humani uultus. si uis me flere, dolendum est
primum ipsi tibi; tum tua me infortunia laedent,
Telephe uel Peleu; male si mandata loqueris

aut dormitabo aut ridebo. tristia maestum   105
uultum uerba decent, iratum plena minarum,
ludentem lasciua, seuerum seria dictu.
format enim natura prius nos intus ad omnem
fortunarum habitum; iuuat aut impellit ad iram
aut ad humum maerore graui deducit et angit;   110
post effert animi motus interprete lingua.
si dicentis erunt fortunis absona dicta,
Romani tollent equites peditesque cachinnum.
    intererit multum diuusne loquatur an heros,
maturusne senex an adhuc florente iuuenta   115
feruidus, et matrona potens an sedula nutrix,
mercatorne uagus cultorne uirentis agelli,
Colchus an Assyrius, Thebis nutritus an Argis.

*The choice and presentation of material: characters (119–27),
characters and themes (128–30), treatment (131–5), organisation
(136–52)*

aut famam sequere aut sibi conuenientia finge,
scriptor. †honoratum† si forte reponis Achillem,   120
impiger, iracundus, inexorabilis, acer,
iura neget sibi nata, nihil non arroget armis.
sit Medea ferox inuictaque, flebilis Ino,
perfidus Ixion, Io uaga, tristis Orestes.
si quid inexpertum scaenae committis et audes   125
personam formare nouam, seruetur ad imum
qualis ab incepto processerit, et sibi constet.
difficile est proprie communia dicere; tuque
rectius Iliacum carmen deducis in actus
quam si proferres ignota indictaque primus.   130
publica materies priuati iuris erit, si
non circa uilem patulumque moraberis orbem,
nec uerbo uerbum curabis reddere fidus
interpres, nec desilies imitator in artum,

unde pedem proferre pudor uetet aut operis lex,   135
nec sic incipies ut scriptor cyclicus olim:
'fortunam Priami cantabo et nobile bellum.'
quid dignum tanto feret hic promissor hiatu?
parturient montes, nascetur ridiculus mus.
quanto rectius hic qui nil molitur inepte: 140
'dic mihi, Musa, uirum, captae post tempora Troiae
qui mores hominum multorum uidit et urbes.'
non fumum ex fulgore, sed ex fumo dare lucem
cogitat, ut speciosa dehinc miracula promat,
Antiphaten Scyllamque et cum Cyclope Charybdin.   145
nec reditum Diomedis ab interitu Meleagri,
nec gemino bellum Troianum orditur ab ouo;
semper ad euentum festinat et in medias res
non secus ac notas auditorem rapit, et quae
desperat tractata nitescere posse, relinquit,   150
atque ita mentitur, sic ueris falsa remiscet,
primo ne medium, medio ne discrepet imum.

II DRAMA: PRECEPTS AND HISTORY

Credibility of characters

tu quid ego et populus mecum desideret audi.
si plosoris eges aulaea manentis et usque
sessuri donec cantor 'uos plaudite' dicat,   155
aetatis cuiusque notandi sunt tibi mores,
mobilibusque decor naturis dandus et annis.
reddere qui uoces iam scit puer et pede certo
signat humum, gestit paribus colludere, et iram
concipit ac ponit temere et mutatur in horas.   160
imberbis iuuenis, tandem custode remoto,
gaudet equis canibusque et aprici gramine campi,
cereus in uitium flecti, monitoribus asper,
utilium tardus prouisor, prodigus aeris,

sublimis cupidusque et amata relinquere pernix.   165
conuersis studiis aetas animusque uirilis
quaerit opes et amicitias, inseruit honori,
commisisse cauet quod mox mutare laboret.
multa senem circumueniunt incommoda, uel quod
quaerit et inuentis miser abstinet ac timet uti,   170
uel quod res omnes timide gelideque ministrat,
dilator, spe lentus, iners, pauidusque futuri,
difficilis, querulus, laudator temporis acti
se puero, castigator censorque minorum.
multa ferunt anni uenientes commoda secum,   175
multa recedentes adimunt. ne forte seniles
mandentur iuueni partes pueroque uiriles,
semper in adiunctis aeuoque moraberis aptis.

Propriety of stage presentations

aut agitur res in scaenis aut acta refertur.
segnius irritant animos demissa per aurem,   180
quam quae sunt oculis subiecta fidelibus et quae
ipse sibi tradit spectator. non tamen intus
digna geri promes in scaenam, multaque tolles
ex oculis quae mox narret facundia praesens;
ne pueros coram populo Medea trucidet,   185
aut humana palam coquat exta nefarius Atreus,
aut in auem Procne uertatur, Cadmus in anguem.
quodcumque ostendis mihi sic, incredulus odi.

Precepts on dramaturgy

neue minor neu sit quinto productior actu
fabula, quae posci uult et spectanda reponi.   190
nec deus intersit, nisi dignus uindice nodus
inciderit; nec quarta loqui persona laboret.
   actoris partes chorus officiumque uirile

defendat, neu quid medios intercinat actus
quod non proposito conducat et haereat apte.   195
ille bonis faueatque et consilietur amice,
et regat iratos et amet †peccare timentes†;
ille dapes laudet mensae breuis, ille salubrem
iustitiam legesque et apertis otia portis;
ille tegat commissa, deosque precetur et oret,   200
ut redeat miseris, abeat fortuna superbis.

The music of drama

tibia non ut nunc orichalco uincta tubaeque
aemula, sed tenuis simplexque foramine pauco
adspirare et adesse choris erat utilis atque
nondum spissa nimis complere sedilia flatu;   205
quo sane populus numerabilis, utpote paruus,
et frugi castusque uerecundusque coibat.
postquam coepit agros extendere uictor et urbem
latior amplecti murus uinoque diurno
placari Genius festis impune diebus,   210
accessit numerisque modisque licentia maior.
indoctus quid enim saperet liberque laborum
rusticus urbano confusus, turpis honesto?
sic priscae motumque et luxuriem addidit arti
tibicen traxitque uagus per pulpita uestem;   215
sic etiam fidibus uoces creuere seueris,
et tulit eloquium insolitum facundia praeceps,
utiliumque sagax rerum et diuina futuri
sortilegis non discrepuit sententia Delphis.

Satyr drama

carmine qui tragico uilem certauit ob hircum,   220
mox etiam agrestes Satyros nudauit, et asper
incolumi grauitate iocum temptauit, eo quod

illecebris erat et grata nouitate morandus
spectator, functusque sacris et potus et exlex.
uerum ita risores, ita commendare dicaces   225
conueniet Satyros, ita uertere seria ludo,
ne quicumque deus, quicumque adhibebitur heros,
regali conspectus in auro nuper et ostro,
migret in obscuras humili sermone tabernas,
aut, dum uitat humum, nubes et inania captet.   230
effutire leues indigna Tragoedia uersus,
ut festis matrona moueri iussa diebus,
intererit Satyris paulum pudibunda proteruis.
non ego inornata et dominantia nomina solum
uerbaque, Pisones, Satyrorum scriptor amabo;   235
nec sic enitar tragico differre colori,
ut nihil intersit Dauusne loquatur et audax
Pythias emuncto lucrata Simone talentum,
an custos famulusque dei Silenus alumni.
ex noto fictum carmen sequar, ut sibi quiuis   240
speret idem, sudet multum frustraque laboret
ausus idem: tantum series iuncturaque pollet,
tantum de medio sumptis accedit honoris.
siluis deducti caueant, me iudice, Fauni
ne uelut innati triuiis ac paene forenses   245
aut nimium teneris iuuenentur uersibus umquam,
aut immunda crepent ignominiosaque dicta.
offenduntur enim quibus est equus et pater et res,
nec, si quid fricti ciceris probat et nucis emptor,
aequis accipiunt animis donantue corona.   250

The iambic metre in drama

syllaba longa breui subiecta uocatur iambus,
pes citus; unde etiam trimetris accrescere iussit
nomen iambeis, cum senos redderet ictus

primus ad extremum similis sibi. †non ita pridem†
tardior ut paulo grauiorque ueniret ad aures,   255
spondeos stabiles in iura paterna recepit
commodus et patiens, non ut de sede secunda
cederet aut quarta socialiter. hic et in Acci
nobilibus trimetris apparet rarus, et Enni
in scaenam missos cum magno pondere uersus   260
aut operae celeris nimium curaque carentis
aut ignoratae premit artis crimine turpi.

The need to study Greek dramatic models

non quiuis uidet immodulata poemata iudex,
et data Romanis uenia est indigna poetis.
idcircone uager scribamque licenter? an omnes   265
uisuros peccata putem mea, tutus et intra
spem ueniae cautus? uitaui denique culpam,
non laudem merui. uos exemplaria Graeca
nocturna uersate manu, uersate diurna.
at uestri proaui Plautinos et numeros et   270
laudauere sales: nimium patienter utrumque,
ne dicam stulte, mirati, si modo ego et uos
scimus inurbanum lepido seponere dicto
legitimumque sonum digitis callemus et aure.

Survey of Greek drama

ignotum tragicae genus inuenisse camenae   275
dicitur et plaustris uexisse poemata Thespis,
quae canerent agerentque peruncti faecibus ora.
post hunc personae pallaeque repertor honestae
Aeschylus et modicis instrauit pulpita tignis
et docuit magnumque loqui nitique coturno.   280
successit uetus his comoedia, non sine multa

laude. sed in uitium libertas excidit et uim
dignam lege regi; lex est accepta chorusque
turpiter obticuit sublato iure nocendi.

Roman drama: its achievements and shortcomings

nil intemptatum nostri liquere poetae,   285
nec minimum meruere decus uestigia Graeca
ausi deserere et celebrare domestica facta,
uel qui praetextas uel qui docuere togatas.
nec uirtute foret clarisque potentius armis
quam lingua Latium, si non offenderet unum   290
quemque poetarum limae labor et mora. uos, o
Pompilius sanguis, carmen reprehendite quod non
multa dies et multa litura coercuit atque
praesectum deciens non castigauit ad unguem.

III   THE POET: HIS AIMS AND HIS CALLING

Mad poet and sane critic

ingenium misera quia fortunatius arte   295
credit et excludit sanos Helicone poetas
Democritus, bona pars non ungues ponere curat,
non barbam, secreta petit loca, balnea uitat.
nanciscetur enim pretium nomenque poetae,
si tribus Anticyris caput insanabile numquam   300
tonsori Licino commiserit. o ego laeuus,
qui purgor bilem sub uerni temporis horam;
non alius faceret meliora poemata. uerum
nil tanti est. ergo fungar uice cotis, acutum
reddere quae ferrum ualet exsors ipsa secandi.   305
munus et officium nil scribens ipse docebo,
unde parentur opes, quid alat formetque poetam,
quid deceat, quid non, quo uirtus, quo ferat error.

Duty and character

scribendi recte sapere est et principium et fons.
rem tibi Socraticae poterunt ostendere chartae,   310
uerbaque prouisam rem non inuita sequentur.
qui didicit patriae quid debeat et quid amicis,
quo sit amore parens, quo frater amandus et hospes,
quod sit conscripti, quod iudicis officium, quae
partes in bellum missi ducis, ille profecto   315
reddere personae scit conuenientia cuique.
respicere exemplar uitae morumque iubebo
doctum imitatorem et uiuas hinc ducere uoces.
interdum speciosa locis morataque recte
fabula nullius ueneris, sine pondere et arte,   320
ualdius oblectat populum meliusque moratur
quam uersus inopes rerum nugaeque canorae.

The Greeks aimed at glory, the Romans aim at wealth

Grais ingenium, Grais dedit ore rotundo
Musa loqui, praeter laudem nullius auaris.
Romani pueri longis rationibus assem   325
discunt in partes centum diducere. 'dicat
filius Albini: si de quincunce remota est
uncia, quid superat? poteras dixisse.' 'triens.' 'eu.
rem poteris seruare tuam. redit uncia, quid fit?'
'semis.' an haec animos aerugo et cura peculi   330
cum semel imbuerit, speremus carmina fingi
posse linenda cedro et leui seruanda cupresso?

Poets wish to be of service, or to please, or both

aut prodesse uolunt aut delectare poetae
aut simul et iucunda et idonea dicere uitae.
quidquid praecipies esto breuis, ut cito dicta   335

percipiant animi dociles teneantque fideles;
omne superuacuum pleno de pectore manat.
ficta uoluptatis causa sint proxima ueris,
ne quodcumque uelit poscat sibi fabula credi,
neu pransae Lamiae uiuum puerum extrahat aluo.   340
centuriae seniorum agitant expertia frugis,
celsi praetereunt austera poemata Ramnes;
omne tulit punctum qui miscuit utile dulci,
lectorem delectando pariterque monendo.
hic meret aera liber Sosiis, hic et mare transit   345
et longum noto scriptori prorogat aeuum.

Tolerance and its limits

sunt delicta tamen quibus ignouisse uelimus.
nam neque chorda sonum reddit quem uult manus et mens
[poscentique grauem persaepe remittit acutum]
nec semper feriet quodcumque minabitur arcus.   350
uerum ubi plura nitent in carmine, non ego paucis
offendar maculis, quas aut incuria fudit
aut humana parum cauit natura. quid ergo est?
ut scriptor si peccat idem librarius usque,
quamuis est monitus, uenia caret; ut citharoedus   355
ridetur chorda qui semper oberrat eadem;
sic mihi qui multum cessat fit Choerilus ille,
quem bis terue bonum cum risu miror; et idem
indignor quandoque bonus dormitat Homerus;
uerum operi longo fas est obrepere somnum.   360

Poems and pictures

ut pictura, poesis: erit quae, si propius stes,
te capiat magis, et quaedam, si longius abstes;
haec amat obscurum, uolet haec sub luce uideri,
iudicis argutum quae non formidat acumen;
haec placuit semel, haec deciens repetita placebit.   365

The poet's is a demanding calling

o maior iuuenum, quamuis et uoce paterna
fingeris ad rectum et per te sapis, hoc tibi dictum
tolle memor, certis medium et tolerabile rebus
recte concedi. consultus iuris et actor
causarum mediocris abest uirtute diserti   370
Messallae nec scit quantum Cascellius Aulus,
sed tamen in pretio est: mediocribus esse poetis
non homines, non di, non concessere columnae.
ut gratas inter mensas symphonia discors
et crassum unguentum et Sardo cum melle papauer   375
offendunt, poterat duci quia cena sine istis,
sic animis natum inuentumque poema iuuandis,
si paulum summo decessit, uergit ad imum.

    ludere qui nescit, campestribus abstinet armis,
indoctusque pilae disciue trochiue quiescit,   380
ne spissae risum tollant impune coronae:
qui nescit uersus tamen audet fingere. quidni?
liber et ingenuus, praesertim census equestrem
summam nummorum, uitioque remotus ab omni.

    tu nihil inuita dices faciesue Minerua: 385
id tibi iudicium est, ea mens. si quid tamen olim
scripseris, in Maeci descendat iudicis aures
et patris et nostras, nonumque prematur in annum,
membranis intus positis; delere licebit
quod non edideris, nescit uox missa reuerti.   390

The poet's is a noble calling

siluestres homines sacer interpresque deorum
caedibus et uictu foedo deterruit Orpheus,
dictus ob hoc lenire tigris rabidosque leones;
dictus et Amphion, Thebanae conditor urbis,
saxa mouere sono testudinis et prece blanda   395

ducere quo uellet. fuit haec sapientia quondam,
publica priuatis secernere, sacra profanis,
concubitu prohibere uago, dare iura maritis,
oppida moliri, leges incidere ligno.
sic honor et nomen diuinis uatibus atque   400
carminibus uenit. post hos insignis Homerus
Tyrtaeusque mares animos in Martia bella
uersibus exacuit. dictae per carmina sortes,
et uitae monstrata uia est, et gratia regum
Pieriis temptata modis, ludusque repertus   405
et longorum operum finis; ne forte pudori
sit tibi Musa lyrae sollers et cantor Apollo.

*The poet's art must be accompanied by talent; and it requires long
and arduous training*

natura fieret laudabile carmen an arte
quaesitum est. ego nec studium sine diuite uena
nec rude quid possit uideo ingenium; alterius sic   410
altera poscit opem res et coniurat amice.
qui studet optatam cursu contingere metam
multa tulit fecitque puer, sudauit et alsit,
abstinuit uenere et uino; qui Pythia cantat
tibicen, didicit prius extimuitque magistrum.   415
nec satis est dixisse 'ego mira poemata pango,
occupet extremum scabies; mihi turpe relinqui est,
et quod non didici sane nescire fateri.'

The poet needs candid criticism

ut praeco, ad merces turbam qui cogit emendas,
adsentatores iubet ad lucrum ire poeta   420
diues agris, diues positis in faenore nummis.
si uero est unctum qui recte ponere possit
et spondere leui pro paupere et eripere artis

litibus implicitum, mirabor si sciet inter-
noscere mendacem uerumque beatus amicum.   425
tu seu donaris seu quid donare uoles cui,
nolito ad uersus tibi factos ducere plenum
laetitiae; clamabit enim 'pulchre, bene, recte',
pallescet super his, etiam stillabit amicis
ex oculis rorem, saliet, tundet pede terram.   430
ut qui conducti plorant in funere dicunt
et faciunt prope plura dolentibus ex animo, sic
derisor uero plus laudatore mouetur.
reges dicuntur multis urgere culillis
et torquere mero quem perspexisse laborent,   435
an sit amicitia dignus; si carmina condes,
numquam te fallent animi sub uulpe latentes.

   Quintilio si quid recitares, 'corrige sodes
hoc' aiebat 'et hoc'; melius te posse negares,
bis terque expertum frustra, delere iubebat   440
et male tornatos incudi reddere uersus.
si defendere delictum quam uertere malles,
nullum ultra uerbum aut operam insumebat inanem,
quin sine riuali teque et tua solus amares.
uir bonus et prudens uersus reprehendet inertes,   445
culpabit duros, incomptis allinet atrum
transuerso calamo signum, ambitiosa recidet
ornamenta, parum claris lucem dare coget,
arguet ambigue dictum, mutanda notabit;
fiet Aristarchus, nec dicet 'cur ego amicum   450
offendam in nugis?' hae nugae seria ducent
in mala derisum semel exceptumque sinistre.

Caricature of the mad poet

ut mala quem scabies aut morbus regius urget
aut fanaticus error et iracunda Diana,
uesanum tetigisse timent fugiuntque poetam   455

qui sapiunt; agitant pueri incautique sequuntur.
hic, dum sublimis uersus ructatur et errat,
si ueluti merulis intentus decidit auceps
in puteum foueamue, licet 'succurrite' longum
clamet 'io ciues', non sit qui tollere curet.   460
si curet quis opem ferre et demittere funem,
'qui scis an prudens huc se proiecerit atque
seruari nolit?' dicam, Siculique poetae
narrabo interitum: deus immortalis haberi
dum cupit Empedocles, ardentem frigidus Aetnam   465
insiluit. sit ius liceatque perire poetis;
inuitum qui seruat idem facit occidenti.
nec semel hoc fecit, nec si retractus erit iam
fiet homo et ponet famosae mortis amorem.
nec satis apparet cur uersus factitet, utrum   470
minxerit in patrios cineres, an triste bidental
mouerit, incestus: certe furit, ac uelut ursus,
obiectos caueae ualuit si frangere clatros,
indoctum doctumque fugat recitator acerbus;
quem uero arripuit, tenet occiditque legendo,   475
non missura cutem nisi plena cruoris hirudo.

COMMENTARY

The Epistle to Augustus (*Epistles* 2.1)

1 sustineas: the *negotia* are a kind of burden.

solus: the final position adds emphasis. No despot, however bene-
volent, is flattered by the suggestion that someone else has been help-
ing him; so it is a mistake to look for an allusion to the death of
Augustus' general Agrippa in 12 B.C.

2–3 These lines illustrate the many great administrative burdens.
Three operations are listed – without connectives, just as Augustus
himself often catalogues his achievements in the *Res Gestae*; e.g. *pa-
triciorum numerum auxi ... senatum ter legi ... censum ... egi ... lustrum
...feci* (8).

armis tuteris: the material cited in *OLD* suggests that *tutari* had
earnest, even solemn, overtones; e.g. *di penates ... uobis mando meum
parentum rem bene ut tutemini* (Plaut. *Merc.* 835). H. was enough of a
realist to recognise that the blessings of the *pax Augusta* depended on
military power; cf. *C.* 4.5.25–32; 15.17–20.

moribus ornes, | legibus emendes 'equip with morals, improve
with laws'. While *mos* is sometimes thought of as a traditional, un-
written, code of behaviour as distinct from *lex*, here the two concepts
are combined; for the *mores* which H. has in mind are those which
Augustus was trying to promote by the *lex Iulia de maritandis ordinibus*
and the *lex Iulia de adulteriis coercendis* (18 B.C.); see *CAH* x 443–52. In
C. 3.24.33–6 H. does distinguish *mores* from *leges*, but he implies that
they should support each other: *quid tristes querimoniae, | si non supplicio
culpa reciditur, | quid leges sine moribus | uanae proficiunt ...?* Cf. *C.* 4.5.22
mos et lex maculosum edomuit nefas.

3–4 'I would damage the public interest if I wasted your time with a
lengthy discourse.'

5 Hercules, Castor and Pollux, Aesculapius, Bacchus, and Romulus
are mentioned as deified heroes in Cic. *DND* 2.62; cf. Hor. *C.* 3.3.9–
16. Caesar (4), i.e. Augustus, the second founder, is followed immediately by the original founder, Romulus.

6 post ingentia facta 'after their mighty acts', a phrase explained in the next two lines.

recepti: the participle has a concessive force: 'though welcomed'.

7–9 'While they dwelt . . . and served . . . brought to an end . . . distributed . . . and founded . . . they complained bitterly . . . ' The activities mentioned all had parallels in the career of Augustus; see, e.g., *Res Gestae* 3, 16, 18.

colunt is used in two different senses, as indicated in the preceding note.

plorauere: in one or more passages of Latin literature, now lost, a hero may have complained of human ingratitude. But H. may be inventing.

10–11 Being the result of Jupiter's union with Alcmena, Hercules was hated by Juno. She drove him to murder his wife Megara and his children in a fit of madness. Seeking to make atonement, Hercules went to Delphi, where he was told that if he performed the tasks set by Eurystheus of Tiryns he would eventually become immortal. The twelve labours are listed by Rose 211–16. One was the destruction of the Hydra, a many-headed snake that dwelt in the swamps of Lerna in the territory of Argos. Hercules smashed the heads with his club; hence *contudit* (10). (In the end, however, he had to call for help on Iolaus, who burned the roots of each head; see Apollodorus 2.5.2.)

fatali 'assigned by fate'.

12 supremo fine 'only at last by death'; cf. *E.* 2.2.173 *morte suprema.*

domari: for the sense of 'destroy', rather than 'tame', cf. *Orion . . . uirginea domitus sagitta* (*C.* 3.4.71–2).

13 urit . . . fulgore 'sears with his fiery brilliance'.
praegrauat 'oppresses with his weight'.
artes 'talents'.

14 exstinctus continues the metaphor of *urit.*

15 praesenti tibi 'to you [on the other hand] while you are still with us'.
maturos 'in good time'.
largimur 'we gladly bestow'.
honores: divine honours, one of which is mentioned in 16.

16 Juvenal (3.144–5) uses the construction *iurare aras*, 'to swear on the altars' (cf. our swearing on the Bible); 'Tibullus' (4.13.15) says *Iunonis numina iuro*, 'I swear by Juno's divinity'. H. here combines both expressions 'altars on which oaths can be sworn by your divinity'. The altars are those erected in the crossroads shrines, with statues of the *Lares Augusti* and the *Genius Augusti*. See Taylor 185–6. By now Augustus had obtained 'quasi-divine status' (B. III 55); he was not officially consecrated as a god until after his death in A.D. 14.

17 nil oriturum ... nil ortum: the repetition, without connective, adds emphasis.

   alias 'at any other time' – in the future with *oriturum*, in the past with *ortum*.

   fatentes 'acknowledging', as one acknowledges a truth.

18 tuus hic populus 'this people of yours'. After identifying himself with it (*largimur, ponimus*), H. now prepares to dissociate himself from it.

   uno: if this is neuter ('in this one respect'), it should be followed by a comma; 19 is then in apposition to *uno* ('i.e., in preferring'), and *cetera* is contrasted with it. But what does *uno* emphasise? That this is the only matter in which the people is *sapiens* and *iustus*? Or that Augustus is pre-eminent over earlier heroes? The first is unlikely, especially in view of 63 (the masses are sometimes right, sometimes wrong). The complimentary context supports the second idea. So *uno* is masc. and goes with *te* (19) 'in preferring you alone'.

19 nostris ducibus: i.e. Roman leaders, starting with Romulus.

21–2 terris semota ... | temporibus defuncta: in English the reverse order would be more natural, but Latin often has a less 'linear' structure; cf. 95. The neut. pl. *quae semota* is prepared for by *nil* (17) and *cetera* (20). See further on *cum* (25) and *in* (31).

23–7 The construction is *sic fautor ueterum, ut* [result] *dictitet Musas locutas* [*esse*] *tabulas ... foedera ... libros ... uolumina.*

23–4 The Twelve Tables were drawn up in two stages, each presided over by a board of ten. The whole set was approved in 449 B.C. For the text see *ROL* III 424–514.

25   Gabiis: supply *cum* from the next phrase. For the postponement of the prep. cf. *in* (31). Dionysius of Halicarnassus (in Rome from *c.* 30 B.C.) says he saw in the temple of Jupiter Fidius on the Quirinal a treaty made by Tarquinius Superbus with Gabii, an old town of Latium; it was written on an ox-hide shield (*Ant. Rom.* 4.58.4; cf. Liv. 1.54.10, with Ogilvie's note). The authenticity of the shield is highly doubtful, but there is no doubt about the peaceful absorption of Gabii by Rome, which took place in the 6th cent. The first treaty with the Sabines was earlier still; see Liv. 1.13.4–8.

aequata 'made on equal terms'; probably a new Horatian usage based on the phrase *foedus aequum*, a treaty between equals; *OLD foedus* 1b.

26   pontificum libros: books containing records and regulations connected with religious ritual.

uolumina uatum 'scrolls of seers' (Loeb). By way of illustration Porph. mentions the prophecies of a certain Marcius (Liv. 25.12.3; Plin. *NH* 7.119); Cicero speaks of the brothers Marcii (*De div.* 1.89). The prophecies were written in Saturnians, allegedly an old Italic metre; and according to Livy they foretold the disaster of Cannae.

27   dictitet: *dictito* is a frequentative verb indicating repeated action; hence 'insists'.

Albano ... in monte: a rocky mountain in Latium, E. of the Alban lake. On its western slopes was the old Alba Longa; on its summit stood the temple of *Iuppiter Latiaris.* In April this was the site of the great festival of the Latin League (Scullard 111–15). It was therefore a holy place for all things Latin, and a suitable Roman counterpart of the Greek Helicon or Parnassus.

Musas ... locutas: what the Muses spoke was the product of pure inspiration; cf. Gellius, *NA* 1.24.2 (Naevius' epitaph), Quint. *IO* 10.1.99 (on Plautus). The lines are, of course, a sarcastic attack on literary chauvinism.

28–33 Stripped of its irony, the argument is as follows: in Greek literature the oldest writing in every genre is the best; the same is not true of Roman literature. False comparisons lead to absurd conclusions. Moreover, just because the Romans are world conquerors, it does not follow that they must be better than the Greeks at painting, music, and wrestling.

29   uel optima 'quite the best'; *OLD uel* 5c.

29–30   If Roman writers are weighed in the same balance (i.e. assessed in the same terms), there is no reason why we should say much (i.e. discussion is pointless). For the subjunctive of tendency, see G–L 631.2.

31   The construction is *in olea nil duri est intra; in nuce nil duri est extra.* For the postponement of *in* cf. *quae nemora aut quos agor in specus* (*C.* 3.25.2), and see on 25 above.

The MSS read *oleam.* Ben., to whom the emendation is due, wrote out the construction required by the text as transmitted (*nil duri est intra oleam, nihil extra in nuce*), and then commented on the horrid roughness (*tam foedam porriginem*) of having *intra* as a preposition and *extra* as an adverb.

32–3   H. has selected characteristically Greek arts in which the Romans took no pride; the note of condescension is especially clear in the Greek importation *psallimus.*

Achiuis ... unctis: *Achiuis,* usually associated with Homer's Greeks, has a mock heroic nuance; *unctis,* coming so soon after *luctamur,* recalls the wrestler's practice of putting oil on his body. (H. knew that conservative Romans believed that the nudity of the *gymnasia* encouraged homosexuality (Cic. *Tusc.* 4.70 and Crowther). The adj. may also carry the more general notion of pleasure-loving prosperity.

34   dies 'the passage of time'; *OLD dies* 10.

35   pretium 'value'.

quotus ... annus: the hypothetical answer would have been an ordinal, e.g., fiftieth. Hence 'which year?'

arroget 'confers', 'bestows'.

38   finis 'limit', here a minimum figure.

39   A voice proposes that anyone a hundred years dead is old and respectable. The anonymous interlocutor is a familiar device in H.'s *Satires.*

40   minor ... anno: i.e. who has died less than a century ago by a month or a year; the abls. indicate measure of difference (G–L 403).

uel 'or even'.

41   ueteresne poetas: understand *inter.*

42   quos: understand *inter.*

respuat 'should reject'; perhaps best classified as a subjunctive of design (G–L 630). Of the other readings, *respuet* clashes with *praesens,* and *respuit* with *postera.*

43–4 The anonymous interlocutor, who reveals himself as obtuse and literal-minded, answers.

honeste 'properly'.

44 The abls. indicate measure of difference (G–L 403), as in 40.

45–7 The horse's tail and the dwindling pile are both illustrations of the same logical point, viz. the problem of drawing the line. When the hairs of a tail are plucked out one by one, there comes a point where it ceases to be a tail. But when is that point reached? And does the difference between tail and non-tail depend on a single hair? Similarly, if pebbles are successively removed from a pile, when does the pile cease to exist? (See Cic. *Acad.* 2.49 with Reid's note.) The argument, which is called a 'sorites' (Gk 'pile'), is used today by anti-abortionists against their opponents. 'Working backwards in time, when is one entitled to say that a baby is not a human being?'

45   utor permisso 'I take advantage of your concession'.

permisso: neut. sing. of the perf. participle used as a noun (*permissum*) – a rare occurrence; *OLD permitto* 6b quotes only this and Curtius 10.5.32 (*ex permisso uoluptas*), apart from the *Digest.*

46   unum: understand *annum.*

et item: though perfectly clear Latin, this is a far less common expression than the variant *etiam,* and should therefore be given preference; cf. *asperitas autem uocis fit ab asperitate | principiorum et item leuor leuore creatur* (Lucr. *DRN* 4.542–3). No argument can be based on *adde etiam unum, | unum etiam* (Pers. 6.58–9); for while Persius had H.'s passage in mind, he could have introduced *etiam* as one of his own variations.

47   dum cadat: for *dum* = 'until' with the subjunctive when an idea of purpose is involved, see G–L 572, Wo. 224.

elusus ratione ruentis acerui 'foiled by the argument of the dwindling pile'. Donatus on Ter. *Eun.* 55 says *eludere proprie gladiatorum* *est, cum uicerint.* This, supported by *cadat*, makes it certain that H. is using a metaphor from the arena. Whether there is an intentional play between *cadat* and *ruentis* cannot be decided. Admirers of H. will incline to scepticism.

48 redit ad fastos 'has recourse to the historical records', i.e. to ascertain a writer's dates. The MSS have both *ad* and *in*. There is good support for *ad* in *ad Ianum redeat qui quaerit Agonia quid sit* (Ov. *Fast.* 5.721), where the manuscript tradition is not in doubt; no satisfactory parallel has been adduced for *in fastos redire.* The form *fastūs* is also possible, but the second declension form is better attested here.

uirtutem 'quality'.

49 quod Libitina sacrauit 'what Libitina has hallowed'. Libitina was the Roman goddess of burials. Her temple contained not only records of burials but also undertakers' equipment, including reusable biers.

50 Ennius: Quintus Ennius was born at Rudiae in Calabria in 239 B.C. After serving for a time in the Roman army, he was brought to Rome by M. Porcius Cato in 204. He wrote in several genres, including tragedy and comedy, but his greatest work was the *Annals*, a year-by-year account of Rome's history in 18 books of hexameters.

et sapiens et fortis et alter Homerus: these names are attached to Ennius (i) as a poet of wide-ranging ethical wisdom, (ii) as an epic poet, by the convention which credits epic poets with the valour of their heroes (cf. *S.* 1.10.43–4), and (iii) because he was thought of as the Roman counterpart of Homer (see further below, 51–2n.).

51 ut critici dicunt: the critics are not named, but one may safely assume that H. was thinking mainly of M. Terentius Varro, who had died in 27 B.C. at the age of 90. We know that Varro cited the *Iliad* and the *Annals* as examples of *poesis* (*Sat. Menipp.* 'Parmeno' 398 Astbury); which shows that he put Ennius at least in the same class as Homer, even if he did not go so far as to claim equality for him.

Is H. contesting the critics' judgement? He would probably have accepted *sapiens* and *fortis*; for he respected Ennius, as may be seen from *S.* 1.4.60–2; *C.* 4.8.13–20; and *AP* 57–8. Even in the ironical context of *E.* 1.19 he mentions Ennius immediately after Homer as an allegedly wine-loving poet (6–7). Nevertheless, he is here writing in a polemical context. In appealing for a fairer attitude to modern writers, H. claims that in *stylistic* terms (as distinct from spirit) Ennius and the earlier poets have been over-valued. So his respect stopped well short of regarding Ennius as *alter Homerus*.

51–2 †leuiter† curare uidetur ... somnia Pythagorea: since 18, H. has been describing the Roman reader as a *fautor ueterum* (23). The same thought continues in *adeo sanctum est uetus omne poema* (54), and in *habet hos numeratque poetas* etc. (61–2). What is said of Ennius and Naevius ought, therefore, to form part of this sequence. (The explicit *criticism* of the public's attitude and of the older poets does not begin until *est ubi peccat* in 63.) There is no problem about the sentence on Naevius (53–4), provided we take *non* = *nonne*, as Ben. advocated, and punctuate with a question-mark. That is, in 53–4, H. is talking, with some indignation, of Naevius' standing.

There is, however, a problem with the lines on Ennius. If H. had said, in the same tone of irritation, 'Ennius' claims and Pythagorean dream appear to be amply vindicated', all would be well. But, in spite of Porph.'s gloss (*securus iam de prouentu suae laudis*), it does not seem possible to coax this meaning, or its equivalent, from the Latin.

The natural sense is '[To judge from his clumsy style] Ennius appears to have little concern as to whether his claims and Pythagorean dream are vindicated.' That was the interpretation of ps.-Acr. But, as we have just seen, that does not fit the sequence of thought.

In this dilemma we need either a new interpretation or a conjecture. White (234) has suggested 'Ennius ... seems frivolous for worrying about the upshot of his pronouncements and Pythagorean dreams.' Shackleton Bailey (76–8) has proposed *Ennius ... uiget et curare uidetur* etc., 'Ennius ... is all the rage and held to take good care how his promises and Pythagorean dreams turn out.' Since neither of these ideas seems quite satisfactory, the text has been printed with daggers, as in SB.

promissa ... et somnia Pythagorea may be a hendiadys ('the expectations raised by his Pythagorean dream'). If the two ideas are separate, they go closely together. The Pythagorean dream came in Book 1 of the *Annals* (see below); therefore the *promissa* probably refer to the confident prediction made in the same book: *perque Italos populos terrasque poemata nostra* | *... clara cluebunt* (*ROL* 1 2–3; Skutsch 12. The point is not affected by the uncertainty of the text.). Some scholars refer to the later boasts in Book 7: *scripsere alii rem* etc. (*ROL* I 231–5; Skutsch 206–10).

somnia Pythagorea: at the beginning of the *Annals* Ennius told how Homer had appeared to him in a dream on the Mountain of the Muses. (He probably did not specify Helicon or Parnassus.) As part of his exposition of the *rerum natura* (Lucr. *DRN* 1.126) Homer declared that by the process of transmigration his soul had passed into Ennius' body (Porph. on *E*. 2.1.51). This story implied that Ennius was an *alter Homerus* in a much more special sense; it might also have implied a claim to poetic equality (or near equality). Lucilius, the second-century satirist, apparently referred to Ennius as a *Homerus alter*. Although Lucilius had a good deal of respect for Ennius' achievement as a pioneer, he did not hesitate to make fun of his stylistic lapses (Hor. *S*. 1.10.54); and so *Homerus alter* was probably a satirical reference to Ennius' dream. The irony does not come through clearly in the passage of Jerome which contains the information: *poeta sublimis, non Homerus alter, ut Lucilius de Ennio suspicatur, sed primus Homerus apud Latinos* (*ROL* III 130). Here Jerome refuses to regard Ennius as the poetic equal of Homer, but grants that he is the nearest thing to him in Roman literature. See further on 58 below.

Pythagoras, who was born in Samos, emigrated to Croton in S. Italy about 531 B.C. Apart from his mathematical studies, he taught metempsychosis (the transmigration of souls), according to which the soul is confined within a succession of earthly bodies (whether plant, animal, or human) until it achieves release by the cultivation of purity. See Guthrie I 146ff. Pythagorean ideas were well known both in Ennius' native district and in Rome.

53–4 Even more absurd, *Naevius* is still quite widely read! Gnaeus Naevius, who came from the neighbourhood of Capua, served in the first Punic war (264–241 B.C.). He was therefore twenty years or more older than Ennius. He started his career by writing tragedies and comedies; but H. is thinking of his last work, the *Bellum Punicum*, written in Saturnians and containing some mythological material. This was the first Roman epic, and although even Ennius in his day affected to despise it (*ROL* I frs. 231–5), it marked an important step in the development of Latin poetry.

in manibus ... et mentibus: i.e. he is read and known by heart.

non = *nonne*, as Ben. saw.

paene recens 'almost [as if] contemporary'.

55   ambigitur 'there is a dispute'.

prior: i.e. in worth.

aufert 'carries off', as if it were a kind of prize.

56   Pacuuius: Ennius' nephew, M. Pacuvius, was born in Brundisium in 220 B.C. and died about 130. He wrote tragedies on Greek themes, of which over a dozen titles are known; see *ROL* II. We are not in a position to assess the significance of the epithet *doctus*; nor, it seems, was Quintilian: *Pacuuium uideri doctiorem qui esse docti adfectant uolunt* (*IO* 10.1.97). Like H., Quintilian refers to the comparison between Pacuvius and Accius, which must have been traditional.

Accius: L. Accius was born at Pisaurum in Umbria in 170 B.C. He wrote more than forty tragedies and lived beyond the age of 80; see *ROL* II.

alti: referring to his elevated and passionate style. The word *senis* should be supplied again with *alti*. Although both Pacuvius and Accius lived long lives, that is not the point of *senis*. The word indicates that for someone writing in the first cent. B.C. both men lived a long time ago. (The fact that Accius was born half a century after Pacuvius is irrelevant.) For *senex* in this sense see *S.* 2.1.34 (Lucilius) and Persius 1.124 (Aristophanes).

It turns out, then, that when the critics in question debate whether Pacuvius is superior to Accius, or vice versa, no straight answer is given. We might see this as a reluctance to pronounce simplistic judgements; but that is not H.'s point. According to him, the critics hand out prizes all round because they cannot bear to admit that any old poet is inferior; each must be excellent in his own way. The same attitude is seen in the comparison of Caecilius and Terence; see further on 59 below.

57   Afrani: L. Afranius, born *c.* 150 B.C., composed *togatae*, 'comedies dressed in the *toga*', i.e. realistic plays about Italian life; see Beare, chap. 15 and the Budé edn of Daviault. These were distinguished from 'comedies dressed in the Greek *pallium*' (*palliatae*), as written by Plautus and Terence. There is therefore a word-play on *toga*.

conuenisse Menandro: in order to take account of the poets' relative periods this has to be translated rather loosely 'was the same
size as Menander's'. According to Macrobius (*Sat.* 6.1.4), Afranius
admitted that he borrowed what suited him (*conueniret quod mihi*) from
Menander and others. It makes little sense, however, to imagine that
H. is referring to that expression.

Menander, who was born in 342/1 B.C. and died *c.* 290, was the
leading representative of the Greek New Comedy; see the edition by
F. H. Sandbach (Oxford 1973) and the new Loeb edition by W. G.
Arnott (1979).

58 Plautus: born in Umbria, Plautus died some time after 184 B.C.
Varro compiled a list of 21 comedies which were generally agreed to
be authentic; many others were attributed to him. In adapting his
Greek originals, Plautus introduced Roman material, expanded the
roles of slave and parasite, and contributed elaborate lyrical passages
(*cantica*) in various metres.

ad exemplar 'following the tradition of'.

properare 'moves briskly', a reference to the various kinds of pace
found in comedy.

Epicharmi: Epicharmus was a Sicilian who wrote Greek comedies
in the late 6th and early 5th cent. B.C. For a survey of his varied style
and subject-matter, see Lesky (1) 237–40.

Lines 57 and 58 illustrate, in an intentionally glib form, the habit of
setting Latin authors beside Greek forerunners in kindred genres. In
the same way Lucilius was set beside Aristophanes – a comparison
echoed by H. for tactical reasons, and with important qualifications,
in *S.* 1.4.1–8. More frequently, comparisons were conducted within
the same genre. Thus Cicero spoke warmly of Terence as an adapter
of Menander, without implying any inferiority (Suet. *Terence*, Loeb II
461), and Varro thought the opening of Terence's *Adelphi* superior
to the original (Suet. *Terence*, Loeb II 456). Julius Caesar, however,
would only allow that Terence was a 'half Menander' – *o dimidiate
Menander* (Suet. *Terence*, Loeb II 461); and Aulus Gellius, writing in
the 2nd cent. A.D., quoted passages of Caecilius' *Plocium* ('The Neck-
lace') to show how far it fell short of Menander's (*NA* 2.23). The same
method was used on a much larger scale by Quintilian; see, e.g., his
remarks on Roman elegy, comedy, and history (*IO* 10.1.93, 99, 101).

59 Caecilius: born in N. Italy about 220 B.C., Caecilius Statius had a successful career as a writer of comedies, of which over 40 titles are known. He died about 168. For his fragments see *ROL* I, and cf. Beare 86–90.

Terentius: Publius Terentius Afer was born about 185 B.C. in Carthage and came to Rome as a slave. He was encouraged as a writer by Scipio Aemilianus and his aristocratic friends. His six plays were produced between 166 and 160 B.C., and he is said to have died in 159. Terence had more of the classical virtues than Plautus, e.g. coherence, elegance, and restraint; but he was less lively and funny, and therefore less popular.

The business of grading the Roman comic playwrights, without reference to the Greeks, is seen in the canon of Volcacius Sedigitus, written about 100 B.C. There Caecilius comes first, Plautus second, Naevius third, and Terence only sixth (Gell. *NA* 15.24). In Varro's *Parmeno* Caecilius is said to have the best plots, Terence the best-drawn characters, and Plautus the best style (*Sat. Men.* 399 Astbury). In his *De sermone Latino* Varro asserts that no one managed to maintain characters (ἤθη) except Titinius, Terence, and Atta; but Trabea, Atilius, and Caecilius were adept at rousing emotions (πάθη); this is attested by Charisius, *Gram.* 2.16, p. 315 Barwick. In a more general classification, Varro selects Pacuvius as the best exponent of the full style (*uber*), Lucilius for the plain style (*gracilis*), and Terence for the middle (*mediocris*); see Gell. *NA* 6.14.6. A glance at this comparative method is found in Petronius, *Sat.* 55, where Trimalchio asks *quid putas inter Ciceronem et Publilium interesse? ego alterum puto disertiorem fuisse, alterum honestiorem.* (For Publilius Syrus, writer and actor of mimes, see Beare 157–8.)

60 ediscit: *in scholis*, Porph.

arto stipata theatro 'packed into the confined space of the theatre'. There were three permanent theatres in Rome at this time: those of Pompey (55 B.C., restored in 32), Balbus (13 B.C.), and Marcellus (13 B.C. or possibly 11). See Platner and Ashby 513–17.

61 potens: the extent of Rome's power is contrasted with her limited taste, which is perhaps symbolised by her watching antiquated plays in too small a theatre.

habet . . . numeratque poetas 'counts and reckons as poets'.

62 Liui scriptoris: Livius the writer or poet (as distinct from the aristocrats who belonged to the Livian gens) is Livius Andronicus, a freedman who in 240 B.C. composed the first adaptations of a Greek comedy and a Greek tragedy for the Roman stage. He also wrote a free translation of the *Odyssey* in Saturnians. For the fragments, see *ROL* II.

63 est ubi peccat: *est ubi* = ἔστιν ὅτε or 'sometimes', corresponding to the earlier *interdum*; hence the indic. was possible. But the subjunct. was also used, and was in fact more common in prose.

65 illis: dat. with both *anteferat* and *comparet*; cf. *quis huic deo | compararier ausit?* (Cat. 61.64–5).

66 pleraque: not 'most things' here, but 'a large number of things', parallel to *multa* (67).

67 ignaue 'in a flat or spiritless manner', the opposite of *(g)nauiter*.
multa: object of *dicere*.

68 mecum facit 'is on my side', 'agrees with me'; cf. *E.* 2.2.23.
Ioue ... aequo 'with the favour of heaven', i.e. soundly.

69 equidem 'for myself'.
delendaque: -*que*, if right, may be taken as specifying what is meant by *insector*; -*ue*, however, is a well-attested variant and could be the true reading.

70 plagosum: active in sense, from *plaga* 'blow'. As it occurs nowhere else in this sense, it may be H.'s coinage, or it may even perpetuate Orbilius' nickname 'Whacker'.

71 Orbilium: according to Suet. *Gram.* 9, L. Orbilius Pupillus, on losing his parents, worked as a magistrate's clerk and then served in the army before returning to his native Beneventum as a teacher. In 63 B.C. he moved to Rome, where he taught *maiore fama quam emolumento*. His fame is attested by the statue erected in his home town (a seated statue, like that of Dr Johnson in Lichfield). His attacks on scholars, parents, and pupils suggest that he was a somewhat cantankerous character. A point in his favour is the fact that he took pride in having rescued M. Pompilius Andronicus' *Criticisms of Ennius' Annals*, and in having had them published under their author's name

(Suet. *Gram.* 8). If Orbilius took a critical interest in Ennius, there is no reason why he should not have devoted a few lessons to Livius Andronicus, whose works would have been less than 200 years old in H.'s schooldays.

dictare: verses were sometimes read out for the class to learn by heart; cf. *E*. 1.1.55 *haec recinunt iuuenes dictata*, and *E*. 1.18.12–14 *sic iterat uoces . . . | ut puerum . . . credas dictata magistro | reddere*. Sometimes, however, they were dictated in order to be written down: *nonnunquam hoc quoque erit utile, ipsum* [*magistrum*] *totas dictare materias, quas et imitetur puer* (Quint. *IO* 2.4.12). It is not certain which method is meant here.

71–2   emendata ... | pulchraque 'finished and beautiful'. The former word suggests the removal of blemishes.

exactis minimum distantia 'little short of perfect'. For *exactus* see B. III, Appendix 5, 421–4; the original connection may have been with stonework.

73   uerbum ... decorum 'a strikingly appropriate word'.

73–5   emicuit si ... ducit: for the tenses used when one action is repeated before another, see G–L 567. In cases like this English normally uses two present tenses.

73–4   The text, as printed here, presents asyndeton, as in 66. One branch of the manuscript tradition, followed by SB, links the two *si*-clauses by *et* at the end of 73.

74   unus et alter: we say 'one or two'.

75   ducit: the required sense seems to be 'carries', as when a captain is said to 'carry' his team; but parallels are lacking.

uenditque 'and sells', as in our modern idiom; *OLD uendo* 4.

76–7   indignor ... nuper: one can imagine the direct form as *reprehenditur, non quia crasse compositum esse putetur, sed quia nuper compositum est*. There the subjunctive *putetur* is used because the reason is rejected (Wo. 243), whereas the indicative *compositum est* signifies that the reason is endorsed by H. Here, however, the acc. and infin. construction (*indignor quicquam reprehendi*) makes both reasons indirect. So there is a double explanation for the subjunctive *putetur*.

crasse ... illepideue: these terms remind us that H. shared many of Catullus' opinions about style; cf. Cat. 1.1; 22.14–15. These opinions were derived from Callimachus; cf. fr. 398 Λύδη καὶ παχὺ γράμμα, where παχύ is close to *crassum*, and *Aet.* 1.24 τὴν Μοῦσαν ... λεπταλέην, where λεπταλέην is like *lepidam*. For a general comparative study, see Cody.

79–80   The construction is *si dubitem recte necne fabula perambulet, patres clament pudorem periisse*, 'If I expressed [or were to express] doubts . . .'

recte ... perambulet 'remained upright as it walked', as opposed to falling on its face.

crocum floresque 'saffron and flowers'. Saffron here is a perfume, prepared from crocus, and sprayed on the stage. Since, apart from ps.-Acro's note, which may be just a guess, there is no evidence that flowers were strewn on the stage, it is worth asking whether *flores* also refers to perfumes; Plin. *NH* 13.5 speaks of perfumes made from roses, irises, and wild vine-flowers.

Attae: T. Quinctius Atta, who died in 77 B.C., wrote *comoediae togatae* of which 11 titles survive (Beare, 130); fragments in Ribbeck. Since, according to Festus (late 2nd cent. A.D.), Atta was a nickname applied to one who was lame (see *OLD atta*), H. had a special reason for using the expression *recte necne perambulet*; cf. 176 below.

80   **periisse pudorem** 'that a sense of propriety was dead'.

81   **patres** 'the older generation'.

cum reprehendere coner 'since I would be attempting to run down'.

82   **Aesopus:** Claudius Aesopus, a celebrated actor in the first half of the first cent. B.C. H.'s *grauis* suggests that he is thinking of Aesopus primarily as a tragic actor.

Roscius: Quintus Roscius Gallus was made a knight by Sulla and was on friendly terms with Catulus and Cicero. The adj. *doctus* may refer to his being equally accomplished in both tragedy and comedy. For both actors see Garton's index.

83   **rectum:** referring back to *recte* (79), but in the sense of 'right'.

84   **parere minoribus** 'to heed their juniors', a paradoxical idea, especially in Rome.

et quae: the satirists not uncommonly ended their lines with two monosyllables. Since the first monosyllable probably took the stress off the second, coincidence of ictus and accent was preserved. Examples are *et quae* (as here, and in *AP* 181), *et pater et res* (*AP* 248, cf. 270, 309), *per quae* (*E.* 2.1.106, cf. 175, *E.* 2.2.13, 153), *non ut* (*AP* 12, cf. 89), *lis est* (*AP* 78), *quod petis hic est* (*E.* 1.11.29). But ictus and accent are quite often separated, as in *Democritus, seu* (*E.* 2.1.194), *lutulenta ruit sus* (*E.* 2.2.75), *audieras, cui* (*E.* 2.2.151), *ridiculus mus* (*AP* 139), *in medias res* (*AP* 148), *officium, quae* (*AP* 314). Sometimes H. begins a new clause at the start of the sixth foot (as in *et quae* here, and in *ex quo* at *E.* 2.2.153), or in the middle of the sixth foot (*fidem, si* in *AP* 52 and *officium, quae* in *AP* 314), with the result that the construction flows over into the following line (enjambment).

86   iam 'besides'; *OLD iam* 8.

Saliare Numae carmen: Numa Pompilius, second king of Rome (715–673 B.C.?), was renowned for his piety. According to tradition, he reformed the calendar and instituted various priesthoods, including the Salii, or priests of Mars. As time went by, the chants of the Salii became more and more difficult to understand. The scholar Aelius Stilo, who edited Ennius and Lucilius, and taught both Varro and Cicero, had tried to elucidate them (Varro, *LL* 7.2); but by Quintilian's time (2nd half of 1st cent. A.D.) they were *uix sacerdotibus suis satis intellecta* (*IO* 1.6.40). For the dress and function of the Salii see *OCD*; for the fragments see *FPL* 1–5.

87   quod mecum ignorat 'of which he knows as little as I'.

89   liuidus: the colour of bruised flesh, 'black and blue'; used to denote jealousy and spite. The English 'livid' had this sense until the 19th cent., when it began to be associated with 'white' (Dickens) and 'pale'. The sense 'furiously angry, as if pale with rage' appears only in the *OED Supplement*.

90–2 Everything that is now old and admirable was once new. We Romans have our Greek classics only because the Greeks were less hostile to novelty.

91   haberet: parallel to *esset*; 'what would the public [now] have etc.?'

92   quod legeret: the question *quid haberet* (91), which is by implication negative, makes the expression grammatically equivalent to *nil habeo quod legam*; for the subjunctive of tendency see G–L 631.2.

tereret: the equivalent of our 'thumb', implying constant use.

publicus usus: a quasi-legal phrase, which nevertheless retains a personal force. Perhaps 'what would the public have as its property, to read and thumb, each man for himself?'

93   positis . . . bellis: i.e. after the Persian wars. The Persians were driven from Greece in 479 B.C. after the battle of Plataea. Actually several important works had been written before that date. There is a similar looseness on the Roman side of the comparison (162).

nugari: with a disparaging overtone 'to turn to idle amusements'.

94   in uitium . . . labier 'to lapse into frivolity'. *labier* is an archaic form of the infin. *labi*. The possible nuances of the form are discussed by B. III, Appendix 6, 424–6.

fortuna . . . aequa 'as Fortune smiled upon her'; cf. 68 above.

95   studiis: abl. with *arsit*; cf. note on 31. The construction of a Latin sentence is often non-linear; prepositions and verbs may come after, as well as before, the nouns to which they belong.

97   'She let her eyes and soul hang intent on the painter's panel' (Wk.).

98   est gauisa: from *gaudeo*, with abl.

99   sub nutrice: 'under [the authority of] a nurse'. H. widens this use from kings and generals to fathers (*S.* 1.2.17), mistresses (*E.* 1.2.25), and guardians (*E.* 1.16.77).

Up to this point Greece has been portrayed as a skittish girl; H. now takes a step further back and sees her as a child. Cf. the words of the Egyptian priest to Solon ' Ἕλληνες ἀεὶ παῖδές ἐστε' (Plato, *Timaeus* 22B), 'You Greeks are always children.'

100   The subject of the verse is *Graecia*.
mature 'soon'.
plena: the same metaphor as our, more colloquial, 'fed up'.

101   The assertion that everything is subject to changes of taste makes little sense with 100 and none with 102. If the line is genuine, it is therefore misplaced. Unfortunately, scholars have not been able to find a home for it. Whether it is put after 102 (Vollmer), 107 (Lachmann), or 110 (Campbell), it weakens the force of H.'s argument. Nor, although it was known to the scholiasts, does it have the neatness expected of a Horatian *sententia*. It has therefore been bracketed as a marginal comment which has been wrongly incorporated into the text.

102 'This was the result of blessed calm and favourable breezes.' The line, which may owe something to *uentorum . . . paces animasque secundas* (Lucr. *DRN* 5.1230), here takes on a hint of the old metaphor of the ship of state. It was chosen as an epigraph by L. P. Wilkinson for his *Horace and his lyric poetry*, published 1945.

After the sketch of the Greeks as gifted but frivolous, H. goes on to portray the Romans as serious but philistine. Surely, one infers, there must be the possibility of a fruitful, Augustan, synthesis. So Fraenkel 389–91.

103   **dulce . . . et solemne** 'agreeable and time-honoured'.

104   **promere iura** 'to give out legal advice (from their store of knowledge)'. For the patron–client relationship see Saller.

105   **cautos . . . nummos:** for the meaning 'secured' cf. *quo mulieri res esset cautior, curauit ut in eo fundo dos conlocaretur* (Cic. *Caec.* 11).

nominibus rectis: the interpretations proposed are (i) 'to upright names', i.e. 'to honest debtors' (*OLD nomen* 22d), dat. with *expendere*; (ii) 'by honest debtors', abl. with *cautos*; (iii) 'by proper bonds', abl. with *cautos*. While *nomen* can certainly mean the heading in a ledger, one needs evidence to show that it could have the sense of a bond or legal document. There is little to choose between (i) and (ii). The position of the phrase between *cautos* and *nummos* tells slightly in favour of (ii). But the quotation from Cicero (above) indicates that *cautos* here can stand on its own; and the sequence of personal objects, direct and indirect, represented by *clienti . . . maiores . . .* and *minori*, might point to (i).

106   **maiores audire** = *a maioribus audire*, followed by the indirect question *per quae posset*. The parallel *maiores audire* and *minori dicere* signify a continuous oral tradition.

107   **damnosa libido:** W. drily remarks that 'the reference is here only to the injury which self-indulgence may cause to one's fortune'. Gambling, drink, and sex are all included in *libido*.

108   leuis 'capricious'.

108–9   uno | scribendi studio 'one passion – that of writing'; for the gen. of definition see Wo. 72.1 (5).

110   comas uincti: for the Greek acc. of respect see Wo. 19 (ii), G–L 338 n.1. The context implies poetic pretensions; so the leaves are probably ivy or bay.

   carmina dictant: at dinner the Romans, or at least those with literary tastes, would improvise and recite verses, which would be taken down in writing by a slave. Quintilian regards such dictation as a slovenly habit (*IO* 10.3.19–22); cf. Hor. *S.* 1.4.9–10 of the careless Lucilius, and Pers. 1.51–2 *siqua elegidia crudi | dictarunt proceres.* Similarly, in Petron. *Sat.* 55 the *codicilli* are probably used by a copyist, though it is possible that Trimalchio recites (*recitauit*) what he himself has written down.

**111   In *E.* 1.1.10 (*nunc itaque et uersus et cetera ludicra pono*) H. had ostensibly abandoned lyric. Shortly afterwards, in *E.* 2.2 (published in 19 B.C.) he had reaffirmed his decision. Yet in 17 B.C. he had written the *CS* and had gone on to compose *C.* 4, a work which was probably completed only a few months before the present poem. Hence *Parthis mendacior* (112).

112   Parthis mendacior: like Rome's other major enemies, e.g. the Greeks and the Carthaginians, the Parthians were supposed to be untrustworthy. Similarly Napoleon referred to England as *perfide Albion.*

112–13   prius orto | sole uigil: is this an intentional reminiscence of *mane ... uigilare* (104)? If so, H. is implying that in this respect at least he is like the old Romans. In any case, one suspects a considerable degree of rhetorical exaggeration; early rising is not part of H.'s poetic personality.

113   scrinia: *scrinium* was a box or container for holding writing-sheets, letters, and other documents.

   posco: neither this verb nor *adfirmo* (111) refers to the immediate present; see note on 111 above. In view of *calamum* and *chartas* (113) and *scribere* (111) one assumes that H. is not speaking of dictation here. Nor is he referring to the use of *stilus* and wax tablets. For writing with a pen, as we do, cf. Pers. 3.10–14, especially *inque manus chartae nodosaque uenit harundo* (11), and H. *S.* 2.3.7.

114   habrotonum 'southernwood' (*Artemisia abrotanum*), an aromatic plant of the wormwood genus, used in the treatment of coughs, asthma, and other ailments; see Plin. *NH* 21.160–2.

115   dare: with both *audet* and *didicit*.
     medicorum 'the province of doctors'; possessive gen., Wo. 72. 1 (1) n. 3, G–L 366 R1.

115–16 When the skill of the *medicus* is equated with that of the physician, as described in 114–5, one is left with a rather inelegant repetition. This could be removed by adopting Ben.'s ingenious *melicorum . . . melici* and understanding *melicus* in the sense of 'musician'. Unfortunately *melicus* is extremely rare as a noun, and when it does occur it means 'a lyric poet', not 'a musician'. Keeping the MS reading, one can either argue that H. was less troubled about the repetition than we are, or else (following Palmer's suggestion, as reported by W.) assume that having specified one kind of medical procedure (the physician's) H. is now including the other (i.e. the surgeon's) as well. In Juv. 2.13, e.g., a surgical operation is performed by a *medicus*; cf. Celsus, *Prooem.* 43.
     promittunt 'undertake' or 'practise' as professionals.
     fabrilia 'things pertaining to a smith or carpenter'.

117 As the line represents a contrast, we might have expected *nos* 'whereas we . . .'
     indocti doctique 'qualified and unqualified'.
     passim 'without distinction'.

118   error 'aberration'; of mentally abnormal behaviour, e.g. *S.* 2.3.63.
     et . . . insania: this goes a stage beyond aberration – 'lunacy'.
     leuis 'mild'. Poetic inspiration was often thought of as a kind of madness; cf. *S.* 2.7.117, *AP* 296–301, and *OLD furor* 1b.

119   uirtutes 'merits'.
     collige 'consider'; the object is the indirect question *quantas . . . habeat.*
     uatis: a noble word, 'bard', used with a touch of humour but with no real intention to belittle.

120 **non temere** 'not readily', hence 'hardly'.

121 The three types of disaster, presented in long, impressive words, are diminished by the brief *ridet*; cf. *E.* 2.2.208–9.

122 **socio** 'partner'.

122–3 **pueroue . . . | pupillo:** the child who is legally in his charge as a minor or orphan, hence his 'ward'.

123 **siliquis:** from *siliqua*, 'a pod'; hence 'pulse', e.g. peas, beans, or lentils.

  pane secundo 'inferior bread'; *OLD secundus* 11c. *secundus* here may be the equivalent of *secundarius*, which probably referred to 'the inferior flour produced by a second grinding' (Moritz 181). See B. III, Appendix 9, 428–9.

124 **militiae:** 'In the poets and later prose-writers a genitive is used with many adjectives . . . to denote that with respect to which the adjective is applicable' (Wo. 73. II (6) under *Genitive of Reference*).

  quamquam: with *piger et malus*, no verb being supplied; Wo. 249 *Note* ii.

  piger et malus 'idle and incompetent'.
  utilis urbi: understand *est*.

125 'If you grant this, that great enterprises are assisted even by small services.' The expression has a proverbial ring (but see on 220); cf. 'Every little helps' and 'Tall oaks from little acorns grow.' The services mentioned subsequently are not really small, but H. is modestly understating the poet's role.

126 Lit. 'the poet shapes the soft lisping mouth of a child'. *balbum* here refers to the inaccuracies of the very young. (Contrast *E.* 1.20.18, where *balba senectus* denotes the toothless quavering of old age, and *S.* 2.3.274, where *balba uerba* means lovers' baby-talk.) 'Lisping' will do as a translation, provided the word is not confined to the mispronunciation of 's'. H. is talking of the use of poetry to teach children how to speak.

127–8 'Even in those tender years poetry has, in a negative and indirect way, a moral influence in giving the ear a bias against coarse subjects and ways of speaking; presently it directly educates the heart by the precepts and examples which it conveys' (Wk.).

praeceptis ... amicis: i.e. precepts for living on friendly terms with one's fellows. The idea is illustrated in 129.

130   recte facta 'good deeds'.

orientia tempora 'the rising generation' (W.); cf. Vell. 2.99.2 *orientium iuuenum initiis*.

131   instruit exemplis: the Latin words may not have conveyed a distinction between 'furnishes with examples' and 'instructs with examples'. Suetonius tells us that Augustus in his reading was always on the lookout for *praecepta et exempla publice uel priuatim salubria* (*Aug.* 89).

inopem ... et aegrum: probably 'helpless and sick at heart' rather than 'poor and sick'; cf. *o laborum | dulce lenimen* of the lyre (*C.* 1.32.14–15) and *deformis aegrimoniae dulcibus alloquiis* of wine and song (*I.* 13.18).

132–3   For a choir of boys and girls singing hymns cf. *C.* 1.21; *C.* 4.6.29–44; and *CS.*

disceret unde 'from what source was she likely to learn?' See Wo. 199 for the use of the impf. subj. in past unreal conditions.

134   praesentia numina sentit 'senses the divinities' benign presence'.

135   docta prece blandus: lit. 'winning favour by means of the prayer which it has been taught'. The punctuation adopted here allows the phrase to go both with what precedes and with what follows.

137   pacem: i.e. the *pax deorum*, the gods' blessing; *OLD pax* 2.

138   carmine ... carmine: 'Horace is not a writer to use anaphora idly. Wherever he uses it he does so to stress something which he has very much at heart.' So Fraenkel 206, citing *C.* 1.17.13–14; 3.4.21; 4.6.29–30, which have to do with the gods, the Muses, and Apollo.

Manes: the gods of the underworld, e.g. Dis, Proserpina, and Hecate.

For the sentiment of the line, cf. another impressive conclusion: *superis deorum | gratus et imis* (*C.* 1.10.19–20).

This warm description of Roman choral lyric (132–8) occupies the central place in the poem.

139-55 As observed in the Introduction (essay on the *AP*, pp. 28–32), a number of writers, following Varro, saw the germ of native Italian, as of Greek, drama in the verbal exchanges which took place at rural festivals of Bacchus. A glimpse of the kind of thing Varro said can be obtained from the 4th-cent. grammarian Diomedes. 'Comedy', he writes, 'received its name ἀπὸ τῶν κωμῶν ("from the villages", i.e. the places where rustic folk gather together). And so the young men of Attica, as Varro says, used to go round villages and deliver this kind of poetic composition for money. Or it received its name from village games (*ludis uicinalibus*); for after people came into Athens from the countryside and these games were established, like the crossroads games (*compitalicii*) in Rome, they stepped forward to sing, and from the κώμηι καὶ ὠδῆι ("village" plus "song") that took place in the city "comedy" received its name' (*Gramm. Lat.* 1 488 Keil).

In the present passage H. speaks of rustic merrymaking which gave rise to the interchange of banter in verse – banter which became more and more insulting until it had to be controlled by law. Although he sees such exchanges as an early forerunner of Roman comedy, he does not attempt to argue that the Fescennine verses were a counterpart of Greek Old Comedy, or that they were the genetic ancestor of the *palliata*. All he is concerned to establish is that early Italian altercations were crude. The same charge is then levelled at the Saturnians of Livius Andronicus, Naevius, and others. Artistic writing only developed when Greek influence made itself felt. But even then progress was slow. Some of the old coarseness persisted up to H.'s own day (160).

139 **fortes** 'sturdy'; for 'sturdy peasantry' cf. Virg. *Georg.* 2.533 *sic fortis Etruria creuit*, and also Hor. *S.* 2.2.114–15 *uideas metato in agello | cum pecore et gnatis fortem mercede colonum*.

140 **condita post frumenta** 'after the gathering in of the harvest'. In strict logic *post* governs the idea in the participle rather than the noun; cf. *C.* 1.3.29–30 *post ignem aetheria domo | subductum*. The rhythm of the line, with its combination of a weak caesura in the 3rd foot and a bucolic diaeresis at the end of the 4th, is unusual; but no particular effect is observable.

Aristotle speaks of tribes and demes meeting to offer sacrifices and enjoying periods of relaxation. Such occasions 'seem to take place after harvests as a kind of first fruits; for people had most leisure at those times' (*Nic. Eth.* 8.9.1160a23–8).

141   ipsum adds emphasis, 'yes, and the mind too'.

ferentem: best taken as = *qui ferebat*, 'which used to put up with drudgery'.

142   cum sociis operum: the *socii* are defined by *pueri* and *coniunx*. The *et* which appears in some MSS before *pueris* spoils the picture of family self-sufficiency by implying that there might also be outside helpers; cf. *I.* 2.39 and *S.* 2.2.115.

143–4   The mention of Tellus, Silvanus, and the Genius together should not be taken as referring to any specific ceremony or festival.

Tellurem: Tellus, the Roman earth-goddess, was associated with various rituals in the calendar; see Ov. *Fast.* 1.657ff. and 4.629ff. with Frazer's comments.

Siluanum: Silvanus, 'he of the woods', was a god of the wild, un-cultivated, land. It was important that he should be propitiated by farmers, who occasionally made inroads on his domain; cf. *E.* 2.2.186. When his help had been enlisted, he could be addressed as *tutor finium* (*I.* 2.22).

Genium: the Genius was 'the idea of the man's self projected from himself and divinized' (Wk.). It was supposed to be born with the in-dividual and to function as his guardian spirit; when the individual died, the Genius lost its distinctive existence and returned to the world soul. See B. III, Appendix 19, 441–4. By offering wine and flowers to his Genius a man indicated that he was enjoying himself. Only the more reflective revellers would have come within the scope of Porph.'s note: *qui indulgent genio suo, memores sunt uitam humanam non esse diuturnam*; cf. the city mouse's exhortation in *S.* 2.6.97, *uiue memor quam sis aeui breuis*.

145   Fescennina ... licentia: in the epitome of Festus (late 2nd cent. A.D.) made by Paulus (8th cent. A.D.) fescennine verses are said to be so called either (i) because they were brought in *ex urbe Fes-cennina* or (ii) because they were believed to ward off the *fascinum* or evil eye (cf. the Gk. βάσκανος and the Eng. 'fascinate'). (i) is supported by Servius on *Aen.* 7.695, who adds *Fescenninum oppidum est ubi nuptialia inuenta sunt carmina*, and by Porph., who says *dicta autem Fescennina ab* *oppido Fescennino, unde primum processerunt et Atellanica nominata sunt,* thus connecting the verses with Atellan farces. Pliny calls the town *Fescennia* (*NH* 3.52); it was in Etruria, close to the Tiber. (ii), or rather a variation of it, has commonly been favoured by scholars who link the account on which H. is basing himself with *Poet.* 4.1449a4, where Aristotle says that one type of man came to write comedies instead of lampoons (ἴαμβοι); he goes on to add that comedy arose from the leaders of the phallic songs. Such boisterous songs are therefore seen by some modern scholars as the Greek counterpart of the fescennine verses, which are supposed to be named from the *fascinum*, a phallic emblem worn round the neck as a protection against malevolent forces (cf. Fascinus in Plin. *NH* 28.39). Whatever its etymology, fescennine raillery was associated with occasions of great success and rejoicing, e.g. harvests, weddings (Cat. 61.119–20), and triumphal processions, when it was most necessary to turn away the evil eye. (For Festus, who himself abridged the *De verborum significatu* of Verrius Flaccus (fl. 10 B.C.) see Sandys I, index.)

per hunc ... morem 'as a result of this custom'.

inuenta: speaking of the evolution of laws, H. says *iura inuenta metu iniusti fateare necesse est* (*S.* 1.3.111). Lucretius writes in similar terms about the emergence of property: *posterius res inuentast* (*DRN* 5.1113). *inuenta* here is the reading of the MSS and scholiasts. Ben.'s *inuecta*, adopted by B. and SB, would mean that H. was referring to the importation of the fescennine verses; but, as O. says, *per hunc modum* tells in favour of *inuenta*: the old custom gave rise to the new development. If H. had the town Fescennium in mind, he could well have meant the phrase *Fescennina licentia* to have a generic sense: 'the sort of licence associated with Fescennium'.

147 libertasque '[verbal] freedom'.

recurrentes ... per annos 'as the years came round', hence 'year by year'.

accepta: since the straightforward 'accepted' suits the context perfectly well, there is no occasion to look for special nuances, such as 'welcomed' or 'condoned'.

148–50 Good-natured sport turns vicious (*saeuus iocus*) and ends up like a mad dog.

149–50   per ... domos 'to tear through respected houses'.

150–51   'Those who were worried by its bloody teeth suffered keenly.' ('Worry: to tear with the teeth ... to harass ...' Chambers.)

152   condicione super communi 'about the state of society'; *OLD super* 11.

152–4   The law in question was contained in the Twelve Tables, which went back to the 5th cent. B.C. Augustine (*De ciu.* 2.9) cites a passage of Cicero (*De rep.* 4.12) which reports some of the wording *si quis occentauisset siue carmen condidisset quod infamiam faceret flagitiumue alteri* (*ROL* III 474), 'anyone who chanted hostile words or composed a *carmen* so as to bring ill repute or disgrace upon another'. This kind of defamatory verse is what H. means by *malo ... carmine*. The *malum carmen* referred to by Plin. *NH* 28.18 has to do with magical incantations – a different matter. For further discussion see B.

lex poenaque lata: *legem ferre* could mean 'to propose a law' or 'to enact a law (=*perferre*)'. Here the two stages are not distinguished; so one might translate as 'brought in'. Since *poenam ferre* is not normally used in the sense of *poenam statuere* ('to establish a penalty'), there is a slight zeugma, combined with hendiadys. A possible translation would be 'a law involving a punishment was brought in'.

nollet: stronger than 'was unwilling'; 'forbade'. The subjunctive indicates both the purpose and the result of the enactment: 'so as to forbid'.

154   describi: the basic meaning is 'to be presented'; but here, as in *S.* 1.4.3, unfavourable terms are implied.

uertere modum 'they changed their tune', as we would say.

fustis: according to Cic. *De rep.* 4.12, the Twelve Tables considered that the offence of traducing a person in public should be a capital crime *sanciendam* [*capite*] *putauerunt*. This probably meant death rather than exile. Such was the understanding of the Cornutus commentary on Persius 1.123 *lege duodecim tabularum cautum est ut fustibus feriretur qui publice inuehebatur*; cf. Porph., who here talks of *fustuarium supplicium*, a phrase which properly referred to the military punishment of being beaten to death.

155   'They reverted to harmless words and entertainment.'

156–7 Graecia capta: the phrase takes a very long view, telescoping events from the capture of Greek cities in Sicily during the first Punic war (264–241) to the sack of Corinth in 146.

ferum 'rough'.

cepit: the paradox with *capta* is explained in the next sentence.

agresti Latio: not just 'rural Latium' as described in 139–55; to the Roman gentleman *agrestis* and *rusticus* carried the idea of uncouthness, while *urbanus* suggested politeness.

157–8 horridus ... numerus Saturnius: according to Porph., the metre of the very early Latin writers was called Saturnian after Saturn, who reigned in the golden age. Doubtless many shared this assumption; its truth is another question (see *CHCL* II 57). The metre was used by Livius Andronicus in his *Odussia* and by Naevius in his *Bellum Punicum*; a few specimens survive, but their scansion is uncertain. There is little to be said for the view, mentioned by B. III 202, which extends the reference beyond the Saturnian and its users to Ennius *et al.*; see on 161 below.

For *horridus* of a rough surface see *C.* 3.24.40–1 *horrida callidi | uincunt aequora nauitae.* Here it suggests a turbulent and dirty stream.

defluxit 'flowed away'.

158 et probably does not introduce a later event, but describes the same event in different terms; i.e. the Saturnian did not just flow away on its own, it was washed away by what took its place.

158–9 graue ... pepulere 'cleanness got rid of the noisome liquid'. The *munditiae* are the new forms and standards derived from Greece by Ennius and his successors. Their effect, however, was not complete.

aeuum: not in Caesar, rare in Sallust and Cicero; as often, Livy, who has *intra tam breuis aeui memoriam* (26.11.12; cf. 28.35.12, and 28.43.6), marks the transition to silver prose. So the phrase *in longum aeuum* has a poetic ring, 'for many a year'.

160 uestigia ruris: 'traces of the farmyard' (Wk.) were to be found in Ennius and the rest (167), and also in other writers up to H.'s own day; cf. what Catullus says about Suffenus: *idem infaceto est infacetior rure* (22.14), and about Volusius' *Annals: pleni ruris et inficetiarum* (36.19).

161   serus 'it was at a late stage that he . . .', 'he' being the Roman, last referred to as *ferum uictorem* (156).

admouit acumina 'applied his shrewdness'. The thought sequence indicates that we have now left the writers of Saturnians (Livius and Naevius) behind. In the section which follows H. goes on to speak of drama, and we can hardly be expected to jump back again in time in order to think of Livius and Naevius as dramatists. One must rather conclude that the new, hellenising, phase is represented by Ennius, Pacuvius, and Accius. This point is important for the interpretation of 162; it also rules out the idea that H. included any of their work under *Saturnius* (158).

162   et: the sentence confirms 161 and restates it in greater detail: 'and indeed it was not until after the Punic wars . . . that . . .'

post Punica bella quietus: H. is referring to a post-war period when, as in the case of Greece (*positis bellis* in 93), the threat of invasion had been removed. But what wars had he in mind? To be exact, Roman tragedy began with the work of Livius Andronicus and Naevius after the first Punic war (264–241 B.C.), but we have just seen that as dramatists they have not been taken into account. Pacuvius and Accius were still writing after the third Punic war (149–146), but the *beginning* of Roman tragedy could not have been put as late as that (*coepit* in 162), and the threat of invasion had disappeared fifty years before. So H. is talking about the years following the end of the second Punic war in 201 B.C. – years which saw the appearance of plays by Ennius, Pacuvius, and Accius. It was inaccurate and unfair to omit Livius and Naevius, but to maintain the somewhat spurious parallel with Greece H. shaped his account so as to begin Roman tragedy with Ennius. Shortly after, he disregarded Livius and Naevius as comic writers too, and selected Plautus as an example of the old carelessness in comedy. This procedure has frequently caused difficulties for those who impute their own care for historical truth to one with different priorities.

quaerere: as K–H observe, study is the first step, then experiments in adaptation, and finally the building of a literary tradition.

163   Sophocles: *c.* 496–406 B.C. He is said to have written over 120 plays. Seven have survived, of which the most famous are *Antigone* and *Oedipus Tyrannus*.

Thespis: he won the prize for tragedy *c.* 534 B.C. He introduced the actor who spoke the prologue and conversed with the chorus leader, thus taking the first step in the conversion of choral lyric into tragic drama.

Aeschylus: 525/4–456 B.C. Seven of his tragedies survive (if we include *Prometheus Vinctus*). The best known is *Agamemnon*, which with the *Choephoroe* and the *Eumenides* makes up the *Oresteia*.

H.'s order is therefore due, not to chronology, but to metrical convenience. The same factor may explain the omission of Euripides, whose name could not be coaxed into a hexameter; but it is worth remembering that although his plays were frequently adapted by the Romans, he was not responsible for any major innovation in the form of the genre.

utile: tragedies would offer food for thought on the value of piety, the destructive power of passion, the dangers of tyranny, and so on. The practical concern is very Roman.

164 temptauit quoque rem, si ... posset: the *rem* is the *si*-clause; 'he made the experiment to see if he could'.

uertere 'to translate' or, better, 'to adapt'. The examples in *OLD* suggest that an object is needed; it can readily be supplied from 163, e.g. 'them' or 'their plays'. One can hardly understand *rem* ἀπὸ κοινοῦ, for the word would have to be given a wholly different sense.

165 placuit sibi: the satisfaction was not unjustified, as H. proceeds to explain; but the praise is qualified in 167.

natura sublimis et acer: something like 'being naturally dynamic (*acer*) with lofty ideas'.

166 spirat tragicum satis 'he does have plenty of the tragic spirit'. *tragicum* is an extension of the cognate acc.; see G–L 333 2 n. 6.

feliciter audet 'his audacious expressions come off'; cf. Quintilian's verdict on H. *uarius figuris et uerbis felicissime audax* (*IO* 10.1.96).

167 inscite ... lituram 'out of ignorance he is afraid to erase'.

lituram: formed from *lino*, 'I smear'; for the smearing of wax tablets with the broad end of the *stilus* cf. *saepe stilum uertas* (*S.* 1.10.72). This smoothed the surface for corrections. The word here means, not an erasure, but the business of erasing.

168   creditur: the subject is *comoedia* (169).

ex medio 'from daily life'. That which is 'in the midst' is open to, and familiar to, all; *OLD medium* 4c.

res 'subjects'.

habere 'to involve'.

169–70   Actually comedy puts a greater burden on the playwright, because it is judged more critically. People know what everyday life is like and how ordinary characters behave.

170–6   As if he were acting each part, Plautus is criticised for his portrayal of the young lover, the tight-fisted father, the treacherous pimp, and the hungry parasite; his style, moreover, is slipshod. The alleged reason is that he cares for nothing but his fee.

An admirer of Plautus might well maintain that H. had failed to appreciate the over-life-size nature of his characters, his metrical virtuosity, and the exuberance of his comic spirit. Terence, in fact, was much more to H.'s taste. One notes that he was praised for his characters by Varro; see on 59 above; cf. Donatus on *Andr.* 447, who remarks on how he maintains τὸ πρέπον (appropriateness) and τὸ πιθανόν (credibility), and Euanthius 3.4., who commends him for observing the *personarum leges* (*Comicorum Graecorum Fragmenta*, Kaibel, 1 65). His purity of style was noted by Julius Caesar (*puri sermonis amator*, Suet. *Terence* 5). It did not suit H.'s rhetoric, however, to mention Terence; for that would have spoilt the pattern old = crude, new = artistic.

171   quo pacto: *pactum*, from *pacisco*, meant 'arrangement', hence 'method' or 'manner'.

tutetur: *tutor, -ari* = 'preserve'; here 'sustain'.

ephebi: the Greek word is used to recall the feckless young men portrayed in the comedies adapted by Plautus.

172   patris attenti: *attentus*, 'careful', when used in connection with money, can easily move towards 'over-careful', 'close'. Here, the series in which the *pater attentus* occurs requires an unfavourable nuance. The construction is *ut* [*partes*] *patris attenti* [*tutetur*]. Here *ut* = 'how'.

173   quantus ... Dossennus: Dossennus ('Hunchback') was one of a handful of figures which appeared in the old *Atellanae*. These were rustic farces which developed in Campania and are supposed to have received their name from the Oscan town of Atella. See Beare, chap. 16. The meaning, then, will be 'what a buffoon he is in his ravenous parasites', the implication being that parasites were more cleverly and less farcically portrayed in Greek comedies.

174   socco: the *soccus* was a slipper worn by comic actors; hence it came to symbolise comedy as the buskin symbolised tragedy. (See on *AP* 80–1.) The slipshod haste described here has reference to Plautus' dramaturgy (cf. 176) rather than his diction and versification.

175–6   The playwright would sell his comedy to the magistrates responsible for the *ludi*. According to Suetonius (*Terence* 2, Loeb II), Terence's *Eunuchus* was acted twice on the same day and earned an unprecedented 8,000 sesterces. As for Plautus, Varro told a story, recorded by Gellius, *NA* 3.3.14, that he invested his earnings from the theatre in business and lost the lot; he then took a job as a grinder in a bakery and managed to write three plays in his spare time. Such tales, whether true or false, helped to earn Plautus a reputation for improvidence and for careless facility.

175   loculos 'cash-box'.

176   securus 'indifferent'.

   cadat an recto stet ... talo 'falls down or stands on a firm footing'. If one translates *cadat* by 'flops' or the like, one must bear in mind that H. is thinking of artistic failure, not of a failure with the public.

177   H. now goes on to speak of the demands made by a mass audience and of the strains imposed on playwrights.

   tulit: a general statement, to be translated by an English present; Wo. 217 (2) (*c*).

   uentoso 'windy', because variable and unsubstantial.

178   exanimat ... inflat 'deflates ... puffs up', carrying on the underlying idea of *uentoso*. Cf. *C.* 2.10.21, where *animosus* 'full of spirit' prepares us for *uento ... secundo*.

   lentus ... sedulus 'dull ... responsive'.

179   leue 'trivial'.

180   subruit ... reficit 'undermines ... restores', as though the *animus* (179) were a structure.

ualeat res ludicra 'goodbye to show business'.

me: this does not mean that H. had ever thought of becoming a playwright.

181   palma: since there is no evidence that poets were so rewarded, the expression is best taken metaphorically; see on *AP* 250.

macrum ... opimum: the literal senses of 'thin' and 'fat' are not wholly excluded, but as H. has been talking of acclaim, or the lack of it, the words are primarily metaphorical.

reducit: our idiom is 'sends me home'; cf. *quos Elea domum reducit | palma caelestis* (*C.* 4.2.17–18). The verb harks back to *tulit* (177).

182   audacem: i.e. the poet who braves a hostile audience; cf. *S.* 1.10.76–7.

183   uirtute et honore minores 'inferior in merit and status'.

184   depugnare parati 'ready to fight it out'.

185   si discordet eques: if, that is, the knights like something which the masses do not. For the present tense of the generalising subjunctive see Wo. 196. In accordance with the law of L. Roscius Otho (67 B.C.), the *equites* (who had fortunes of 400,000 sesterces or more) sat in the first 14 rows of the stalls. The *orchestra* was reserved for senators. For references to Otho's law see Mayor on Juv. 3.153 (and again in his *addenda*). Refinements were introduced by Augustus, probably in a *Lex Iulia Theatralis* of 18 B.C.; see Rawson.

185–6   Terence (*Hec.* second prol. 29ff.) complained that the first presentation of his *Hecyra* had been spoiled by rumours that boxers (and perhaps a tightrope walker) were about to perform in the theatre; at the second presentation people came flocking in to see a gladiatorial show.

carmina: here of verse drama.

186   ursum: this is H. embroidering on Terence; but bear-baiting certainly took place on a huge scale. 100 were killed at the games in 61 B.C. (Plin. *NH* 8.131) and 300 in 25 (Dio 53.27.6).

pugiles: it was not just the *plebecula* that enjoyed boxing; speaking of Augustus, Suetonius says *spectauit studiosissime pugiles, et maxime Latinos* (*Aug.* 45.2).

plebecula: the diminutive expresses contempt; cf. Pers. 4.6.

gaudet: some MSS read *plaudet*, the *pl-* resulting from the preceding *pl-ebecula*. (The technical name for this is a *Perseverationsfehler* – 'a persistence-error'; i.e. one resulting from the persistence of a letter, or group of letters, in the copyist's mind.) As the tense of *plaudet* was obviously wrong, subsequently copyists wrote *plaudit*, which is found in inferior MSS.

187 uerum ... quoque 'why ... even'.

188 incertos 'restless' and 'shifting', with the added moral sense of 'inconstant' and 'superficial'. This reflects a suspicion of 'spectacle' which goes back to Aristotle: 'Spectacle stirs the emotions, but involves less art than [plot, character, thought, diction, and music], and has least to do with poetry; for a tragedy can achieve its effect even without performance and actors. Indeed spectacular effects belong rather to the skill of the wardrobe-master than to that of the poet' (*Poet.* 6.1450b16–20).

gaudia uana: whatever may be thought of the pageant described in 190ff., it was certainly empty so far as poetry was concerned. Similar feelings were expressed by Cicero in his letter to M. Marius (*Fam.* 7.1.2), in which he described the games held by Pompey to celebrate the opening of his new stone theatre in 55 B.C. *quid enim delectationis habent sescenti muli in Clytaemestra aut in Equo Troiano creterrarum tria milia aut armatura uaria peditatus et equitatus in aliqua pugna?*

189 quattuor ... in horas: i.e. at least twice as long as for a comedy.

aulaea premuntur 'the curtain is kept down'. From at least 56 B.C. (Cic. *Pro Cael.* 65) the curtain was raised to hide the stage and lowered to reveal it. The opposite (i.e. the present) practice was apparently introduced before the time of Apuleius (2nd cent. A.D.). see Beare, Appendix E.

190 fugiunt: the representation seems to be that of a rout. Porph. says 'the play is held up ... while the people are shown a spectacle of war, and at the end a triumphal procession is brought on'. Cf. the passage from Cicero quoted above on 188.

191   mox 'in due course'.

regum fortuna: a lofty (and metrically neat) expression for *reges infortunati*.

192   esseda: two-wheeled war chariots used by the Belgae and Britons.

pilenta: luxuriously upholstered coaches, also used by Roman ladies at religious processions.

petorrita: four-wheeled vehicles said to be of Gallic origin.

naues: in such pageants there may have been models of ships, or beaks of ships, rather than actual ships. But H. says *naues*, and so we must translate 'ships'. Anything else spoils the rhetoric.

193   ebur 'ivory'; i.e. 'ivory statues', or 'elephant tusks'. The former explanation would accord well with the first interpretation of *Corinthus* below.

Corinthus: (i) = Corinthian bronze vessels and statues; this effectively balances *ebur* = ivories. It is true that, unlike *Anticyra*, which in a number of passages = 'hellebore' (e.g. Hor. *AP* 300, Juv. 13.97), *Corinthus* does not seem to occur elsewhere denoting, by metonymy, its most famous product. But examples of the use may have been lost, or possibly this is an original expression of H.'s. (ii) = the treasures of (captured) Corinth; this would not balance *ebur*, but would represent a large rhetorical step beyond it. (iii) = a model or painting of Corinth; such models are well attested (*simulacra oppidorum* in Cic. *Pis.* 60; *ante suos currus oppida uicta feret* in Tib. 2.5.116; *cum simulacro captarum Syracusarum* in Liv. 26.21.7); but the idea does not combine well with *ebur*. For further discussion see B. III, Appendix 12.

The play which H. had in mind must have been one which allowed a display of the booty captured in Corinth in 146 B.C. to be represented as part of the spectacle. Cf. the 3,000 bowls which, though presumably part of Pompey's Asian loot, were shown in *The Trojan Horse* (see on 188 above). One notes the jingoistic repetition of *captiuum . . . captiua*.

194   foret: imperf. subjunctive in a present unreal condition; Wo. 193, no.3.

Democritus: Democritus of Abdera (5th and early 4th cent. B.C.) is supposed to have taken the view that human follies called for laughter rather than anger or despair. The content of his work *On cheerful-ness*, Περὶ εὐθυμίης (Diog. Laert. 9.45 and 46; cf. Cic. *De fin.* 5.87), probably gave rise to his reputation as the laughing philosopher. See Guthrie II 386ff. and the notes of Mayor and Courtney on Juv. 10.28ff. Democritus and Leucippus were the first proponents of atomism, a theory taken over by Epicurus and expounded by Lucre-tius in *De rerum natura*.

195 H. means a giraffe (*camelopardalis*), an animal first seen at Rome in Caesar's triumphal games in 46 B.C. (Dio 43.23.1-2; Varro, *LL* 5.100; Plin. *NH* 8.69). The construction is uncertain. It could be (i) *panthera confusa camelo* (subj.) *diuersum genus* (apposition), (ii) *diuersum genus* (subj.) *panthera confusa camelo* (apposition), (iii) *panthera confusa camelo* (subj.) *diuersum genus* (acc. of respect or retained acc.). Modern editors favour (iii). Perhaps they are right, but the parallels offered are not exact. Virgil could write *Cressa genus Pholoe* (*Aen.* 5.285) 'Pholoe, a Cretan as to her race'. But that is much easier than 'a leop-ard mixed with a camel as to its double species'. As for the retained acc., it is possible to turn *laeuo suspensi loculos tabulamque lacerto* (*S.* 1.6.74) and *delphinum caudas utero commissa luporum* (Virg. *Aen.* 3.428) into the active voice and still produce good sense: 'they would hang their satchels . . . on their left arm', 'she joined dolphins' tails to the bellies of wolves'. But again the present case is more difficult: 'a leop-ard mixed its double species with a camel'. As between (i) and (ii), *genus* seems less likely to be the subject than *panthera*; and also *panthera* is paralleled by *elephans* (196). These considerations point to (i), but one cannot be sure. The intertwined word-order is deliberate.

camelo: a clear case of the dat. after *confusus* is *ubi puluereae fuerint confusa farinae* (Ov. *Med. fac.* 61). The usage presumably arose from the idea of adding one element to another.

196   elephans albus: i.e. a rare albino.

conuerteret ora: the tense of the subjunctive is parallel to that of *foret* (194). The simple verb is used thus in *I.* 4.9-10 *ut ora uertat huc et huc euntium | liberrima indignatio.*

197   ludis . . . ipsis: i.e. *quam ludos ipsos.*

198   ut . . . praebentem gives an explanation, like ὡς + participle.
   nimio . . . plura 'more by a great degree', 'far more'. The variant

mimo gives weak sense, for the audience is said to provide a greater spectacle than the pageant just described (197); to bring in a single actor spoils this sequence of thought.

199   scriptores autem 'as for the writers', i.e. the playwrights.

199–200   H. combines two sayings, (i) *surdo narrare fabulam* 'to tell a tale to a deaf man', and (ii) ὄνωι λέγειν μῦθον 'to tell a tale to an ass'. See Ter. *Heaut.* 222 and Zenobius 5.42 respectively. The nouns *asello* and *fabellam* have a conversational quality appropriate to folk material.

201   eualuere 'have ever succeeded'.
    theatra 'theatres'. The satirically impersonal idea is taken up by *nemus* and *mare* (202).

202   Garganum ... nemus: the woods on the mountainous promontory of Garganus in Apulia, which projects into the Adriatic.
    mare Tuscum: the sea off the west coast of Italy.

203   artes 'works of art', cf. *E.* 1.6.17.

204   diuitiaeque: the wealth included jewellery and embroidered costumes, as we see from what follows.
    oblĭtus: from *oblino*, literally 'smeared' or 'plastered', hence 'over-decorated'; cf. *tua enim* [*uilla*] *oblita tabulis pictis* (Varro, *RR* 3.2.5).

205   cum stetit: as *cum* = 'whenever', the indicative is normal; Wo. 233; G–L 567.
    concurrit dextera laeuae 'right [hand] clashes with left'; *laeuae* is dat. The phrase indicates a mindless response.

206   nil sane 'nothing at all'.

207   laena: according to *OLD*, the word, which means a woollen cloak, was adapted from the Greek χλαῖνα, perhaps through Etruscan. For the purple cloak cf. the *hyacinthina laena* ridiculed by Persius (1.32). *laena* here is a clever conjecture, proposed by Marcilius and made independently by Markland (see B.). The MSS *lana* (wool) makes less good sense, for the audience is looking at the garment rather than the material.
    Tarentino ... ueneno: the Spartans had a long-established ex-

pertise in dyeing (Nisbet on *C*. 2.18.7), and Tarentum was a Spartan settlement. See also Plin. *NH* 9.137, which mentions in particular its red purple. Since *imitari* can sometimes imply 'not genuine' and *uenenum* can sometimes mean 'poison', their combination adds force to H.'s disapproval.

208   quae ... recusem: *illa*, understood before this clause, is the object of both *laudare* and *tractent*. *recusem* is in a subordinate clause in indirect speech; but it would still be a potential subjunctive in the direct construction: 'I would refuse if asked'.

209   recte 'well'.

210   For the difficulties and thrills of tightrope-walking, cf. the following passage from Pliny: *uides qui per funem in summa nituntur quantos soleant excitare clamores, cum iam iamque casuri uidentur, sunt enim maxime mirabilia quae maxime insperata, maxime periculosa ... (Epist.* 9.26.3); see also Manil. *Astr.* 5.653–5.

For *per* denoting motion over, cf. *C*. 2.1.7 *incedis per ignes*, where H. refers to walking over a crust of lava.

211   inaniter 'by illusions', i.e. without any real basis; the word goes with *irritat* and *mulcet* as well as with *angit*.

212   irritat 'stirs up'.

213   ut magus: the magician, too, works with *carmina* or 'spells'. The postponed position of the phrase allows it to influence what follows.

Thebis ... Athenis: the dramatic poet transports his audience to Thebes (as with *Oedipus Tyrannus*) or to Athens (as with *Hippolytus*).

214–6   uerum age et his ... redde: here the *et* probably goes with *his* ('to these writers too'), signalling the introduction of another category of poets. *age* can be followed by another imperative without any connective, as in *age dic Latinum, barbite, carmen* (*C*. 1.32.3–4).

215   fastidia 'disdain'.
superbi 'contemptuous'.

216   redde: not 'give back', but 'give, as is due'.
munus Apolline dignum: the temple of Apollo on the Palatine,

dedicated in 28 B.C., had a portico. Adjoining this portico, or perhaps forming part of it, was the library. It consisted of two sections, one Greek and one Latin, with medallion portraits of famous writers on the walls. It was large enough for senate meetings. See Platner and Ashby 16–19.

217 uis complere: at this point it becomes clear that H. is now addressing Augustus specifically.

218 The idea of the poet as a steed continues from *calcar* (217). The figure of Pegasus may be in the back of H.'s mind.

Helicona uirentem 'the green pastures of Helicon'. Mt Helicon in Boeotia, between Lake Copais and the Gulf of Corinth, was sacred to the Muses. In the course of time, Mt Helicon as the source of inspiration became rather a cliché; hence H.'s tone is half ironical.

219 quidem 'admittedly'.

220 ut uineta ... caedam mea: like 125 above, the phrase has a proverbial ring; but before accepting ps.-Acr.'s statement that it *was* a proverb, we should check how many other instances are extant; in fact there are none. What we do have is the following pair: (i) the fragment of some Greek comedy: τὴν αὐτὸς αὐτοῦ γὰρ θύραν κρούει λίθωι, 'he strikes with a stone on his own door' (*Com. Att. Frag.* Kock III 564), and (ii) Tib. 1.2.100 (addressed to Venus) *quid messes uris, acerba, tuas?* So the idea, in a loose form, was traditional. That is as far as we can go. For roughly similar expressions in English, cf. 'fouling one's own nest', 'digging one's own grave', and 'cutting one's own throat'.

223 loca 'passages'; for this sense the prose form is *loci*.

reuoluimus: lit. 'roll back', in order to read again.

irreuocati: *reuocare* meant 'to call back for an encore'. The form *irreuocati*, however, is without parallel, and may be a coinage. The rhythm of the line, with its absence of strong caesuras, and its sound (the recurring *re-, re-, irre-*) may satirise the idea of tedious repetition.

224 non apparere 'are not noticed'.

labores: for the idea of effort cf. *quemuis efferre laborem* (Lucr. *DRN* 1.141); *operosa paruus | carmina fingo* (*C.* 4.2.31–2). The idea had occurred in the writings of the Alexandrians, e.g. Theoc. 7.51: τὸ μελύδριον ἐξεπόνασα, and πόνος had been used of a poetic work, e.g. Call. *Epig.* 7.1 (cf. Asclepiades, *A.P.* 7.11.1). Sometimes the poet was represented as working late into the night, e.g. Cinna 11–12 *(FPL* 89) *Arateis multum inuigilata lucernis | carmina*; cf. Call. *Epig.* 29.4 = *A.P.* 9.507, and also *noctes uigilare serenas* (Lucr. *DRN* 1.142).

225 tenui ... filo 'with how fine a thread our poems are spun' (Wk.). The idea of delicate craftmanship recalls the Greek λεπτός (Call. *Epig.* 29.3 = *A.P.* 9.509) and λεπταλέος (Call. *Aet.* 1.24). Possibly the metaphor of spinning also occurred in some lost passages of Alexandrian poetry; but, as it is, we have no Greek parallel for Virgil's *deductum dicere carmen* (*Ecl.* 6.5) and H.'s *deducta poemata* here.

227 ultro: i.e. without any previous requests from us.

228 egere uetes: i.e. put an end to our poverty. Apart from playwrights, poets could hope for financial assistance only through patronage, and the Emperor was now the chief patron.

scribere cogas: lit. 'compel us to write'; cf. *haud mollia iussa* (Virg. *Georg.* 3.41, addressing Maecenas). With *arcessas, uetes,* and *cogas* H. has over-emphasised the degree of compulsion exercised on writers by Augustus, just as he has over-emphasised the poets' feelings of humble dependence with *laedimur* and *lamentamur*; the poets, we are told, actually *hope* to be subjected to this high-handed benevolence (*speramus*). Rather than diluting the force of *cogas*, we should (as often with H.) recognise a certain amount of good-humoured exaggeration. By this exaggeration H. implies that the gap between the poets and the Princeps is really not so wide as to be intolerable. Nevertheless, as everyone knew, the wishes of Augustus (whether invitations, exhortations, or straight commands) carried a special weight. Plato's Seventh Epistle states the general truth τὰς τῶν τυράννων δεήσεις ἴσμεν ὅτι μεμειγμέναι ἀνάγκαις εἰσίν, 'we are aware that the requests of tyrants have an ingredient of coercion' (329 D); cf. Cic. *Att.* 9.13.4. See the article by Griffin for further discussion.

229 est operae pretium: *operae* is gen., 'it is a recompense of trouble', hence 'it is worth while'. This formula of transition has a rather grand pedigree going back to Ennius: *audire est operae pretium procedere recte qui rem Romanam Latiumque augescere uoltis* (*ROL* 1 471–2; Skutsch 494–5).

230 aedituos: caretakers, who would act as guides to visitors, retailing the god's works and explaining the rituals in his honour. In Rome the job was done by freedmen or public slaves.

belli . . . domique 'war and peace'.

spectata 'conspicuous'.

231 uirtus: as if the poets were caretakers in the temple of *Virtus Augusti*. In the 2nd cent. B.C. Scipio Aemilianus had built a temple to *Virtus* (Plut. *De fort. Rom.* 5; *Moralia*, Loeb IV); and to judge from H. *S.* 2.1.70 (*scilicet uni aequus Virtuti atque eius amicis*) and *S.* 2.1.72 (*uirtus Scipiadae*) he was addressed in some such terms by Lucilius.

232 Alexander the Great's dates are 356–323 B.C.

ille 'the notorious'.

233 Choerilus of Iasos in Caria attached himself to the retinue of Alexander and wrote second-rate epics in his honour; cf. *AP* 357.

incultis . . . et male natis: dat. 'in return for his uncouth and misbegotten verses'.

234 rettulit acceptos: lit. 'entered as received', a term from bookkeeping.

regale nomisma 'a royal issue'; for occurrences of the rare Greek importation, *nomisma*, see B.

Philippos: the Philippus was a gold piece, coined by Philip II of Macedon, Alexander's father. One side had the head of Apollo, the other a chariot. For illustrations see Jenkins, pl. nos. 232, 234–40; Kraay, no. 565 (pl. XVIII and pl. 171).

235–7 The comparison is very imperfect. In full it would look something like this: 'just as black fluid when used [by an incompetent person] produces blots and stains [on a clean surface], so by means of ugly verses writers as a rule defile illustrious deeds'.

237–8 H. represents Alexander as paying a huge sum for Choerilus' absurd poetry. The intention is to underline the contrast between the king's literary taste and his taste in art (see 239–41). But stories from the scholiasts suggest that H. has distorted the tradition. According to Porph. on *AP* 357, only seven good lines were produced (so ps.-Acr. here); and Alexander said he would sooner be Homer's Thersites than Choerilus' Achilles. Ps.-Acr. on *AP* 357 says that Alexander arranged to give a gold coin for every good line and a blow for every bad one; as a result Choerilus was beaten to death.

239 edicto uetuit: the fullest, and most extreme, form of this story is in Plin. *NH* 7.125 *idem hic imperator edixit ne quis ipsum alius quam Apelles pingeret, quam Pyrgoteles scalperet, quam Lysippus ex aere duceret*; cf. Plut. *De Alex. fort. aut uirt.* 1, *Mor.* 335B, Loeb IV (ἐκέλευε), and *Alex.* 4, Loeb VII (ἠξίου). Cicero's version is less autocratic: *Alexander ille . . . ab Apelle potissimum pingi et a Lysippo fingi uolebat (Fam.* 5.12.7).

Apellen: Apelles of Ephesus painted portraits of Philip and Alexander. (One of the most famous represented Alexander brandishing a thunderbolt.) Other subjects included Artemis and her chorus of maidens, an allegory of Calumny, and a picture of Aphrodite rising from the sea. See Pollitt 163–9.

240 Lysippo: abl. of comparison. Lysippus of Sicyon, who flourished in the last quarter of the 4th cent. B.C., produced outstanding sculptures of gods (Zeus, Poseidon, Apollo), heroes (Hercules), and men (Alexander and his generals). His statues had smaller heads and a more slender physique than those of his predecessors. Amongst his most celebrated works were a statue of Alexander with a spear, and a representation of an athlete scraping himself with a strigil (apoxyomenus). See Pollitt 143–51; Richter 151, no. 202.

duceret 'make' by modelling; *OLD duco* 23a.

aera: not, strictly, the bronze material itself, but rather bronze artefacts, whether heads or full-length statues. When the material is referred to, it is put in the abl., with or without a preposition, e.g. *uiuos ducent de marmore uultus* (Virg. *Aen.* 6.848), *leues ocreas lento ducunt argento* (Virg. *Aen.* 7.634).

242 iudicium ... artibus 'that judgement which was so discriminating in viewing works of art'. The contrast between *artibus* and *libros* indicates that *artes* is being used in the sense of artefacts – *OLD ars* 8b. So to render *uidendis artibus* as 'visual arts' or '*des arts plastiques*' is less satisfactory. For the use of *uideo* cf. *uolet haec sub luce uideri (AP* 363). It is not easy to decide whether *artibus* is dat. or abl. Clear analogies are lacking. The abl. of the gerundive without *in* is usually instrumental; on the other hand it is hard to find the dat. of the gerundive with *subtilis* or similar adjs., e.g. *callidus, doctus, peritus, uersutus*.

243   et 'and in particular'.

haec Musarum dona: the gifts of the Muses are works of poetry;
cf. *munera . . . Musarum*, Cat. 68.10. The type of poetry under discussion (*haec*) is non-dramatic and celebratory.

244   Boeotum: this is best taken as a gen. pl. = Βοιωτῶν, with *in
crasso aere* (*crasso* serving as a contrast to *subtile*). The construction may
perhaps be echoed in Juv. 10.50 *ueruecum in patria crassoque sub aere
nasci*. Boeotia, with its lakes and valleys, had a rather heavy and
misty atmosphere in comparison with that of Athens: *Athenis tenue
caelum, ex quo acutiores etiam putantur Attici: crassum Thebis, itaque pingues
Thebani* (Cic. *De fat.* 7). The belief that climate affected mentality was
widespread in antiquity; see Mayor and Courtney on Juv. 10.50.
The question has been studied in our own century by Ellsworth
Huntington.

K–H point out that with *uocares* the grammatical object (the neuter
iudicium) begins to become personal, and that *natum* at the end of 244 is
felt to be masculine referring to Alexander, the judgement's owner.
This process is rendered more abrupt if *Boeotum* is taken as the acc. of a
substantive 'if you had asked that judgement to consider books, you
would have sworn he was a Boeotian'. Nor is it satisfactory to take
Boeotum as an adj. qualifying *iudicium*: 'you would have sworn it was a
Boeotian one, born in a thick atmosphere'.

245   dedecorant 'bring discredit on'; the subj. is *Vergilius Variusque*
(247).

tua . . . iudicia: Augustus' judgement is contrasted with Alexander's.

246   munera: the gifts of the Muses (243) produce in return gifts of
a more material kind. According to ps.-Acr., both poets had received
1,000,000 sesterces from Augustus. At his death Virgil is said to have
had 10,000,000 (Suet. *Virg.* 13); another source (a note found in two
MSS of the late 8th and mid-9th cent.) says that Varius received
1,000,000 for his *Thyestes*; see Jocelyn (2) 387.

multa . . . laude: i.e. the gifts reflected credit on the giver.

247   The subject of the verb is postponed, thus acquiring emphasis.
When it arrives, it turns out to be the pair who started H. on his
career (*Vergilius, post hunc Varius, dixere quid essem, S.* 1.6.55). Here they
appear as the Emperor's friends, and also as poets. The whole unit ex-

actly fills the line, thus lodging in the memory; cf. *S.* 1.4.1 *Eupolis atque Cratinus Aristophanesque poetae.*

Virgil's dates are 70–19 B.C.; so, if we are right in assigning this epistle to the beginning of 12 B.C., he had been dead a little over six years. Varius, along with Plotius Tucca, prepared the *Aeneid* for publication; how much longer he lived is not known.

L. Varius Rufus was a distinguished poet on his own account. His activity as a writer of epic is mentioned as early as *S.* 1.10.43–4 and again in *C.* 1.6.1–2; but the subject of his poem is uncertain. Macrobius (*Sat.* 6.1.39–40; 6.2.19–20) preserves four fragments of his *De morte.* The first two contain what appears to be an attack on Mark Antony; the others are illustrative passages describing a horse and a hound. For text, see *FPL* 100. Was the *De morte* Varius's epic? Or was it, as some think, a didactic poem? There is evidence, of a rather slender kind, that Varius wrote elegies (Porph. on *C.* 1.6.1), and a panegyric on Augustus (ps.-Acr. on *E.* 1.16.25, where the scholiast's text has *Varus*). But his tragedy *Thyestes* is well attested. Quintilian thought it equal to anything by the Greeks (*IO* 10.1.98; cf. Tac. *Dial.* 12.6). For details about the play see Coffey and Jocelyn (2).

248–50 The construction is *nec magis apparent uultus uirorum clarorum, expressi per aenea signa, quam mores animique [eorum], expressi per uatis opus.* For the thought cf. *C.* 4.8.13–20, and Cic. *Pro Arch.* 14 and 30.

nec magis . . . apparent 'are not more clearly visible'.

250   sermones: object of *componere* (251).

251   repentes per humum: H.'s hexameter poems are 'talks' or 'discourses' (*sermones*) on subjects of moral and literary interest. As the pieces themselves are, with a few exceptions, fairly short, and as they do not set out to celebrate heroes and their mighty deeds, they occupy a relatively low position in the hierarchy of genres – certainly below epic, tragedy, and choral lyric. H. accepted this position, maintaining that he lacked the power and stamina to compose an epic. No doubt he was right, but an exaggerated phrase like *repentes per humum* should put us on our guard. First, H. had glorified Augustus in a number of great lyric poems (e.g. *C.* 3.4), which were by no means lacking in nobility, seriousness, or inspiration. Secondly, even the final ode of Book 4, a delightful poem in praise of Augustus, had begun with a

Callimachean claim that the author had been deterred from anything grander by the intervention of Apollo. Thirdly, one must beware of crude generalisations about the *sermones*. Although the style is, in the main, relaxed and conversational, it moves easily up and down according to the requirements of the theme and the poet's mood. In the first 17 lines of this epistle, for example, the tone and language are formal and deferential, for obvious reasons. And as we move on to the description of *res gestae* (251-6), we sense that ideas and diction are at a level quite unusual for the genre; H. is giving us a glimpse of what he cannot, and will not, do, except for short periods.

res componere gestas: i.e. to compose a historical epic or panegyric in honour of Augustus.

252   terrarumque situs et flumina: Velleius (born *c.* 20 B.C.) promises, but postpones, some similar material in praise of Tiberius: *gentes Pannoniorum Delmatarumque nationes situmque regionum ac fluminum numerumque et modum uirium excelsissimasque et multiplices eo bello uictorias tanti imperatoris alio loco explicabimus* (2.96). Descriptions of strange and far-away places were regularly used to enhance the prestige of the conqueror. For later references see Doblhofer 67-79, who reminds us that tableaux of cities and rivers were carried in Roman triumphal processions; cf. Prop. 2.1.31-4; 3.4.15-16; Ov. *AA* 1.219-28.

252-3 arces | montibus impositas: i.e. fortified hill-towns. A comparison with *milite nam tuo | Drusus Genaunos ... | Breunosque ueloces et arces | Alpibus impositas tremendis | deiecit ...* (*C.* 4.14.9-13) shows that H. is thinking of the Alpine victories of Augustus' stepsons, Tiberius and Drusus, in 15 B.C. For an account of the campaigns see *CAH* x 349-50.

barbara regna: see the long list of conquests in *Res Gestae* 26-33.

253-4   tuisque | auspiciis: as a general conducted a religious ceremony before going into battle to ensure that he enjoyed the favour of the gods, the fighting was said to take place under his auspices. In the case of Augustus, since he was Commander-in-Chief, all campaigns took place under his auspices, even those which he did not lead in person; cf. *milite ... tuo* (on 252-3 above) and *partim ductu, partim auspiciis suis* (Suet. *Aug.* 21.1).

254   totum ... per orbem: at the end of *Georg.* 1, Virgil had hoped that the young (Augustus) Caesar would save a war-torn world *quippe* *ubi fas uersum atque nefas; tot bella per orbem* (505). Here that task is presented as accomplished; cf. Vell. 2.89.3; *Res Gestae* 13. In fact the picture of universal peace was illusory. Late in 13 b.c. Agrippa started his campaign in Illyricum; in 12 operations began in Germany to extend the frontier to the Elbe; and shortly after that came an insurrection in Thrace.

duella: an archaic word, revived by H. on the principles stated in *E.* 2.2.115–18.

255 custodem: H. paradoxically represents the *custos* as behind bars.

Ianum: Janus was the god of gate and arch, of entrances and exits. He was therefore shown with two faces looking in opposite directions. As god of entrances, he presided over beginnings, including the beginning of the day (*S.* 2.6.20–23) and the beginning of the year (Ov. *Fast.* 1.65). In accordance with a custom which was supposed to go back to Numa Pompilius, his temple was closed only in time of peace *ius institutum a Pompilio ... ut sit aperta semper, nisi cum bellum sit nusquam* (Piso in Varro, *LL* 5.165). For an early reference see Ennius, *Ann.* 225–6 with Skutsch's note. The opening of the temple doors presumably signified the beginning of war; they remained open as long as the business was unfinished. Under Augustus they were closed on three occasions: in 29 b.c., in 25 or early 24, and in 8 or 7; see Syme (3) 25.

256 formidatam Parthis ... Romam: this refers to the events of 20 b.c., in particular the ceremony at which Phraates of Parthia restored to Augustus the standards captured from Crassus at Carrhae in 53 b.c. and from Mark Antony in 40 and 36 (see *CAH* x 260–5). Although no violence took place, the standards would not have been handed over without the presence of a Roman army; hence *formidatam* is justified. Augustus' propaganda, however, went a good deal further, encouraging people to think of the episode as a military victory. Thus in the *Res Gestae* (29) Augustus records the recapture of standards from Spain, Gaul, and Dalmatia *deuictis hostibus*; he adds *Parthos trium exercituum Romanorum spolia et signa reddere supplicesque amicitiam populi Romani petere coegi*; and then goes on to speak of the conquest of the Pannonian tribes (*deuictas* in 30). Cf. Suet. *Aug.* 21.3; Hor. *E.* 1.12.27–8 (*ius imperiumque Phraates Caesaris accepit genibus minor*); *E.* 1.18.54–7. See also the figures in the centre of the breastplate on the statue of Augustus from Prima Porta (Taylor 179; Earl pl. 37), and the coins illustrated in Mattingly, pl. 16, no. 20; pl. 17, nos. 1,2,7; and in Sutherland 132, no. 238, and 137, no. 247.

Several scholars have been reminded of the notorious line from Cicero's poem on his consulship *o fortunatam natam me consule Romam*! If the echo was intended, H. has removed the objectionable jingle *-natam natam*, and he has diverted the compliment away from the writer himself to another party. For discussion of the question, and bibliography, see Allen.

257   cuperem: attracted to the mood of *possem*, which is an unreal present condition; Wo. 193 no. 3. 'The verb is most easily attracted when the clause is actually interpolated into the phrase which contains the attracting subjunctive', Handford 161 (b) i. H. excuses himself with a similar plea of inadequacy in *C.* 1.6.5–20 and *S.* 2.1.12–13; cf. *C.* 4.2.27–32; 4.15.1–4. The same sort of evasion seems to have been practised by Lucilius (*ROL* III 691, 702, 703, 704). See also Virg. *Ecl.* 6.3–8; Prop. 2.10; 3.1.15–20; 3.9.1–4. The tactics of the so-called *recusatio* have been studied by Wimmel; see also Hopkinson 98–101.

257–8   neque paruum | ... recipit: Augustus' general policy on this matter is recorded by Suetonius *recitantis et benigne et patienter audiit, nec tantum carmina et historias, sed et orationes et dialogos. componi tamen aliquid de se nisi et serio et a praestantissimis offendebatur, admonebatque praetores ne paterentur nomen suum commissionibus obsolefieri* (*Aug.* 89.3).

maiestas ... tua: the first example of 'your majesty', which was to become formalised as 'Your Majesty'. Being related to *maior*, the word is naturally contrasted with *paruum* (*carmen*).

259   uires ferre recusent: H. is practising what he was to preach in *AP* 38–40 *sumite materiam uestris, qui scribitis, aequam | uiribus, et uersate diu, quid ferre recusent, | quid ualeant umeri.*

recusent: generic subjunctive. Wo. 155 shows how this use arose from the potential subjunctive.

260   The punctuation is Ben.'s. As W. says, to take *stulte quem diligit* together would be inappropriate, for the *quem* could be referred to Augustus.

sedulitas 'zealous attention'.

urget 'causes vexation to'.

261 se ... commendat 'seeks to win approval'.

numeris ... et arte: a hendiadys, 'the art of poetry'. K–H include fine art; but (i) since *nec sermones* (250), H. has been talking only of poetry; (ii) in the present context *numeris* alone would be inadequate for poetry and *arte* for fine art; (iii) the assertion in 260–1 is explained by *discit enim citius* etc. (262), which naturally refers to the learning of poetry.

262–3 A sad comment on human nature. K–H quote Cic. *De orat.* 1.129 *nihil est enim tam insigne, nec tam ad diuturnitatem memoriae stabile, quam id in quo aliquid offenderis.* The subject of *discit* is *aliquis*, supplied from *quis* (263), which, after the relative *quod,* = *aliquis*; G–L 107 RI.

264–70 In view of the undignified ending which he has in mind, H. tactfully substitutes himself for the *princeps*.

264 nil moror: lit. 'I do not detain', hence 'away with'.
officium: the same as *sedulitas* (260).

264–5 ficto | in peius uultu: lit. 'with a face fashioned for the worse'. The incompetent artist produces both a bad likeness and an ugly work. It may be misleading to use the word 'caricature' in this context; for a good caricature can somehow distort without sacrificing the likeness.

proponi cereus 'to be displayed in wax', *cereus* being predicative.

266 decorari 'to be glorified or embellished'; placed within the phrase *praue factis ... uersibus*, the word is amusingly sarcastic.

267 ne rubeam: this is usually translated as 'blush [with embarrassment]'; but such a mild idea combines oddly with *porrectus ... deferar*. One might leave open the possibility of a more violent reaction by translating 'flush'. This would allow for mortification and anger, even if the notion of apoplexy is thought too extreme.

pingui: the gift is crass because of its wretched poetry. For the Callimachean background of *pinguis*, see on 76–7.

268 The addressee and the composer of the bad poem are both thought of as symbolically present in its pages. So when these are packed off as waste-paper, donor and recipient are together consigned to oblivion.

capsa ... operta: *operta* is the reading of the best MSS and of Porph. A book-box full of waste-paper can easily be thought of as covered. The coffin (present as a secondary idea) would imply more obscure contents if closed. So there is no justification for reading *aperta*.

porrectus: *OLD porrigo* 2 'to lay prostrate, stretch out (in sleep or death)'; cf. *I.* 10.21–2 *opima quodsi praeda curuo litore | porrecta mergos iuuerit.*

269   uicum uendentem tus: lit. 'the street selling incense', a punning reference to the *uicus Tuscus*, a street originally inhabited by Etruscan settlers. It contained small shops of various kinds, and was situated in the disreputable area of the Subura; cf. *Tusci turba impia uici* (*S.* 2.3.228).

odores: since the goods are dry, the reference must be to aromatic herbs and the like; *OLD odor* 3. (Our 'perfume' or 'scent' is misleading.)

270   quidquid ... amicitur: this seems to be a reworking of *at Volusi annales Paduam morientur ad ipsam, | et laxas scombris saepe dabunt tunicas* (Cat. 95.7–8).

chartis ... ineptis: the sheets are 'fatuous' or 'silly' in virtue of their bad poetry. They are also, by the same token, unfitted for literary purposes, and must therefore be regarded as waste-paper. The idea of 'unfitted' or 'unfitting' is given by the etymology of *ineptus*, i.e. *in* + *aptus*; cf. the *inepta crura* of the bridge in Cat. 17.2–3.

As for the last three lines as a whole, if we take *porrectus* (268), plus *morientur* from the passage of Catullus which H. has in mind, plus Porph.'s comment *quasi mortuus in feretro*, we need not doubt the funeral imagery. It may be that *capsa* is not elsewhere equated with *arca* or *feretrum*; but such an equation is surely the point of the present witticism.

The Epistle to Florus (*Epistles* 2.2)

1   Flore ... Neroni: for the characters see pp. 12–13 above.

bono: of moral character.

claroque: of birth and status.

amice: *amicitia* did not necessarily imply a warm, personal, relationship between equals. Florus would not have been on the same footing as Tiberius in power or status.

2–17 The construction is *si quis uelit ... et agat ... ille ferat.* The seller is probably an owner rather than a dealer; see 13.

3 Tibure: Tibur (Tivoli) stands on the falls of the Anio, 760 ft above sea level, about 18 miles ENE of Rome.

Gabiis: Gabii was an old Latin town about 14 miles E of Rome. The boy (2) is therefore a *uerna* (6), born and reared in a Latin household. The owner is in a position to vouch for his character and abilities.

4 candidus 'fair', referring in a complimentary way to the boy's complexion.

talos a uertice ... ad imos 'from head to toe'.

5 At 8,000 sesterces the boy was expensive in comparison with Davus, who is supposed to have cost 2,000 (*S.* 2.7.43), with the cooks valued at 2,700 by Pliny, *NH* 9.67, and with the slave bought for 1,200 by Habinnas in Petronius, *Sat.* 68. But he was cheap in comparison with those mentioned by Martial as costing 20,000 (8.13, 11.38) and 100,000 (1.58, 3.62, 11.70). See Duncan-Jones, Appendix 10.

6 aptus: with *ministeriis*; the phrase is amplified by *ad nutus eriles.*

7 litterulis ... imbutus: both words have a slightly belittling force: 'a smattering of basic Greek'. A literate slave could be employed as a reader, copyist, or secretary.

8 argilla ... uda 'as the clay is wet, you will be able to mould it into whatever shape you please'.

9 indoctum ... dulce: adverbial acc., G–L 91.1c.

bibenti: i.e. when you are having your evening drink. Since this was the usual time for such entertainment there is no reason to regard *bibenti* as hinting at a further disparagement: 'at any rate over your wine'.

10 fidem ... leuant 'reduce credibility'.

11 extrudere 'to get rid of'.

12   meo . . . aere 'though poor, I am in funds'.

13–14   faceret . . . ferret: potential subjunctives of the 'present unreal' type; Wo. 193.3.

13   temere 'readily'.

14   semel . . . cessauit 'he once shirked his work' (W.). The shirking and the subsequent hiding constituted the *fuga* (16). There was some debate about the definition of *fuga*. In the *Digest* of Roman law the question is raised 'What of the man who hid in the house with a view to absconding when the opportunity occurred?' According to certain authorities, even if he did not actually leave, he was still a runaway because of his intention. But if he hid only until his master's anger simmered down, he was not a runaway (21.1.17.4). The seller, then, is perhaps being over-scrupulous in using such a term, but he is anxious to protect himself against any come-back on the part of the purchaser.

15   in scalis latuit: as the punctuation indicates, these words probably go together. The other possibility is to take *in scalis* with *pendentis habenae*; but (i) it is more relevant to know where the boy hid than where the strap was hanging. (Possibly it was not hanging at all, for *pendentis* might mean 'uplifted'.) (ii) *in scalis latuit* gives more precision than *latuit* alone to *ut fit*. The stairs as a customary hiding place is supported by Cic. *Pro Mil.* 40 *cum se ille fugiens in scalarum latebras abdidisset*, and *Pro Corn.* fr. *correpsit in scalas* (quoted by Schol. on Juv. 7.118). (iii) The view adopted here gives a smoother and more natural word-order.

   metuens: as often, an adj. followed by an objective gen.; 'fearful'.

16 excepta . . . fuga: in the sale of slaves and cattle, the usual principle of *caueat emptor* did not apply. The vendor had to declare any defect in his goods. Thus the curule aedile's edict read 'see to it that the sale-ticket of every slave is written so as to make clear what ailment or fault each one has, which is a runaway (*fugitiuus*) or given to wandering off (*erro*), or is still undischarged for some offence' (Gell. *NA* 4.2.1; cf. Cic. *De off.* 3.71, *Digest* 21.1.1.1–2, and Crook 181–7).

   laedit 'puts you off'.

17   poenae securus: gen. of reference (Wo. 73.6).

18   prudens 'with your eyes open'.

dicta ... est lex 'the terms were stated'.

19   moraris 'detain', 'trouble'.

20   dixi ... dixi reinforce *dicta* (18).

21   talibus officiis: it is not surprising that, like *aptus* 'efficient' or 'capable', its opposite *mancus* could be used not only with *ad* + acc., as in *ad mandata ... mancus* (Plaut, *Merc.* 630), but also with the dat., though this is the only recorded instance.

prope mancum 'pretty well incapacitated'.

mea: though placed early, this goes with *epistula nulla*, 'no letter of mine'.

23   tum: whether H. means 'What did I achieve then?' or 'What, then, have I achieved?', the word carries only a light stress.

mecum facientia 'on my side'; see *OLD facio* 29a. The force of the participle is concessive.

24   attemptas 'contest'.

super hoc: the main possibilities are: (i) 'in regard to this matter', *OLD super* prep. B (with abl.) 11, (ii) 'besides', *OLD super* adv. 3 (then *hoc* goes with *quereris*), (iii) 'in addition to this', *OLD super* prep. A (with acc.) 7. Of these (i) seems slightly weaker rhetorically; (ii) and (iii) are equally balanced. H. would have indicated his preference in reciting the poem; but one wonders how the ordinary Roman reader could have decided the matter.

25   carmina: here 'lyrics' rather than 'poems'; see 76 (*canoros*) and 77–80.

mendax 'false to my promise'. The position of the word enhances its force.

26 Luculli miles: L. Licinius Lucullus conducted a number of campaigns against Mithridates of Pontus and Tigranes I of Armenia in the period after 74 B.C. (Plut. *Lucull.* and App. *Mith.*). He won several victories, but the discipline of some of the legions which he took over was poor. (Porph. on 26 mentions the soldiers who had served under Valerius Flaccus and Servilius Isauricus.) He himself lacked diplomacy; and because of his fair administration of the cities of Asia

Minor he made enemies in Rome. He was relieved of his command in
64 B.C. See *CAH* IX 365–71.

uiatica: originally *uiaticum* (sing. or pl.) meant 'travel-money'.
By H.'s time it could also mean, as here, 'savings'. Since the misfortune is related of only one soldier, and since the theft took place
while he was asleep, we may assume he had his money with him and
had not deposited it at the camp.

28 perdiderat: this happened before the main action took place.
For the pluperfect introducing a story cf. *E.* 1.7.29–30 *forte ... uulpe-
cula ... | repserat in cumeram.*

30 regale 'belonging to the king', whether Tigranes or Mithridates.

31 summe 'in the highest degree', hence 'very strongly'.
diuite rerum: *diues* takes a gen. by analogy with *plenus*; Wo. 73. II
(3) n. 1.

32 donis ornatur honestis: Roman military decorations included
various kinds of crown, a special spear and banner, neck-rings, arm-
lets, badges, and horse-trappings; see Maxfield, chap. 4.

33 bis dena sestertia 'twice ten thousands-of-sesterces'.
nummum: gen. pl. 'in cash'.

34 sub hoc tempus 'shortly after this'.

36 timido quoque 'even to a coward'.
mentem 'resolution'.

37 i pede fausto 'go, and good luck to you'.

38 laturus: the participle is here the equivalent of a main verb,
cf. *S.* 2.1.10–12 *aude | Caesaris inuicti res dicere, multa laborum |
praemia laturus.*

39 catus, quantumuis rusticus 'shrewd, for all his rusticity'.

39–40 ibit, | ibit mimics the commander's *i ... i* (37); *quo uis* varies
quo uirtus ... uocat.
zonam 'money-belt'.

41–52 This section presents autobiographical material, condensed and processed so as to support H.'s argument. In saying that it 'is not factual autobiography', B. (III 289) may give the misleading impression that certain incidents have been fabricated; but he is right to describe the argument as 'charming and self-satirizing'. H. presents himself as the passive plaything of fortune. For further comment see the introductory essay, p. 14.

41-5 The lines overlap with, and provide a sequel to, the account of H.'s education in *S.* 1.6.71-84.

42 This recalls the opening of the *Iliad* Μῆνιν ἄειδε, θεά, Πηληϊάδεω Ἀχιλῆος | οὐλομένην, ἥ μυρί' Ἀχαιοῖς ἄλγε' ἔθηκε 'Sing, Goddess, of the wrath of Achilles, Peleus' son, that baneful wrath which brought countless woes to the Achaeans.'

43   artis: a partitive gen. (G–L 367–72).
    bonae ... Athenae: an unusual phrase. The adj. is taken as 'kind' (W.), *liebe*, i.e. 'dear' (K–H), 'my *alma mater*' (Wk.). But perhaps, in view of what follows, it refers to Athens as the home of moral philosophy, hence 'Athens the good'. The other possibility is to take *bonae* with *artis*; but while *bonae artes* is a common phrase for the liberal arts, it is hard to find instances of the sing. *bona ars* used in a general sense. If, then, Athens the good added a little more *ars*, what does *ars* mean? Probably that which is imparted by training, as distinct from what is inherited; hence, generally, 'education'; what kind is specified in 44.

44   scilicet ut uellem: either (i) 'so that, of course, I was eager' or (ii) 'in the sense that I was eager'. On the first view, the further education which H. acquired in Athens stimulated him to study philosophy; on the second, the further education *was* philosophy, see *OLD scilicet* 5. View (i) is the more common, but (ii) is to be preferred as giving neater sense; so Villeneuve (Budé edn). The reading *possem*, altered from the corrupt *possim* to maintain the correct sequence, gives an unwanted note of confidence.

45   siluas Academi: after the death of Socrates (399 B.C.) Plato travelled to a number of places in the Mediterranean, including Magna Graecia. On his return he began to teach in a gymnasium called the Academy, which was situated on the river Cephisus about a mile NW of Athens. The area is supposed to have belonged to the old

Attic hero Hecademus, who revealed to the Dioscuri the whereabouts
of their sister Helen after Theseus had carried her off (Plut. *Thes.* 32).
For this reason the Spartans, who revered the Dioscuri, always spared
the Academy when they invaded Attica. It was walled in by Hip-
parchus, and adorned with trees by Cimon (Plut. *Cimon* 31), who be-
queathed it to the Athenians as a public park. Plato subsequently
bought a piece of property nearby, and he taught either in the park or
in his garden until his death in 348 B.C. (see Glucker, chap. 5). The
famous trees were cut down by Sulla in the siege of 87–86 (Plut. *Sulla*
12), but they were probably replanted long before Brutus attended
the Academy in 44 (Plut. *Brut.* 24.1). Like Brutus, H. doubtless heard
the lectures of Theomnestus.

46   dura ... tempora: the period in which Brutus and Cassius
struggled against Antony and Octavian. H. was recruited by Brutus
in Athens, probably followed him to Asia (*S.* 1.7.18–19), and fought
for him at Philippi (42 B.C.) as a *tribunus militum* (*S.* 1.6.48). Although
the tone of the passage is light, we are made aware of the terrible experiences which Horace shared with his fellow students. The classes of
1914 and 1939 would understand.

47   arma 'army'.

48   Caesaris Augusti: it was complimentary to apply retro-
spectively the title 'Augustus', which Octavian accepted in 27 B.C. But
with H., a deferential gesture is often accompanied by a smiling bow
which preserves his self-respect. Here the sonorous title is qualified by
the prosaic *lacertis* 'brawny arms'; but many readers would have been
aware that it was Antony who won the battle of Philippi; Octavian
was indisposed. (See Vell. 2.70.1; Suet. *Aug.* 13.1; Plut. *Brut.* 41, *Ant.*
22.1–4.)

   non responsura 'destined to be no match for'.

49–52   The humorous parallel between H. and Lucullus' soldier
consists in the following points: both had lost their money through
misfortune; both reacted energetically (the soldier by leading an
assault, H. by writing iambics and satires); both retrieved their fortunes; and both were reluctant to make further efforts. We are not
supposed to think of the fact that H. did not *immediately* recover his
fortune through his writing. In fact he managed to obtain a post in

the treasury. Also, since there were no contracts or royalties, no author could expect to make money directly from the book trade. H. could not have been sure that his early verse would attract a patron who would provide him with an income. No doubt he would have continued to write, though perhaps even less frequently, had no patron come forward. But because his writing *had* eventually led to enrichment, H. could now pretend that money had been his only motive.

49   simul primum = *simulac.*

50–1   inopemque ... laris: H.'s father had presumably died, and the estate had been confiscated because of H.'s supporting Brutus. *laris* is an extension of the partitive gen. See G–L 374 n. 1, Wo. 73. II (3).

52   quod non desit: the subjunctive is generic, 'such as to be sufficient'.

53   quae poterunt ... expurgare cicutae: the health of the human body was thought to depend on a proper mixture of the four humours: blood, black bile, yellow bile, and phlegm (Hippocrates, *De nat. hom.* 4). Sickness implied that the proportions had been disturbed, and so treatment aimed to reduce whichever element had become excessive. In the case of madness, the humour in question was black bile, and hellebore was thought to be the most efficacious remedy. See O'Brien-Moore, chap. 2. Hemlock, however (*cicuta*), was also used for this purpose. The fruits of hemlock, and to a lesser extent its leaves, contain the alkaloid conine, hence its scientific name *Conium maculatum*. While large doses of the substance cause vertigo, nausea, paralysis, and eventually death, in smaller quantities it has a sedative action on the nerves. Various uses are listed by Plin. *NH* 25.151–4. He also speaks of external application to relieve gout, swellings, and nosebleeds (26.101, 122, 131). *expurgare*, therefore, means 'to cure, by cleansing of excessive black bile'. The pl. *cicutae* implies doses.

53–4   poterunt ... ni ... putem: the basic sense is 'I would be incurably mad if I did not think sleep preferable'. For the main clause H. has substituted a rhetorical question; and instead of a verb in the subjunctive he has used the indicative of *possum*. See Wo. 125.

54   For the idea of the dedicated poet working at night cf. Cinna *haec*

tibi Arateis multum inuigilata lucernis | *carmina* (*FPL* 89) and Call. *Epig.*
29.4 = *A.P.* 9.507 Ἀρήτου σύμβολον ἀγρυπνίης. See also Lucr. *DRN*
1.142 *noctes uigilare serenas*, and Juv. 7.27 *uigilataque proelia*.

57   tendunt extorquere 'are straining to wrest'.
   quid faciam uis? 'What would you have me do?' A rhetorical
question. By itself, however, the question allows another possibility:
'What do you want me to compose?' This idea prompted the next excuse, perhaps as the result of a second reading.

58   denique 'moreover'; *OLD denique* 2b.

59   carmine: lyric, i.e. odes.
   iambis: i.e. epodes.

60   Bioneis sermonibus 'Bionean talks', i.e. satires. Bion was a
fishmonger's son from a Greek city on the N. coast of the Black Sea,
which the inhabitants called Olbia and other Greeks Borysthenes.
After an unsuccessful attempt at tax evasion the whole family was sold
into slavery. Bion was lucky enough to be bought by a rhetorician
who gave him an education and eventually left him enough money to
move to Athens. Arriving there about 315 B.C., he studied philosophy
with a succession of teachers. His διατριβαί, 'diatribes', were lively
informal homilies on ethical topics, and included such features as
character-sketches, animal similes, and dialogues with imaginary opponents. The English 'diatribe' has now come to mean an abusive
harangue. For a study of Bion see Kindstrand.
   sermones, as noted above, refers to the *Satires*. The *Epistles* can
hardly be included; for (i) an epistle is what H. is actually writing, (ii)
the *Epistles* are not characterised by *sal niger*, even allowing for some
exaggeration. Nevertheless, we are not in a position to say how close a
resemblance there was between H.'s *Satires* and Bion's diatribes.
   et: in a hendiadys with *Bioneis sermonibus*; best translated here as
'with'.
   sale nigro: literally 'black', therefore 'coarse' salt, as distinct from
sal candidus. Here the expression is used for pungent wit, cf. *S.*
1.10.3–4. Our 'coarse wit' has a rather different sense.

61   prope softens the boldness of the analogy, 'as it were'. The idea
of food may have been suggested by the literal meaning of *sal*.

62 uario ... palato: the position of the phrase is in favour of taking it as dat. with *poscentes* rather than as an abl. of quality with *conuiuae*.

63 renuis: refusal was indicated by throwing the head back, rather than by shaking it.

Ben. preferred the variant *quod tu* to *tu quod*; but this upsets the chiastic balance of main verb, *quod*-clause, *quod*-clause, main verb.

64 sane emphasises either the whole statement, 'you may be sure', or the adjs. *inuisum acidumque*.

67 sponsum 'to act as a guarantor'; for the supine see G–L 435.

67–8 Strictly speaking, to attend a recitation was itself an *officium*; but rather than understanding *aliis* with *officiis* we may prefer to think that the writer flatters himself by assuming that it is a pleasure rather than an *officium* to hear him recite – or at least a very different *officium* from the tedious kind; cf. *S*. 2.6.23–4 *Romae sponsorem me rapis: 'eia, | ne prior officio quisquam respondeat, urge'*.

cubat hic 'so-and-so is [ill] in bed'.

Quirini: the gen. of the proper name enables H. to achieve variety in the abl. *Auentino* (69).

69 uisendus: *uiso* was used of visiting the sick at least as early as Lucilius (*ROL* III fr. 189); cf. Hor. *S*. 1.9.17 *quendam uolo uisere non tibi notum*.

70 haud sane commoda: the transmitted text reads *humane commoda*, which must be taken ironically. Ps.-Acr. explains it as *probe commoda* 'jolly convenient'. Others think *humane* = φιλανθρώπως, 'considerately' or ἐπιεικῶς, 'reasonably'. But it is hard to find another instance of *humane* with an adj.; and the ironical effect, though regarded as *sonnenklar* ('clear as daylight') by K–H, sounds strained and un-Horatian. Of the various conjectures proposed (e.g., Ribbeck's *homini uni*, Schmidt's *naturae*, Jeep's *insane*) Froehlich's *haud sane commoda* is perhaps the most plausible: 'jolly inconvenient'. The excuse, of course, is H.'s, and it is countered by *uerum . . . obstet*.

71 purae 'clear'.

meditantibus 'working out verses'. This use, in which

meditari = componere, recurs in 76 below; cf. *S.* 1.9.2 *nescio quid meditans nugarum.* For other examples see *TLL* VIII 576.

72   calidus 'in hot haste'.

gerulisque 'porters'. The omission of *cum* is unexpected; contrast *C.* 3.1.35–6 *caementa demittit redemptor | cum famulis . . .* H. may be parodying the quasi-proverbial phrase *equis uirisque* (Cic. *De off.* 3.116).

redemptor 'contractor'.

73   torquet 'heaves', with a comic notion of menace, as if a siege were in progress. The 'huge contraption' is a crane. Some take *ingens* with *tignum*, understanding *ingentem* with *lapidum.* But, if H. had intended that, he could have written *nunc lapidum ingentem torquet nunc machina tignum*; whereas if he wanted *ingens* to go with *machina* he would naturally have written the line as printed. In a passage based on this Juvenal also has *tignum* without an adjective: *hic tignum capiti incutit, ille metretam* (3.246).

74   The 'golden line' (adj., adj., verb, noun, noun) is in mock-heroic vein (Wk.).

tristia implies, not decorous silence, but lamentation.

robustis 'massive'. For a similar scene cf. *S.* 1.6.42–3 *si plaustra ducenta | concurrantque foro tria funera.* The only vehicles allowed into the city in daylight were builders' waggons and carts for removing filth. See Friedländer IV, Appendix 6, 28–31.

75   There is a high degree of correspondence between the two halves of this dactylic line. The monosyllabic ending breaks the coincidence of ictus and accent in the fifth and sixth feet. The resulting abruptness, combined with the muddy sow, produces a comic effect. See B. on *AP* 139 and Fordyce on *Aen.* 7.592.

76   nunc 'now', i.e. 'in view of the conditions just described'. *i nunc* is a set phrase; cf. Virg. *Aen.* 7.425; Hor. *E.* 1.6.17; Prop. 3.18.17.

77–8   For the picture of the inspired poet, at leisure in the country-side, enjoying nature cf. Juv. 7.58–9. The commonplace is solemnly pondered by Quintilian in *IO* 10.3.22–4.

rite cliens Bacchi 'duly following their patron deity, Bacchus'. As a nature deity, Bacchus/Dionysus was frequently associated with poetic inspiration; see *C.* 2.19 and 3.25.

80   contracta ... uestigia uatum: the bards' narrow tracks are contrasted with the broad and busy highway trodden by others. Cf. Call. *Aet.* 1.1.25–8, and *Epig.* 30.1–2 = *A.P.* 12.43. Callimachus, however, is distinguishing good from bad poetry; H. has a more general purpose, viz. to contrast poetic seclusion with the hubbub of the city.

81   ingenium 'the intellect', here used to denote a comic figure. The present tense of *exit* (83) and *quatit* (84) indicates that H. is generalising.

uacuas: not 'uninhabited' but 'quiet'.

desumpsit: the perf. generalises (Wo. 217 (2) (c)); so translate by a present, 'chooses'.

82   insenuitque 'grows [prematurely] old'.

83   libris et curis 'bookish concerns', a hendiadys; abl., to judge from *E.* 1.7.85 (*amore senescit habendi*) and Quintilian, *IO* 8 pr. 18 (*quodam inani ... studio senescunt*).

exit 'emerges' preserves the ambiguity of the Latin.

85   The construction is *in mediis rerum fluctibus et in mediis urbis tempestatibus.*

86   lyrae: gen. with *sonum*.

motura 'capable of exciting'; cf. *o mutis quoque piscibus | donatura cycni, si libeat, sonum* (*C.* 4.3.19–20).

digner: deliberative subjunctive. The nuance is 'Am I to think it worth the effort?'

87   fautor: the MSS have *frater*, but then the consecutive *ut* can hardly be defended. The closest parallel seems at first to be H.'s description of the spring on his estate *fons etiam riuo dare nomen idoneus, ut nec | frigidior Thracam nec purior ambiat Hebrus, | ... fluit ...* (*E.* 1.16.12–14). But there the construction is not (*tam*) *idoneus ut*; rather, as K–H remark, we have to understand *frigidus et purus* before the *ut*. Nothing similar can be done here. Moreover, if the two brothers exchanged compliments, one might expect X to be called 'Tiberius' by Y (cf. *S.* 2.3.173), and Y to be called 'Gaius' by X. But here the orator X is called 'Gracchus' and the lawyer Y is called 'Mucius'. The fraternal relationship seems irrelevant. *fautor* (Schütz) is the most attractive conjecture. This word, which has the sense of the substantival *studiosus*, can more readily dispense with *tam* before *ut*, as happens with the adjs. *diues* (*S.* 1.1.95), *capitalis* (*S.* 1.7.13), and *inaequalis* (*S.* 2.7.10). Admittedly, however, *fautor* does have *sic* in *E.* 2.1.23.

There have also been doubts about *Romae* because H. commonly supplies a location for non-Roman, but not for Roman, anecdotes (*S.* 1.1.64; 2.5.84; *E.* 2.2.128). But since he has just spoken about philosophers making themselves ridiculous in Athens (81ff.) he now indicates that the next anecdote or illustration is set in Rome; cf. *E.* 2.1.103. Granted, this is not necessary, since a change of scene has already been signalled by *hic* (84), but the problem hardly calls for emendation.

88   meros ... honores 'unadulterated praise'.

89   Gracchus ... Mucius: though Gaius Gracchus was perhaps considered a greater orator than his brother (Cic. *Brut.* 125–6), both were admired (Cic. *Brut.* 103). Likewise, there was more than one celebrated lawyer called Mucius, e.g. P. Mucius Scaeuola (cos. 133 B.C.), his cousin Q. Mucius Scaeuola, 'the Augur' (cos. 117 B.C.), and Publius' son Q. Mucius Scaeuola 'the Pontifex' (cos. 95 B.C.). So it is best to take both names as generic.

huic ... ille: the MSS have *hic ... illi*, but this introduces a contradiction. In the first part of the line we have been told that X (*hic*) is a Gracchus in the sight of Y (*illi*); so H. cannot now say that X (*hic*) is a Mucius in the sight of Y (*illi*). The change printed in the text has been almost universally accepted since Britannicus (1516).

90   qui minus 'how less?'
  argutos: with a penumbra of irony, 'warbling'.

91–101   On this scene see Introduction p. 15. The tense of *compono* relates to the supposed time of the scene described, not to the time at which H. is writing the epistle.

91   mirabile uisu: a set phrase, 'wonderful to see'; for the supine in *-u* see G–L 436.

92   caelatumque 'adorned' or 'engraved'.
  Musis: dat. of the agent, see G–L 215.1 and 354.

93   fastu 'lordly expression'.

molimine 'air of massive seriousness', worn by one who *magna molitur*.

93–4 circum- | spectemus: the tmesis gives a deliberately portentous effect.

94 uacuam Romanis uatibus aedem: the Latin library in the temple of Apollo on the Palatine. As several of the older Latin poets were already to be found in the library (*E.* 1.3.16–17), *uacuam* cannot mean literally 'empty'. It rather means 'open to' or 'available for', and that implies that *Romanis uatibus* is dat.

95 procul 'at a [discreet] distance'.

96 ferat 'offers as his contribution'.
   qua re 'how'.
   coronam: a garland signifying poetic excellence; see Mayor on Juv. 7.29.

97–8 The exchange, which is likened to a duel, may be thought of as taking the following form: A recites a piece; B pays a compliment and recites a piece in return; A pays a compliment and recites another piece; and so on.

97 consumimus 'wear down'.

98 Samnites: in apposition to the subject of *consumimus*; the Samnite was a type of gladiator armed with a large oblong shield, a vizored helmet with crest and plumes, a greave on the left leg, a padded right sleeve, and a sword or lance. See Grant 55–6.
   ad lumina prima 'until lighting-up time', hence 'until daylight fails'.

99 discedo 'I come off'.
   puncto: before individual voting tablets were introduced, the official would ask each voter whom he was supporting and then record his answer by pricking a tablet.

101 optiuo: the word occurs only here in classical Latin. Does it mean 'received by adoption', i.e. = *adoptiuo*, or 'chosen'? Probably the former, for the other poet does not actually choose the name Mimnermus; it is conferred on him by H., who has cleverly divined his further wishes (*apposcere* in 100). But the distinction is fragile.

crescit 'his stature is enhanced', cf. *C.* 3.30.7–8 *usque ego postera* | *crescam laude recens*. The ironical objectivity (cf. *fit* in the same line) makes this preferable to 'he swells with pride'.

102–3   multa fero ... | cum scribo et ... capto: the statement is made in general terms 'I put up with a lot when I am writing'. The time, again, is that of the scene just described. How far that scene is factual cannot, of course, be determined.

105   obturem ... aures 'I would block ... my ears'. The statement looks forward from the time of the vignette to the time when H. will have stopped writing. That time has now come.

impune: with *obturem*, 'without fear of reprisal'.

107   ultro 'on their own account'.

108   si taceas 'if one says nothing'; for the generalising 2nd sing. see Wo. 119.

beati 'happy souls' (Loeb); going with the whole sentence and deriving added point from its position.

109   legitimum: i.e. in accordance with the rules of art. The idea of legitimacy is developed in the description of the censor.

fecisse: probably an aoristic infin. with no idea of past time, cf. *E.* 1.17.5 and B. on *AP* 98. W. says 'the result rather than the process is the object of desire'; for this view (which appears over-subtle) see Wk. on *C.* 3.4.51–2.

110   censoris: one of two magistrates, appointed every five years for a period of eighteen months to revise the lists of senators and equites. Anyone who had proved unqualified or unworthy was struck off the roll; new names would be added.

111   splendoris 'lustre', both of language and (in the metaphor) of men, especially equites.

112   sine pondere 'without weight', both of language and (metaphorically) of men (referring to their substance and consequence).

honore: i.e. a position of respect (in political life).

fruentur: the best MSS read *feruntur*, which breaks the chain of future indicatives; other MSS have corrected this fault and read *ferentur*. But as Horkel pointed out, *ferentur* is still out of keeping with *habebunt* and *erunt* because it introduces the idea of opinion. These objections are removed by reading *fruentur* (easily corrupted to *feruntur*), which along with *indigna* governs *honore*.

113 mouere loco: (i) of words from their place in the poem, (ii) metaphorically, of men from their place in their order or tribe.

114 uersentur adhuc 'still linger'.

inter: virtually = *intra*; see *TLL* VII 1.2127.28ff.

penetralia Vestae: the train of thought seems to demand a two-fold meaning: (i) of words – 'although they may still linger in a holy place [within the poet's heart?], resisting his decision', (ii) of men – 'although they may still linger in a holy place, resisting the censor's decision'. Unfortunately there is no evidence that the temple of Vesta was a place where one could lodge appeals or claim immunity. The private hearth is no more promising. So the phrase remains unexplained.

115 populo: dat. with *obscurata diu*, 'which have long been unknown to the people'.

bonus eruet 'he will kindly unearth'.

116 proferet in lucem: the censor could restore to the limelight a member of a family which had lapsed into obscurity; the poet could do the same with words and expressions.

117 memorata 'uttered'.

Catonibus atque Cethegis 'men like Cato and Cethegus', dat. of the agent; see G–L 215.1 and 354. Marcus Porcius Cato the Censor (234–149 B.C.), though of peasant stock, rose to the consulship in 195. As censor in 184 he had earned a reputation for moral austerity. Although he adopted a conservative stance and distrusted Hellenic influence, he was not ignorant of Greek. He was a vigorous orator, an authority on agriculture, and a prolific historian. M. Cornelius Cethegus, censor 209, cos. 204, drove Hannibal's brother Mago out of Italy in 203. He died in 196. Like Cato, Cethegus was much admired for his eloquence. Ennius said he possessed 'a sweet-speaking mouth' (*suauiloquenti ore*) and was called 'the marrow of Persuasion' (*Suadai medulla*); see Skutsch 304–8; *ROL* I 300–5.

118   More conveniently rendered by turning the verb into the passive: 'now beset by ugly neglect and lonely old age'.

119   As the censor admits new members, the poet will admit new words. What, then, is meant by *quae genitor produxerit usus?* 'What use has fathered and given to the world' (Wk.; *sim.* W. and Loeb), 'que l'usage, père fécond, aura mis en circulation' (Budé); this is unconvincing because 'use' or 'usage' does not in fact beget, it only perpetuates. 'Proposed by their father, Usage' (Penguin); this is also rather weak, for H. would then be limiting the poet to accepting words already in educated currency. 'Der *usus*, das Bedürfnis der Sprache' (K–H, rightly, though they insist that *usus* in *AP* 71 has the same sense). So the meaning is 'which father Need has begotten'. In language, as in other areas, necessity is the (father or) mother of invention; cf. *utilitas expressit nomina rerum* (Lucr. *DRN* 5.1029).

120   **uemens:** the two adjs. which follow remove the idea of wildness and violence and leave only the power.

121   The great poet does a service to his country – a remark which comes quite naturally after the historical and political ideas used in the previous lines. The patriotic function of poetry is treated at greater length in *E.* 2.1.124ff.

122   **luxuriantia:** of rank, excessive growth. The double dactyl, a rare form, 'illustrates the fault of which Horace speaks' (McGann (1) 354 n. 32).

122–3   See the Introduction, pp. 15–16.
        sano | cultu 'beneficial attention'.

124   **et torquebitur** 'at the same time, he will be under intense strain'. The first five words of the line were adopted by Pope as an epigraph for his *Imitation* of *E.* 2.2.

125   **mouetur:** in this middle use *mouetur* has the same sense as the transitive *saltat* (*S.* 1.5.63); cf. 'she danced Giselle', and see on *AP* 232. A contrast is implied between the nimble satyr and the clumsy Cyclops.

126   **praetulerim:** potential subjunctive, '[if given the choice] I should prefer'.

inersque: here 'without *ars*', hence 'incompetent'.

127 denique 'at least'.

128 sapere et ringi 'to have all my wits and to bare my teeth in frustration', i.e. to know I was third-rate and to be unable to do anything about it.

haud ignobilis 'a man who was not unknown'.

Argis: in the *sermones* H. used the usual Latin form *Argi*, but in *C.* 1.7 (i.e. in a lyric) he used the Greek neuter *Argos*.

131 cetera … munia: the natural run of the words connects *cetera* with *munia*. Some scholars would separate them (taking *cetera* = 'in other respects') on the grounds that attendance at the theatre in Greece was not a duty. But that assumes that *munia* = 'moral duties'. In fact it has a much vaguer and lighter force. Being a good neighbour or a likeable host is a very general sort of obligation; many instances of each would simply be thought of as socially desirable. But going to the theatre in Greece was also considered socially desirable, even though the theatre would not have accommodated all those eligible to attend; and so it could rank as a *munus* in this weaker sense. Goldhill (58–68) has described the civic ideology of the Great Dionysia. No doubt many elements were specifically 5th-cent. Athenian; nevertheless, later performances in Argos would still have been civic occasions.

seruaret: generic subjunctive; cf. *posset* (133, 135).

132 sane 'certainly'.

134 non insanire: this lunatic did not 'go crazy' or 'get mad' when the seal on a flagon of wine had been tampered with. Fury at the minor misdemeanours of slaves is seen as a sign of insanity in *S.* 1.3.80–83 *si quis eum seruum patinam qui tollere iussus | semesos piscis tepidumque ligurrierit ius | in cruce suffigat, Labeone insanior inter | sanos dicatur.*

135 patentem 'without a cover'. By now the moral colouring of *munia* has completely faded.

136 opibus curisque: we might render the plurals by saying 'by the constant help and attention'. When a man was judged insane (*furiosus*), the praetor deprived him by an *interdictum* of the control of his property and handed him over to the care of his *agnati*, i.e. those who were related to him through the male line. If there were no *agnati*, the duty devolved upon his *gentiles*, or fellow clansmen.

137 elleboro ... meraco 'undiluted hellebore'. There were two types of hellebore, one white and one black. Pliny (*NH* 25.56) says the white was much the more terrible; but the black must have been bad enough. According to the *U.S. Dispensatory* (1955) 1712, in overdoses it produces inflammation of the gastric and intestinal mucous membrane, with violent vomiting, hypercatharsis, vertigo, cramp, and convulsions which sometimes end in death.

138 pol: an old-fashioned interjection: 'By Jove!'
occidistis 'you have done for me' (B.).

139 cui: for the dat. of disadvantage with verbs of taking away see G–L 345 ʀɪ; Wo. 156.

139–40 Supply *sit*, rather than *est*, with *extorta* and *demptus*, since the relative clause gives a reason; Wo. 156 and 157.1 (*b*).

141 sapere: after the story of the lunatic we take it = 'to be sane', but in the new section it turns out to mean 'to be wise'.
nugis 'childish frivolities', in particular his lyric poetry; cf. *E*. 1.1.10 *nunc itaque et uersus et cetera ludicra pono*.

142 pueris: with both *concedere* and *tempestiuum*.

143 sequi 'search for'.

144 numerosque modosque: i.e., not musical and lyric, but moral *numeri* and *modi*. Cf. *nil extra numerum fecisse modumque | curas* (*E*. 1.18.59–60) 'you take care to do nothing out of time and tune'. Music was frequently used as a moral metaphor in Pythagorean and Platonic texts; see B. ɪɪɪ, Appendix 17, 438–9.

146 tibi: H exhorts both himself and his readers. The condition described is dropsy, i.e. an accumulation of fluid ('lymph') usually caused by a malfunction of the heart, liver, or kidneys. In spite of *C*. 2.2.13 (*crescit indulgens sibi dirus hydrops*), Ov. *Fast*. 1.215–16, and other passages, dropsy does not in fact cause thirst. But since, in their efforts to reduce the fluid, doctors would withhold drink, it was natural that thirst should be associated with the condition; see Celsus, *De med.* 3.21.2, 4, 6.

147   quod 'the fact that x is the case', x being the whole clause *quanto . . . cupis.* Both *quod* and the following clause are objects of *faterier.*

148   faterier = *fateri*; cf. *curarier* (151). Such infins. are archaic. Is H. being deliberately old-fashioned and sententious?

149   monstrata radice uel herba 'by means of the root or herb indicated'.

150–1   fugeres . . . curarier 'you would refuse to be treated'.
proficiente nihil 'ineffective'.

151   audieras: i.e. you heard at an earlier point in time that prosperity banished folly. You proceeded on that mistaken assumption and made money. But in the light of new knowledge you ought to reject what you were told. Cf. Virg. *Ecl.* 9.7–11 (Lycidas) *certe equidem audieram . . . omnia carminibus uestrum seruasse Menalcan* | (Moeris) *audieras, et fama fuit; sed . . .*
cui: see on 75 above; there is no comic effect here, but there may be a hint of archaism. See B. and his references.

153–4   et . . . tamen 'and yet'; *OLD tamen* 2a.

153   ex quo = *ex quo tempore.*

154   plenior 'richer', but with down-to-earth associations of a fuller belly.

156   nempe ruberes 'why, you would blush'.

157   uno emphasises the singularity of *te*; cf. Cic. *Fam.* 7.16.3 *constat . . . neminem te uno . . . iuris peritiorem esse,* and Cat. 107.7 *quis me uno uiuit felicior?*

158   si 'while it is true that . . .'; lit. 'if, as is the case'.
proprium 'one's own'.
libra . . . et aere 'by balance and bronze'. H. is referring to an ancient process of conveying property (*mancipatio*) which is described by Gaius (the Roman jurist of the 2nd cent. A.D.) as follows: 'In the presence of at least five adult Roman citizens, and a sixth who holds the

balance, the purchaser, holding a bronze piece, says "I declare that this man is mine and that he has been purchased by me in virtue of this bronze piece and this bronze balance." Then he strikes the balance with the bronze piece and gives the latter to the vendor as a price' (1.119, abridged). Originally the balance was used to weigh the price; bronze alone was used for coinage.

159 quaedam ... mancipat usus 'in certain cases *possession* confers ownership'.

    si credis consultis: H. does not pose as an expert.

    usus refers to the uninterrupted and unchallenged possession which could confer ownership (*OLD usus* 5; cf. *usucapio*). The assertion made in 159 is (ostensibly) illustrated in 160–71. Some editors supply *si* before *quaedam* and take 160 as the apodosis. It is not easy to see what is gained by this.

160 Having employed *usus* (159) in the sense of *usucapio*, H. now continues as if he were talking about *usus* in the sense of *usus fructus*, i.e. the right to use the property of another (*OLD usus* 4). The argument is specious, for actually the land you are working for your own benefit is *not* yours, regardless of what the bailiff may think.

    Orbi: the owner is Orbius.

161 occat 'harrows'.

    daturas: as the field feeds the man for whom it is worked (*pascit ager* in 160), so the crops will provide him with grain. This sequence is spoilt by reading *daturus*. Also the grain is not the bailiff's to give.

163 cadum temeti: an archaic phrase meaning 'a jar of strong drink'.

163–5 By paying a small rent and using the produce, says H., you are gradually buying a farm which originally cost the owner a lot of money. The introductory *nempe* may be a sign that the argument is rather thin; for there is no question of purchase by instalments.

166 numerato: abl. with *uiuas*. The true emphasis would be given by saying 'What matter whether you paid just recently or long ago for what you live on?'

167–74 The man who purchased a property quite a long time ago does not think of himself as consuming 'bought', but rather 'home-

grown', produce; the vegetables etc. are 'his own'. But H. argues that
in fact the man is *still* eating 'bought' produce; the fact that he paid a
long time ago is neither here nor there. Moreover, the idea that the
property is 'his own [in perpetuity]' is merely an illusion. Ownership
can never be more than temporary.

167 emptor and **quondam** go together. *quondam*, which takes up
olim (166), is necessary to the argument as summarised above.
quoniam, found in most MSS, fails to bring out the required sense. It
also obliges us to put a question-mark after *putat* (168) instead of after
olim (166), thus weakening the force of the single-line rhetorical question (166) and interrupting the sequence *emptum ... emptis* (168). The
mention of Aricia and Veii, 'two municipia of long standing' (B.), is
in keeping with the long time-span suggested by the passage.

170 usque ... qua 'up to the point where'.

170–1 assita certis | limitibus 'planted along the fixed bounda-
ries'. The boundary consisted of a strip of unploughed land.

171 refringit 'breaks', in the manner of a breakwater (*OLD refringo*
3). This is Horkel's conjecture for *refugit*, which means 'has avoided'.
Despite what several editors say, the use of *refugit* is not defended by Varro, *RR* 1.15 *fines praedii sationibus notis arborum tutiores
fiunt, ne familiae rixentur cum uicinis*, for there, too, the planting of trees
prevents disputes, it does not avoid them. The tense of *refugit* is also objectionable. It is not justified by *E.* 1.19.48 *ludus genuit certamen*, for
there *genuit* is gnomic (i.e. generalising), whereas here the context is
specific. The neighbours' *iurgia* are allegations that X is encroaching
on their land. The force of such allegations is broken by the line of
trees, which shows that the boundary has been there for generations.

172 proprium 'permanently one's own'; cf. *S.* 2.6.5 *propria haec mihi
munera faxis*.

173 prece 'as the result of a request'. i.e. by gift.
   pretio 'by purchase'; the sound effect with *prece* is notable.
   morte suprema 'finally, by death'; cf. *S.* 1.7.13 *ultima mors*.

174 cedat in altera iura 'passes into someone else's control'.

176 alternis 'by turns'; the MSS read *alterius*, which stretches the

succession over three generations. But *unda ... undam* suggests a sequence of pairs: AB, BC, CD; so Ben.'s conjecture is an improvement.
Cf. *alterna iactamur in unda*, Prop. 2.12.7. The whole of the preceding
passage, from 158–79, has strong Lucretian overtones. See e.g.
Kenney's note on *DRN* 3.971 *uitaque mancipio nulli datur, omnibus usu*.

177 uici: in this context *uicus* means a collection of workers' dwell-
ings on a large estate.

177–8 Sheep which grazed on the plains of Calabria during winter
were driven into the hills of Lucania for the summer. It was therefore
advantageous to own adjoining estates in the two areas.

178 metit: the landowner falls to a greater reaper, just as the acquisitive builder in *C.* 2.18.29–32 falls victim to a greater *auarus*.

179 grandia: although *grandis* eventually passed into the Romance
languages (a fact which indicates a popular level of style) in the sense
of 'big', there is no reason to think that when used by classical writers
in the senses of 'distinguished' and 'exalted' (*OLD* 5 and 6) it was anything other than a dignified word.

non exorabilis auro: in *C.* 2.18.34–6 H. refers to an attempt on
the part of Prometheus to get out of Hades by bribing the *satelles Orci*
(Charon? Mercury?); *non exorabilis auro* may possibly allude to the
same episode.

180 Tyrrhena sigilla: these were Etruscan figurines made of
bronze.

181 argentum 'silver plate'. There are some splendid examples of
Roman silver plate in the British Museum.

Gaetulo murice: purple dye manufactured from shellfish on the
coast of N. Africa.

182 habeant: generic, hence subjunctive.

curat: specific, hence indicative. This prepares us for the entrance
of H. himself in 190.

183 ungui 'to have an oil massage'.

184 Herodis: Herod the Great of Judaea (*c.* 73–4 B.C.) was an able
administrator, but as a devotee of Greek literature and a loyal friend
of Rome he was often unpopular with his own people. He was sup-

ported by Antony in the early 30s, and until his later years he retained
the confidence of Augustus. To attribute to Herod the massacre of the
innocents (the folk-tale found in Matthew 2.16) was chronologically
possible because the birth of Christ was put about 6 years too late
by Dionysius Exiguus, the scholar who, in the first half of the 6th
cent. A.D., was commissioned to standardise the calendar of church
festivals.

palmetis pinguibus: fertile and profitable groves of date-palms,
like those of Jericho; cf. Plin. *NH* 5.70 *Hiericuntem palmetis consitam.*
The case is dat. after *praeferat.*

185 diues et importunus 'rich and unrelenting'; there is no need
to take *et* as adversative; the two characteristics are far from
incompatible.

186 'Subdues the wooded country with fire and steel.' In the phrase
flammis et ferro (and the like) the *ferrum* is regularly a sword. Here H.
has in mind the steel of a plough or axe, but the sword is still present
as a metaphor illustrating the man's character.

187 scit Genius ... temperat astrum: for the Genius, see on *E.*
2.1.144. The words are not an expression of bafflement ('goodness
knows'). They indicate, rather, that what makes one man an idler
and his brother a worker is the Guardian Spirit which controls the
fate of each. (This explanation is due to Prof. G. P. Goold.) H. did not
believe that the course of a person's life was determined by the star
under which he was born; the language of *C.* 2.17.13ff. was prompted
by the interests of Maecenas, and is not in any case that of a doc-
trinaire astrologer. See also *C.* 1.11, which remonstrates with
Leuconoe for wasting her time on horoscopes. It must be admitted,
however, that, if analysed, H.'s thought would be close to circularity:
what makes one person different from another? His Genius. And what
is his Genius? That in virtue of which he is different from another
person.

natale ... astrum: the star, or constellation under which a
person is born; hence, loosely, his fate.

188 naturae deus humanae 'the god presiding over human
nature'.

188–9 mortalis in unum | quodque caput: see on *E.* 2.1.144.

189   uultu mutabilis 'varying in countenance'.

   albus et ater: 'light and dark', 'bright and gloomy'. According to one opinion, represented by O., H. is referring to different phases in one man's life: his Genius becomes happy or sad as *he* is happy or sad. But, in view of the contrasted brothers, H. probably means 'if a man is a bright and happy type, so is his Genius; if he is dark and gloomy, so is his Genius'. The general drift of the argument is: 'People's temperaments lead them to behave in many different ways (some of them rather foolish); my own preference is to follow the mean.'

190   utar 'enjoyment will be my motto'; the verb is explained in what follows.

   res 'the occasion'.

191   heres: H. is generalising, we are not to think of an individual.

192   non plura datis 'no more than I have given him'.

   inuenerit: perf. subjunctive, conveying the heir's reason for his adverse judgement.

   idem 'also'; the adj. goes with the subject of *uolam* (193), cf. *C.* 2.10.22–4 *sapienter idem | contrahes uento nimium secundo | turgida uela.*

193   simplex hilarisque 'open and cheerful'; this represents the virtuous mean (i.e. generosity) in the spending of money; *nepoti* represents the vicious excess of the spendthrift.

**194   In the saving of money, thrift represents the mean (*parcus*), miserliness the extreme (*auaro*). The theory of virtue as a mean was expounded by Aristotle in his *Nicomachean Ethics*, 3.6.1115a–4.9.1128b.

195   distat 'it makes a difference'.

**195–6   The good man is not reluctant to spend money and not overkeen to make more.

197   ac potius 'but rather'.

   festis Quinquatribus: the Quinquatrūs (fem. pl.) was a spring holiday held originally in honour of Mars on the fifth day after the Ides of March, i.e., by inclusive counting, 19 March. Later it was extended to five days and became associated with Minerva, the patroness of arts and crafts. Schools, accordingly, were closed. See Scullard 92–4.

puer ... olim 'as you used to do when you were a boy'. So understood, rightly, by the Budé editor.

198 exiguo gratoque: *-que* has the same function as 'and' in our 'short and sweet'; i.e. it can be seen as marking a contrast.

199 pauperies ... absit: in this difficult passage the transmitted text has been, tentatively, retained, but *pauperies ... absit* has been put in brackets, with a strong stop after *absit*. In 195ff. H. has contrasted the spendthrift with the man who uses his money sensibly; but that assumes, of course, that the man has some money to use. So H. adds as a parenthetic afterthought 'let us not *think* of the house suffering from filthy poverty'. The phrase is reminiscent of *C.* 2.10.7, where H. makes it clear that *aurea mediocritas* requires something more in the way of comfort than the squalor of a tumbledown house (*obsoleti sordibus tecti*). This punctuation allows *ego* to begin a new sentence, and avoids the awkward connection of house and ship.

When *pauperies ... absit* is taken with what follows, as is the usual practice, the sequence of thought suffers: 'May squalid domestic poverty be far away; whether my boat be large or small I shall be personally unaffected.' The only other course is to emend the text so as to give the sense 'Provided I am not faced with extreme poverty, I shall remain personally unaffected, whether I sail in a large or a small [financial] boat.' This requires *modo ut* (Jeep) for *domus* (but according to B. *modo ut* is not found between Terence, who died in the middle of the 2nd cent. B.C., and late Latin), or something more radical like *dummodo pauperies immunda procul sit, ego utrum* (Campbell). This last suggestion has some merit, since *domus* and *absit* are omitted in certain MSS; but it has not been printed by either B. or SB.

201–2 That is, I am not driven before strong winds from the north (too strong a following wind could be dangerous), nor do I have to cope with adverse winds from the south, in directing my life.

203 'In physical strength, talent, appearance, character, status, possessions.'

204 extremis usque priores 'always ahead of the last'.

205 abi: a colloquial expression of approval, as K–H say, quoting *abi, laudo: scis ... tractare homines* (Plaut. *Trin.* 830). But since H. has

in a sense been pleading not guilty to the charge of greed, *abi* retains
some of its original force as a formula of dismissal.

cetera: understand *uitia*, a point which becomes clear with *uitio*
(206).

206 fugere: the grammar is given by the metre.

207 ira: is the word to be taken on its own in the usual sense of
'anger'? Or, like *formidine*, does it go with *mortis* – 'the fear and resent-
ment of death'? The second interpretation seems preferable because
(i) the fear of death, as one form of superstition, is continued by others
in 208–9; *ira* = 'anger' would interrupt the sequence; (ii) *ira* =
'anger' anticipates 210–11; (iii) in the series *inani ambitione . . . mortis
formidine* the disyllable *ira* does not carry enough weight by itself; (iv)
satisfactory parallels do exist, though they are not easy to find, e.g. *ira
odioque eius* (Liv. 2.22.4), *stimulataque paelicis irā* (Ov. *Met.* 4.235). Such
cases, where the gen. denotes 'directed at', are misleadingly listed in
TLL vii 363 with the more common cases where it denotes 'caused
by'.

208 terrores magicos 'the terrors of magic' (Wk.).

209 nocturnos lemures '*umbras uagantes hominum ante diem mor-
tuorum et ideo metuendas*' (Porph.).

portentaque: weird phenomena and stories, e.g. men turning into
wolves, and witches charming the moon from the sky.

Thessala: Thessaly, a district of northern Greece, was backward
in comparison with the famous city-states to the south. Hence, like
parts of the Celtic fringe, it was associated with wild and irrational
goings-on. See *OLD Thessalus* 1b.

210 grate: i.e. with gratitude, rather than with sorrow and ap-
prehension.

211 lenior et melior: this optimistic expectation is balanced by the
pessimistic expectation in *AP* 169–74. Both views are found in Cic. *De
sen.*, *passim*.

212 quid . . . leuat: i.e. 'What relief do you get?' In the MS tradition *iuuat* is more strongly supported, and it gives quite adequate
sense: 'What good does it do you?' The letter *l*, however, in Porph.'s

lemma shows that he read *leuat*. It is more likely that the corruption
went from *leuat* to *iuuat* than vice versa; for *quid iuuat* was a very
common phrase, e.g. *S*. 1.1.41; Prop. 1.2.1. H. should be credited with
the less usual expression.

spinis: for 'thorn' = 'moral fault' cf. *E*. 1.14.4–5 *certemus, spinas an-
imone ego fortius an tu | euellas agro.*

213–16 These lines pose a difficult problem. Early in the poem H.
said that the years had taken away laughter, sexual pleasure, parties,
and fun, and were now trying to wrench away poetry too (55–7).
Later he claimed it was time to give up an amusement (*ludum*) fit for
youngsters, i.e. lyric poetry, and to study moral philosophy (141–2).
If the last three lines of the epistle are taken on their own, they can
readily refer back to these ideas: you have had enough amusement
(*lusisti*), enough food and wine; it's time to take your leave, for fear
that, having had too much to drink, you may be pushed away by the
younger generation. That is, it is time to leave the banquet of youth,
the life-style associated with love and lyric poetry, and to devote
yourself to philosophy. In that case the end of the epistle reiterates one
of H.'s reasons for not sending *carmina* to Florus. This view is strongly
advocated by B.

But the last three lines are not on their own. We approach them
after a passage of interrogation: are you free from ambition, and the
fear of death? Do you scoff at superstition? Are you growing mellower
as old age approaches? If you can't live properly, *decede peritis*. What
does *decede peritis* mean? If it could mean 'attend to those who *can* live
properly, i.e. the philosophers,' the difficulty would be greatly eased.
But it is very doubtful if the phrase can bear that sense. It naturally
means 'make way for those who can', i.e. there is no moral point in
continuing to live. In that case the last three lines would be a metaphor of life.

This second view derives support from the passage's Lucretian prove-
nance, which is very evident in the remarks about ambition, death,
and the supernatural (206–9). It seems likely that after writing *decede
peritis* H. brought in the idea of a banquet because he recalled *cur non
ut plenus uitae conuiua recedis?* (*DRN* 3.938), *ante | quam satur ac plenus pos-
sis discedere rerum* (959–60), and *agedum dignis* (?) *concede* (962). But
Lucretius' verbs *recedis*, *discedere*, and *concede* all have to do with leaving

the banquet of life; which suggests that in 214–16 H. too is referring to the banquet of life. In this final metaphor *lasciua decentius aetas* stands for those who enjoy what life puts before them and are not made miserable by anxieties over money, power, and death.

214   lusisti ... edisti ... bibisti: all the parallels have a different order from this, viz. 'to eat and to drink and to be merry' (Eccles. 8.15); φάγε, πίε, εὐφραίνου, 'eat, drink, and be merry' (Luke 12.19); ἔσθιε πῖνε, ὄχευε (or ἀφροδισίαζε, or παῖζε) – renderings of the inscriptions on the tomb of the Assyrian Sardanapallus (see B.'s note); *affatim edi, bibi, lusi* (Livius Andronicus, *ROL* ii 22). H. may have changed the order simply for metrical reasons. *lusisti* includes sexual pleasure; whether it also includes the pleasure of writing poetry depends on the interpretation of the lines as a whole.

215   potum: the perf. participle *potus* from *poto, -are* is frequently active and intrans. 'having drunk'; the idea of excess, usually implied, is here made explicit by *largius aequo*.

216   pulset: the context suggests 'push you roughly towards the door' (*OLD pulso* 8b) rather than simply 'punch' (*OLD pulso* 5a).

   lasciua decentius aetas 'a generation in which frivolity is more becoming'.

The Epistle to the Pisones ('*Ars Poetica*')

1   Adjectives and nouns form a chiasmus. The human head turns out to be that of a woman (4).

2   uarias: of more than one colour, but not of more than one bird. H. has in mind a (generic) bird's feathers.

   inducere 'to put on'. Up to now we have human head, horse's neck, bird's feathers. So on what does the painter put the coloured feathers? Surely on the body and wings of a bird. These are not mentioned, but they can be understood without great difficulty and are implied by *undique* (see next note).

3   undique collatis membris: the parts of the creature are drawn from each division of the animal kingdom: man, quadruped, bird, and fish; cf. *ex diuersis naturis* (Quint. *IO* 8.3.60), where this passage is referred to. It is best to take the phrase as an abl. abs., placing a comma after *plumas.* If *membris* were dat. with *inducere,* the horse's neck and fish's tail would be covered in feathers. Clearly that is not what H. means. (Apart from anything else, the force of *atrum* would be destroyed.) The *membra* here make up the whole body, including the trunk; cf. *OLD membrum* 2.

3–4 The *ut*-clause ('in such a way that') completes the picture, explaining *undique collatis membris* and adding greater detail.

turpiter: probably with *desinat* ('ended horribly') rather than with *atrum* ('horribly black'). This gives a better balance with *mulier formosa superne* and with *atrum . . . in piscem,* which does not need further elaboration (see next note).

atrum: the word often carries overtones of 'ugly', 'sinister', and the like.

4 piscem: the writer of the note in ps.-Acr. remembered Virgil's Scylla, whose lower half was an *immani corpore pistrix* (*Aen.* 3.427), and so explained *in piscem* as *in beluam marinam, hoc est in pistricem.* But the fish, like the woman, the horse, and the bird, is normal in itself. It is the combination that is monstrous. So there is no justification for altering *piscem.* Moreover, to accommodate a sea-monster in the hexameter we would have to turn to *pristim,* which is not in ps.-Acr. The word is used of Triton in *Aen.* 10.211, and probably for this reason appears in inferior MSS of H. The adoption of *pristim* would involve the further change of *atrum* to *atram.*

5 spectatum: supine expressing purpose after *admissi* (G–L 435).
amici: voc., as indicated by the punctuation.

6 Pisones: see Introduction pp. 19–21.

7–8 cuius . . . uanae | . . . species 'whose features are conceived fantastically'. *species* includes the shapes of the pictures, the visions of the feverish dream, and the images of a poem.

fingentur: the Latin tense corresponds to that of *fore* (6).

8–9 ut . . . formae: lit. 'in such a way that neither foot nor head is assigned to a shape so as to make it a unity'; i.e. so that the form lacks the most basic principles of unity. *uni* is proleptic.

9–10 An objection is stated: poets and painters alike (*aequa*) have always been given the right to dare anything. This rather extravagant assertion is partly accepted (11), partly modified (12–13). If *aequa* is taken in the sense of 'fair' or 'reasonable', then *quidlibet audendi* sounds slightly odd, and the subsequent qualifications in 12–13 seem to have been anticipated.

11 *'petimus' quasi poetae, 'damus' quasi critici*, ps.-Acr.

12–13 H. is still talking of unity in visual terms; so he means 'not so as to show wild mating with tame, snakes pairing with birds, lambs with tigers'.

14 'Works with noble beginnings and grand promises' (Loeb edn).
plerumque: here 'often', not 'usually'.

15–16 purpureus ... pannus: the purple patch is a form of decoration; it has a conspicuous sheen (*late splendeat*); and H. sees it as incongruous and distracting. In view of *unus et alter* it cannot mean a stripe (*clauus*) or a piece of material tacked onto the hem (*instita*). *pannus* is therefore best taken as a piece of fabric sewn onto the outside of the garment. Such flounces, or *segmenta* (Ov. *AA* 3.169; Juv. 2.124), could also be strips of gold (Val. Max. 5.2.1) or silver (*CIL* xiv 2215).

15 splendeat: subjunctive of purpose.
unus et alter 'one or two'.

16–18 Such descriptive scenes figured in the exercises of the rhetorical schools. *uix possum credere quemquam eorum uidisse siluas uirentesque gramine campos, quos rapidus amnis ex praecipitio uel, cum per plana infusus est, placidus interfluit; non maria umquam ex colle uidisse lenta, aut hiberna cum uentis penitus agitata sunt* (Papirius Fabianus in Sen. *Contr.* 2.1.13). Such pictures had presumably become commonplaces in the poetry of H.'s contemporaries (cf. *S.* 1.10.37, though there *Rheni* is a noun). The ridicule of such scenes became, in its turn, a commonplace of satire; cf. the grove of Mars in Juv. 1.7–8.

17 The largely dactylic line echoes the speed of the swift-flowing water.

19 non erat ... locus: the impf. implies that something has happened which ought not to have happened.

19–20 According to the scholiasts, there was an incompetent artist who could paint only cypress trees; one day a seaman asked him to paint the shipwreck from which he had escaped. The painter asked if he wouldn't like a bit of a cypress tree put in. Hence a Greek proverb μή τι καὶ κυπάρισσον θέλεις;

20–1 What use is this, if the subject of the painting is a man swimming for his life? H. throws *enatat* etc. forward for graphic effect. The man shown in the painting (*qui pingitur*) also commissioned it (*aere dato*).

fractis . . . | nauibus: the pl. is the poetic equivalent of a sing. To take it as describing several ships is possible, but that would imply a more elaborate painting in which the main figure was less prominent.

21   coepit: the rule that *coeptus est* is used with a pass. infin. (G–L 423 n. 3) is not invariable; for early exceptions see B.'s note.

22   urceus: '*urcei* are vases . . . with very short necks and two small handles barely large enough for the hands . . . The mouth is wider than the bottom.' That description, in *CIL* xiii 3.1.86, is accompanied by an illustration. The difference between an *urceus* and an *amphora* is illustrated by Hilgers, Tafel 1; cf. pp. 36 and 84–5. H.'s point is that an incompetent craftsman lacks control of form. But when an object's form changes, its name and function may change too.

23   denique 'in a word', 'in short'.

quiduis 'anything you like'; a variant reading adopted by Ben. It is superior to *quod uis*, which = *quod instituis* and is therefore rhetorically weak, and to *quoduis*, which as an adj. requires the noun *opus* to be understood – an awkward construction.

dumtaxat: this limits *quiduis* 'but at least [let it be] a single homogeneous whole'. The meaning in the end is virtually the same as *dummodo* + the subjunctive, but the grammar is different; for in spite of *OLD dumtaxat* 3, the word is not established as a conjunction.

25–7 The brevity of the plain style may give rise to obscurity; the smoothness of the middle style to limpness; and the amplitude of the grand style to pomposity. For the three styles see *Ad Herenn.* 4.11 (*grauis, mediocris, extenuata*); Cic. *Orat.* 69–99; Quint. *IO* 12.10.58–65.

25   specie recti 'by the appearance of what is right'. The virtues of style are recognised as such, but contrary to appearances they are not easy to attain. Every virtue, in fact, has an attendant vice. So the good writer must have taste. Cf. *Ad Herenn*. 4.15 (*specie grauitatis falluntur nec perspicere possunt orationis tumorem*) and 16; Varro in Gellius (*NA* 6.14); Longinus 3.1–4. This traditional idea, like so many others, is applied to an amatory context by Ovid in *Rem. am*. 323 *et mala sunt uicina bonis*.

26   nerui: not 'nerves' but 'sinews'. In *Ad Herenn*. 4.16 the vicious counterpart of the middle style is called *dissolutum, quod est sine neruis et articulis*; cf. S. 2.1.2.

27   animi que 'spirit', 'vigour'.

28   serpit humi: cf. *repentes per humum*, used of his own *sermones* in *E*. 2.1.251, a passage of deliberate self-depreciation.

   nimium: with both *tutus* ('careful', cf. *C*. 2.10.6) and *timidus*. At some point the poet has to trust himself to the air; cf. *C*. 4.2.25–7 *multa Dircaeum leuat aura cycnum, | tendit, Antoni, quotiens in altos | nubium tractus*, though few can fly as high as Pindar.

29   A writer who is eager to lend variety to a simple, homogeneous, theme by bringing in marvels ends up by depicting absurdities.

31   This is an example of how H.'s argument is always on the move. In 24–7 he was talking of the *species recti* and the pitfalls of following what you believe to be right. Here he is referring to the *culpae fuga* and the pitfalls of shunning what you think is wrong. This new emphasis begins almost imperceptibly in 28 with the idea of avoiding danger. Then we have the writer who is anxious to avoid monotony; finally comes the *sententia* (31), which recalls *dum uitant stulti uitia in contraria currunt* (*S*. 1.2.24). The clause *si caret arte* at once concludes the maxim and prepares us for the clumsy workman who follows.

32   Aemilium ... ludum: the scholiasts say this was a gladiatorial school, run by a certain Aemilius Lepidus. According to one tradition, preserved by Cruquius, it was not far from the Circus Maximus. (Cruquius, a professor at Bruges, had access to four MSS in the Benedictine abbey of St Peter near Ghent. All four, including the oldest and most valuable, designated as V, were destroyed when the abbey was burnt by iconoclasts in 1566.)

32–3   faber imus ... | exprimet: the futures *exprimet, imitabitur*, and *nesciet*, along with the slightly vague *circa*, probably indicate that H. had no specific person in mind. If right, *imus* means 'the lowest in esteem' (cf. *C.* 3.1.14–15: *Necessitas | sortitur insignis et imos*). The sense then is 'A smith of the poorest kind, from the area near Aemilius' school, will represent you nails and imitate wavy hair in bronze.' Another explanation offered by the scholiasts is that *imus* means at the end of the school premises. This is unlikely for the reasons just given. Ben. and several others read *unus*, with some manuscript authority. Palaeographically there is nothing to choose between the two readings, but *imus* is printed here because (i) the context points rather to any smith, (ii) *unus*, as well as being specific, would be complimentary – 'surpassingly well', but H.'s argument seems rather to be that a half-competent smith (continuing *si caret arte* from 31) will get a part right, but it takes an artist to get the whole right; (iii) *unam* has just been used in a different sense (29). Nisbet (3) 233 suggests that the original reading was *optimus*, and that the *et* was added when *opt-* dropped out. If that line is followed, *infimus* (Kenney) seems the most likely possibility; cf. *OLD infimus* 3.

34   infelix 'unsuccessful'.

operis summa 'because of his work as a whole'. (The sense 'in regard to' would call for the gen., not the abl. of respect.)

ponere 'represent', *OLD pono* 19.

36   prauo 'crooked'.

37   spectandum: lit. 'worth looking at', hence 'while deserving admiration'.

38   aequam: i.e. not too much for.

39   uersate 'turn over in your mind', hence 'ponder', 'consider'.

40   cui: dat. of the agent; G–L 354.

potenter 'within his capabilities'. This interpretation, which is adopted by the scholiasts, gives excellent sense. There is, apparently, no exact parallel in *TLL*. If we wish to play safe we can translate 'effectively' – a sense for which there *are* parallels (*OLD potenter* 2). But after what H. has just said, the natural explanation of 'effectively' will be 'within his capabilities'; and so that nuance will remain implicit. Editors who will not allow H. even this degree of freedom either distort the sense or emend the text.

40–1   For the thought, cf. Cato's famous dictum *rem tene, uerba sequentur* (80.15 Jordan).

42 uirtus (fem.) is in origin a man's quality; *uenus* (neut.) is a woman's. Being both disyllables starting with *u-* and ending in *-us*, they make an effective and untranslatable pair.

aut ego fallor: this does not imply diffidence.

45–6 With some hesitation the order of these lines as given by the MSS and the scholiasts has been retained. To support this decision one has to consider the train of thought from 40 on: choose the sort of subject or topic that you're capable of handling; then you'll have no problem about fluency or organisation. The essence of good organisation is to say A when A is called for, B when B is called for, and to postpone P, Q, and R. (Here A, B, etc. are left vague; they may be descriptions, episodes, or points of information.) 45: the person responsible for writing a poem (i.e. the person committed to producing it) should embrace this, but wave away that. ('This' and 'that' are still unspecified.) 46: you should also be subtle and careful in stringing your words together. 47: you will achieve distinction if, by a clever collocation, you make a familiar word new. (Clearly H. is now talking of words.) This seems an acceptable argument; it does not have to be defended by maintaining that *auctor* provides a subject for *dicat*, *differat*, and *omittat* (the subject could, if necessary, be taken from *hunc* in 41). The transposition of 45 and 46, advocated by Ben. and many others, seems less convincing; for in its new place *hoc amet, hoc spernat* etc. would refer to the choice of words, and it would be awkward to put the choice of words in between *serendis* and *iunctura*, which both have to do with the *combination* of words. Those who wish to explore the problem in greater detail should consult B., who follows Ben. SB retains the traditional order, but starts a new paragraph with 45.

45 promissi carminis auctor: both 'the author of a promised poem' and 'the guarantor of a promised poem'. The idea is that, to produce a poem to which one is committed, one has to be selective.

46 in uerbis ... serendis: i.e. in stringing his words together, from *OLD sero*² (cf. *series iuncturaque* in 242), not from *sero*¹ 'I sow or plant'. B.'s examination of the materials of *TLL* suggests that, as distinct from *sermones/orationes/colloquia serere*, *uerba serere* is an original expression of H.'s.

47 dixeris: the fut. perf. could be rendered 'you will succeed in'.

47–8 callida ... iunctura 'a clever collocation'. The *Odes* provide abundant examples, e.g. *uxorius amnis* (*C.* 1.2.19–20), *simplex munditiis* (*C.* 1.5.5), *carpe diem* (*C.* 1.11.8). See also 242. This is perhaps the most striking feature of Persius' style. See Harvey's note on *iunctura callidus acri* (Pers. 5.14).

49 Some MSS (though not B.'s important B, C, K, and R) have *rerum et*. Retaining *et*, Klingner construes *si necesse est monstrare et fingere, continget*. But it is weak to say 'if it is necessary to do x and y, you will have the chance to do them'. Also x and y are not parallel; rather y is a response to x. K–H and others, putting a comma after *rerum*, take *et continget* and *habebunt fidem* (52) as parallel assertions. But in the resulting construction (*si*-clause, *et fingere continget ... et habebunt fidem*, *si*-clause) *habebunt fidem* is not the logical apodosis of the first *si*-clause, nor is *fingere continget* qualified by the second *si*-clause. It is better to omit *et* (49) and to place a semicolon after *pudenter* (51). The sequence then is: 'If it is necessary to use new *indicia* to elucidate obscure subject-matter, you will have the chance to invent new terms.'

There were three main ways of inventing new terms: (i) to use an already-existing Latin word in a new, technical, sense by analogy with its Greek equivalent; e.g. *indicia* (49) 'signs' could be used to mean 'verbal symbols' by analogy with the Greek σημεῖα; (ii) a new Latin word could be constructed on an existing root, e.g. *cinctutis* (50) from *cinctus–us*; for other cases see Bo III 391–5; (iii) a Greek word could be imported, e.g. *amystis* (*C.* 1.36.14), *hydropicus* (*E.* 1.2.34); for other cases see Bo III 351. In 48–51 H. is probably thinking mainly of (i), but (ii) is glanced at in passing (*cinctutis*), and (iii) is not excluded. In 52–3 (ii) is excluded, but (i) and (iii) are both possible.

abdita rerum 'obscurities of things' = 'obscure things', especially the subject-matter of Greek intellectual inquiry. The phrase is not Lucretian; but the construction (neut. pl. + *rerum*) occurs twice in *DRN*, viz. *uitalia rerum* (2.575) and *textaque rerum* (6.997). The phrase *terrai abdita* is found in 6.809. With H.'s *abdita rerum* cf. *uanis rerum* (*S.* 2.2.25) and *fictis rerum* (*S.* 2.8.83).

50 cinctutis 'kilted', i.e. wearing old-fashioned dress. Porph. says *cinctus est genus tunicae infra pectus aptatae*. The illustrations in Daremberg–Saglio 1173, figs. 1469 and 1470 show the garment to have been wrapped round the body from the waist to above the knees.

This is what Asconius had in mind (Giarratano 33, on Cic. *Pro Scauro*) when speaking of Cato, *sine tunica exercuit, campestri sub toga cinctus*.

Cethegis: see on *E.* 2.2.117.

51   continget: the nuance required seems to be 'you will have the chance' (so, in effect, Wk., Loeb, and Russell). 'You will succeed' (O. and K–H) does not give the required sense; 'you will be allowed' (W.) renders *dabiturque licentia* otiose, and is not supported by his references (*E.* 1.17.36 and 2.2.41). Exact parallels to the present case are hard to find. In *E.* 1.17.36 (*non cuiuis homini contingit adire Corinthum*) and Virg. *Aen.* 6.108–9 (*ire ad conspectum cari genitoris et ora | contingat*) 'to have the chance to' merges with 'to have the good fortune to'.

sumpta pudenter 'provided it is exercised with discretion'.

52   et 'moreover'.

noua ... fidem 'new and recently formed words will find acceptance'.

53   cadent: the stream comes down from its source, *OLD cado* 2c.

parce detorta: the channels must be opened sparingly. The *uerba* are not altered (as the classification in *OLD detorqueo* 3b seems to imply), but derived.

53–5   And indeed (*autem* amplifies and defends the previous sentence) why should Roman critics grant to Caecilius and Plautus what they deny to Virgil and Varius? The desired equality of treatment is represented by putting the modern pair directly under the ancient, in the same position in the line. One might have expected the emphasis to lie the other way: i.e. why deny to Virgil and Varius what is granted to Caecilius and Plautus? But H.'s arrangement allows a chiasmus with 55ff. – past, present, present, past – which sets H. beside his two friends (*ego cur*).

54   Caecilio: see on *E.* 2.1.59.

Plautoque: see on *E.* 2.1.58. Since Plautus was a popular playwright, with little concern for doctrines of stylistic purity, his language, and in particular his use of Greek, was freer than that of Terence.

55   Vergilio: since we have to use Virgil as a means of learning

Latin, we tend to accept his diction as a kind of poetic norm, ignoring the extent of his innovation. In antiquity, readers noticed his archaisms (Quint. *IO* 8.3.24–8). His unusual combinations of ordinary words were criticised by a Vipranius (Vipsanius Agrippa ?) as a *noua cacozelia*, something like 'an affectation of stylistic novelty' (Suet. *Virg.* 44). And his practice of introducing new words ran counter to the principles of Julius Caesar, who had taken a strong line on such matters: 'you should avoid a strange and unfamiliar word as you would a rock' (Gell. *NA* 1.10.4); cf. the position of Cornelius Celsus as recorded by Quint. (*IO* 8.3.35). A brief account of such criticisms can be found in Conington–Nettleship I xxix–liii.

Varioque: see on *E.* 2.1.247.

ego: in so far as H.'s own work is relevant, we should think of the lyrics rather than the *sermones*. In the *Odes* he had allowed himself greater latitude in regard to Greek adaptations (see Bo III 351–3); and so here he takes his stand alongside Virgil and Varius. H.'s coinages in both *Odes* and *sermones* are not negligible (Bo III 391–5). This is one of the few places in the *AP* where we catch an echo of contemporary quarrels.

acquirere: a word with commercial associations; it prepares for *ditauerit* (57).

56 inuideor '[why] am I grudged the right?' Since *inuideo* takes the dat., the personal passive is abnormal. Perhaps H. is practising his own precept in a small way by using a form analogous to the Greek φθονοῦμαι.

Catonis: see on *E.* 2.2.117.

Enni: see on *E.* 2.1.50. For his style in the *Annals* see Skutsch, *Index Rerum* under Style, 841. For his tragic vocabulary see Jocelyn (1), Index 1, 445–64.

57 sermonem patrium ditauerit: is H. deliberately reversing Lucretius' *patrii sermonis egestas* (*DRN* 1.832; 3.260)?

59 'To introduce words bearing the mint-mark of the day.' The metaphor was already latent in *habebunt uerba fidem* (52).

60–2 Initially a twofold comparison is presented: words, like forest leaves, have a life-cycle. Then a third element is introduced, metaphorically in *uetus . . . aetas* (61b) and literally in *iuuenum ritu* (62). H.

dwells on the idea of human transience in 63–8, before returning to his main topic, viz. words.

foliis ... mutantur 'change in regard to their leaves'; *foliis* is an abl. of respect (G–L 397).

priuos ... in annos: the MSS have *pronos ... in annos*; but while such phrases as *in annos, in dies*, and *in horas* are found with the numerical adjectives *singulus* and *priuus*, the use with *pronus* has no parallel. Ben. therefore wrote *priuos ... in annos* 'year by year', with which one may compare *priuas mutatur in horas* (Lucr. *DRN* 5.274) and *inque dies priuos* (Lucr. *DRN* 5.733). The fact that in two other occurrences of *priuus* in H. the word means 'own' rather than 'single' need not inhibit us from emending the text. The word *illacrimabilis*, for instance, is used only twice by H.; but in *C.* 2.14.6 it means 'unweeping' and in *C.* 4.9.26 it means 'unwept'.

In 61a a lacuna has been assumed, and Lehrs's supplement (p. ccxix of his edn of 1869) has been printed *exempli gratia*. The difficulty of the transmitted text has to do with the symmetry of the comparison. If we write 'as forests change in their leaves every year, the earliest fall, so the old age of words dies *and ... those recently born flourish and thrive,*' not only do we lack a connective after the as-clause, but we have nothing in the forest image to correspond to the words italicised. K–H brush the point aside, saying that the idea of new growth is understood in 60, and offering as a parallel *primaque dispereunt* (Lucr. *DRN* 4.376). But after the issue of newly minted words (59) we expect an explicit mention of new leaves in 60ff., and in the Lucretius passage such explicitness has just occurred in the previous line *semper enim noua se radiorum lumina fundunt*.

Housman 1 155–6 proposed repunctuation: *prima cadunt ita uerborum. uetus interit aetas*, etc. There is some awkwardness, however, in making the same statement twice about old words – once in connection with leaves and again in connection with men.

A Carolingian commentator (the Tractatus Vindobonensis) paraphrases *prima, scilicet folia, cadunt, noua succrescunt; ita uetus aetas uerborum ... intereunt*. Here *noua succrescunt* supplies the missing idea. The hint was taken by Lehrs in his suggested supplement, and also by Nettleship 177.

We can hardly be meant to imagine a process whereby deciduous trees lose all their leaves in the autumn and gain new ones in the following spring; for that would not supply a convincing analogy to either words or men. We must rather think of a succession of two or three years in which the oldest leaves drop off while the less old are still there and the young ones have already appeared. See Fairclough's note in the Loeb edn 455.

63 debemur morti: cf. θανάτωι πάντες ὀφειλόμεθα, *A.P.* 10. 105.2 (Simonides?).

nostraque extends the range of the Greek epigram and leads into the works which follow.

63-8 As examples of men's works H. chooses the construction of a harbour, the draining of a marsh, and the redirection of a river to prevent flooding. Cicero, talking in an optimistic vein about corporate achievements, had offered a slightly longer list *adde ductus aquarum, deriuationes fluminum, agrorum irrigationes, moles oppositas fluctibus, portus manu factos* (*De off.* 2.14). H., too, is generalising, but there was nothing to prevent a reader from thinking of examples – harbours *like* the *portus Iulius* (see Virg. *Georg.* 2.161-4; Strabo 5.4.5-6; Dio 48.50; and below on 65), drainage-works *like* that projected by Julius Caesar for the Pomptine marshes, the diversion of a river *like* that projected by Julius Caesar for the Tiber (Suet. *Iul.* 44.3; Plut. *Jul. Caes.* 58.4-5).

64 arcet: here with the poetic construction 'defends x (acc.) from y (abl.)'; see *OLD arceo* 4. Neptune defends the fleets because he has been welcomed ashore – an arresting idea.

65 regium opus: a general phrase, meaning 'a work grand enough for a king'. This is Meineke's emendation of the manuscripts' *regis opus*, which ought to mean 'the king's work' or 'a [particular] king's work'. Precision is not wanted here, and anyhow it is not easy to think of a suitable *rex*. As an example of a regal work, readers might have thought of the royal harbour at Alexandria. According to Strabo 17.1.9, this was ἴδιος τῶν βασιλέων, 'for the monarchs' private use', and ὀρυκτός, 'man-made' (see Fraser I 22 and II notes 134 and 146). More likely, people would have called to mind the *portus Iulius* at Puteoli. In the early 30s Octavian had to build a fleet to counter Sextus Pompey. Timber cut in the area of the *lacus Auernus* was sent through a tunnel to Cumae and down a canal to the *lacus Lucrinus*, which was then much larger than it is today. The two lakes thus joined together were used for training the navy. For coastal communication Agrippa built up the shingle bar separating the *lacus Lucrinus* from the sea (the *Via Herculanea*). The exit to the sea was at the *portus Iulius*. See Frederiksen 333–4 and pl. xiv.

Some doubt is attached to Meineke's conjecture, because it introduces a rather uncommon elision in this position. However, *optimum erat* (*S.* 2.1.7), *rancidum aprum* (*S.* 2.2.89), and *integrum edax* (*S.* 2.2.92) are close enough parallels to modify the objection. Less close, but still relevant, are cases like *liberum et erectum* (*E.* 1.1.69) and *non ego inornata* (*AP* 234).

palus prius: this is Ben.'s emendation of *diu palus*, which makes the final syllable of *palus* short. None of the attempts to excuse the anomaly carries conviction (see B.). Nor has any better correction been devised. The hypothesis is that at a very early stage *prius* was omitted after *palus* by haplography; *diu* was then inserted before it.

68   doctus iter melius: when *doceo* is used in the passive, the acc. of the thing taught is sometimes retained in poetry and silver prose; G–L 339 n. 4. The river, like the swamp and the sea, is personified.

69   nedum + subjunctive: the basic idea is 'let x not be thought of', hence 'still less is it true that'; G–L 482.5 R2. This brings us back neatly to the topic of speech.

sermonum 'speech', 'language'. For the pl. B. cites Varro, *Men.* 399 Astbury *in sermonibus Plautus* (*poscit palmam*). There the pl. may be influenced by the preceding pls. *argumentis* and *ethesin*. Here *sermonum* may owe something to the pl. *facta*.

honos et gratia 'glory and charm'.

uiuax: used predicatively with *stet*, and referring to both *honos* and *gratia*.

70–1   The two processes represent an arc swinging upwards from left to right, intersected by an arc swinging downwards from left to right. The pattern is underlined by the chiastic order of the verbs *renascentur . . . cecidere . . . cadent . . . sunt in honore.*

71   usus: usage; i.e. the norms of educated speech; cf. *consuetudinem sermonis uocabo consensum eruditorum sicut uiuendi consensum bonorum*, Quint. *IO* 1.6.45. If he is widely read, a poet can in a small way help to *shape* usage. So, very rarely, can a scholar (one thinks of Dr Johnson with his dictionary). In an age of mass culture the speech-habits of a TV personality may have a disproportionate influence. But in the main, as H. implies, the forces at work are large, imperfectly understood, and beyond the control of any individual.

72 quem penes 'in whose hands'.
    arbitrium 'decision'.
    ius 'authority'.
    norma 'rule'.

73 The line presents the stuff of epic – viz. the deeds of princes and leaders and the grim wars of which they form a part; by avoiding a strong caesura in the third and fourth feet and by the use of *-que . . . -que* (recalling -τε . . . -τε) it may also evoke the rhythm of a Homeric hexameter, though the elision in the fourth foot tells against the idea.

74 quo scribi possent numero: this does not, of course, imply that there were other possibilities; the hexameter was the right metre for the purpose.
    monstrauit: Homer was the first writer of epic; H. does not say he was the inventor of the hexameter, an achievement variously ascribed to Apollo, Orpheus, and others.

75 uersibus impariter iunctis: i.e. hexameter followed by pentameter. *impariter* is apparently a coinage of H.'s.
    querimonia 'lament', i.e. the laments of sepulchral inscriptions; see *A.P.* 7. H. is thinking of the traditional derivation of elegy from εὖ λέγειν (Didymus, see B.; Suet. *Fr.* 3) or ἒ ἒ λέγειν (Suda). See Page 209–10, Harvey 171.

76 inclusa est: i.e. framed in elegiac couplets; cf. *pedibus quid claudere senis, S.* 1.10.59.
    uoti sententia compos: lit. 'thought expressed in possession of prayer', i.e. the grateful acknowledgement of answered prayers. This refers to the votive epigram; see *A.P.* 6. Love is not brought in until 85.

77 exiguos 'tiny'. The epigrams were small in size and importance when compared with epic.
    auctor 'first exponent'.

78 The Alexandrian scholar Didymus 'Chalkenteros' ('Copper-guts'), a contemporary of H., mentioned three candidates: Archilochus, Mimnermus, and Callinus. For ancient testimony on Archilochus, see Edmonds II 82–96; for Mimnermus see I 82–8; for Callinus see I 40–4. For Didymus see Pfeiffer (2) 297.

79 Archilochum: a Greek iambic poet of the 7th cent. B.C. from the island of Paros. For a modern study of him, see Rankin (1).

iambo: the word *iambus* was derived from ἰάπτω, 'I hurl'. So 'Rage armed Archilochus with her proper weapon–the iambus.'

80–1 An attempt may be made to reproduce the pun by translating: 'the foot was found to fit the sock and the stately buskin'. The *soccus* was, more accurately, a slipper worn by comic actors, but Milton renders it by 'sock' in *L'Allegro*, 131–2:

> Then to the well-trod stage anon,
> If Jonson's learned sock be on.

coturni were thick-soled boots worn by tragic actors to increase their height. According to Webster 9, the earliest illustration belongs to the mid-2nd cent. B.C. They were not used in the Greek classical theatre; cf. Beare 373, P-C (2) 204–6.

aptum: gives a reason: because it was suited to dialogue. The predominantly iambic base of conversation was noted by Arist. *Poet.* 4.1449a26–7 πλεῖστα γὰρ ἰαμβεῖα λέγομεν ἐν τῆι διαλέκτωι τῆι πρὸς ἀλλήλους, and by Cic. *Orat.* 189 *magnam enim partem ex iambis nostra constat oratio* (cf. also 191).

81–2 populares | uincentem strepitus 'drowning the noise of the pit'. According to Cic. *De orat.* 3.182, the iambic is a short foot with an insistent beat (*insignes percussiones*); cf. Quint. *IO* 9.4.136.

natum rebus agendis 'naturally suited to action'. Aristotle says that the iambic is a metre of movement (κινητικόν), representing and encouraging action (πρακτικόν), *Poet.* 24.1459b38.

83 fidibus: the strings of the lyre. Lyric poetry fell into two main categories: (i) Dorian (e.g. Pindar), which was public, choral, and rhythmically complex; its subjects were religious or national, and included victories at the games (83–4). (ii) Aeolic (e.g. Alcaeus and

Sappho), which was less formal, more personal, and metrically simpler (85). For the subject as a whole, see Bowra 4–8.

83–5 H. goes beyond the threefold division of gods, heroes (i.e. with one divine parent), and men, as found in Pindar, *Ol.* 2.2 (τίνα θεόν, τίν' ἥρωα, τίνα δ' ἄνδρα) and *C.* 1.12 (*Quem uirum aut heroa . . . quem deum?*). The list is closer to that of *C.* 4.2.13–24.

84 pugilem uictorem 'victorious boxer', balanced by winning horse.

85 curas 'heart-aches'; *OLD cura* 5a.

libera uina referre: i.e. to compose uninhibited drinking-songs. As Dionysus was Λυαῖος, Bacchus was *Liber*. For his manifold powers see *C.* 3.21.

86 'To observe the different types and styles of poetic works as laid down' – i.e. the various genres.

88 pudens praue 'from a distorted modesty'. To refuse to learn one's trade is not a sign of true modesty.

90 priuatis 'informal' in regard to diction, rather than ceremonious.

91 cena Thyestae: Thyestes, in his efforts to secure the throne of Mycenae, had seduced his brother Atreus' wife and stolen a golden ram which was the guarantee of sovereignty. By way of revenge, Atreus tricked Thyestes into eating his own sons. The story was adapted from the Greek dramatists by Ennius, Varius (H.'s friend), and Seneca.

92 'Let each thing keep the proper place allotted to it' – a social metaphor; cf. *S.* 1.9.51–2 *est locus uni | cuique suus*. The line gathers up what has just been said about tragedy and comedy into a universal declaration – which is immediately qualified in the following lines. The verse was rejected by Lehrs and Ribbeck on insufficient grounds.

The reading *decentem*, which is found in most of B.'s major authorities including the oldest Blandinian, enables *locum . . . decentem* to be governed by both *teneant* and *sortita*. The other reading, *decenter*, cannot go with *sortita*, and, if pressed closely, gives slightly inferior sense, since the propriety would then reside in the acquiescence rather than in the place.

93 uocem . . . tollit: not just in volume but also in emotional level. According to B., *tollo* in this sense with *uocem* is 'unusual and poetic'. For the opposite idea see *OLD submitto* 9.

94 Chremes: a conventional comic father.
  delitigat 'declaims away', as if in a lawcourt. The word occurs only here in classical Latin, and may be a coinage.
  ore 'utterance'.

95 tragicus 'in tragedy'.
  plerumque 'often'.
  pedestri: i.e. ordinary, down-to-earth.

96 Telephus, king of Mysia, was wounded by Achilles. In great wretchedness he went to the Greeks in search of a cure. This was eventually supplied by Achilles, who used the rust of the spear which had inflicted the wound. The subject was treated by all the major playwrights, Greek and Roman.
  Peleus experienced many troubles, including exile on two occasions, before marrying Thetis and becoming the father of Achilles.
  pauper et exsul, uterque: it is best to take *pauper* with Telephus, *exsul* with Peleus. Both heroes are the subject of *proicit*.

97 proicit 'casts away', 'abandons'.
  ampullas: *ampulla* was lit. a jar, the diminutive of *amphora*; but the word was applied to bombastic rhetoric, primarily as a result of the jar's corpulent shape, perhaps also because of the hollow boom produced by blowing into it (see the scholiast on Hephaistion, *Ench.* vi, quoted by Pfeiffer on Call. 215). Both ideas may be detected in Virg. *Cat.* 5 *Ite hinc inanes, ite, rhetorum ampullae,* | *inflata rhoezo uerba*. But here the notion of swollen shape predominates; cf. the comments of ps.-Acr. (*inflata, grandia*) and the note which Cruquius found in his Blandinian MSS (*uentricosa*). Porph. says H. has taken the image from Callimachus, cf. μοῦσα ληκυθίζουσα (215 Pfeiffer). Since one type of λήκυθος was round, this also is compatible with the interpretation given above; see Quincey 35ff. Another interpretation, which connects λήκυθοι with paint, is less plausible here.

sesquipedalia uerba: *sesqui-* as a prefix means that the quantity is multiplied by one and a half. Hence the present expression means 'words one and a half feet [i.e. 18 inches] long'. Many examples may be found in the early Roman tragedies.

98   si curat 'if he is concerned to'. Though some distance away, the clause qualifies *dolet* (95). Placed here, it prepares us for the next idea, viz. the effect of poetry on an audience. The strongly spondaic rhythm of the line, without a 3rd-foot caesura, is noticeable, as is the sequence *cur-, cor* ... *quer-*. Is H. showing how the heart may be touched by unpretentious words?

tetigisse: an aoristic infin., without any sense of past time; see on 347, and cf. 435, 455.

99   The distinction between *pulcher* and *dulcis* indicates that *pulcher* means 'formally correct', 'well made', even 'noble'. A work with this quality alone would be impressive in a rather cold and austere way. *dulcis*, however, implies a direct influence on the emotions – perhaps 'affecting'.

sunto: for this imperative, and *agunto* (100), see G–L 267–8, which says that the form is 'chiefly used in laws, legal documents, maxims, and the like'. This suits the prescriptive context here – a context which also helps to account for the rhyme.

100   animum ... agunto: the power which H. has in mind is the Greek ψυχαγωγία – an idea found, e.g., in Plato (*Phaedr.* 271D), Aristotle (*Poet.* 5.1450a33 and b16–17), Eratosthenes (Strabo 1.2.3), and Neoptolemus (see B. I 55).

101   adflent: the MSS have *adsunt*, but this fails to provide a proper contrast to *ridentibus arrident*. Ben. read *adflent*, citing Ov. *Met.* 3.459 *cum risi arrides* and Sen. *De ira* 2.2.5 *arridemus ridentibus*; cf. also Ov. *AA* 2.201 *riserit, adride*. W. and Housman (I 157) found this inelegant in view of *flere* in the next line, but that objection is hypersensitive.

102–3   si uis ... tibi: in this famous saying, as in much of the *AP*, H. is following the Peripatetic tradition of Aristotle and his successors. In the theatre the actor reflects on the fortune and condition of the character he is portraying, and induces in himself the analogous emotion. On the contrary theory, propounded by the Stoics, the actor remains at a distance from the character, and uses his professional technique to *simulate* the appropriate emotion. For the Peripatetic view, see Aristotle, *Poet.* 17.1455a30ff. (with D. W. Lucas's note); Cic. *De orat.* 2. 188–97, *Orat.* 132; Quint. *IO* 6.2.26–31. For the Stoic approach, see Cic. *Tusc.* 4.55; Sen. *De ira* 2.17. The diaeresis at the end of the 2nd foot throws a strong emphasis on *tum*.

103–4 H. is really, of course, addressing the actor playing Telephus or Peleus, and through him the playwright. But in *tua infortunia* he allows actor and character to coalesce.

104 male ... mandata: ineptly assigned, so that what the speaker says is out of character.

106 plena: supply *uerba*.

107 ludentem: here a noun, as in *ludentis speciem dabit* (*E.* 2.2.124).
   lasciua: understand *dictu*.

108 By saying that nature shapes us internally, H. means that nature produces an emotion within us.
   prius: emotion precedes speech; cf. *post* (11).

108–9 ad omnem | fortunarum habitum 'to suit every form [or manner] of experience'. *habitus* is used like the Greek σχῆμα.

111 The whole sequence, therefore, is (i) what happens to us, (ii) the corresponding emotion produced by nature, (iii) the words expressing the emotion through the medium of the tongue.

112 fortunis absona 'out of tune with his experiences [and hence his condition]'. But as *fortuna* can also refer to a person's *social* condition (e.g. his birth and status), the word subtly prepares us for 114.

113 equites peditesque: social divisions were reflected in the seating; see on *E.* 2.1.185. Here H. uses the old military phrase 'horse and foot' as though the audience were organised for war; cf. *OLD pedes* 2b.
   cachinnum 'guffaw'.

114 diuusne ... an heros: the god's tranquillity in tragedies is distinguished from the hero's agitation. Some have thought the distinction too fine and so have emended the text. The earliest and best-known suggestion is *Dauusne ... an heros*. But H. is talking here of different characters *within the same type of play*, whether tragedy or comedy; e.g. *senex* as distinct from *iuuenis, matrona* as distinct from *nutrix*. The contrast of Davus in a comedy with a hero in a tragedy would be too broad and obvious. The interest of the ancients in such matters can be seen in Plutarch's *Comparison of Aristophanes and Menander* (*Mor.* 853, x, Loeb edn).

115–16 *maturusne* is answered by *florente, senex* by *iuuenta; feruidus* reminds us retrospectively that the *senex* is *gelidus* (cf. 171). The *matrona* is powerful (and dignified); the nurse (lowly) and fussily attentive. The suppression of the contrasting adjectives recalls a similar procedure in *C.* 3.13.6–7 *gelidos [purosque] inficiet tibi | rubro [calidoque] sanguine riuos.*

117 The difference between the two men's occupations would be reflected in their talk. The much-travelled merchant would talk expansively about cities visited, dangers survived, money made and lost. The small farmer would be interested in weather, blight, yield etc. In money-matters he would be more likely to talk of what he had saved.

uirentis: not merely decorative. The man is hard-working and successful.

118 Colchus an Assyrius: foreigners, too, have their characteristics. A Colchian, from the E. end of the Black Sea, was supposed to be fierce, like Aeetes, Medea's father. An Assyrian was expected to be soft and luxurious, like Sardanapallus (see Mayor on Juv. 10.362). H. is sketching the broad stereotypes from which the dramatist has to begin. We are not to imagine that he ruled out all variations.

Thebis ... an Argis: the basis of this distinction (between Greek and Greek) eludes us. Boeotians were supposedly slow-witted (*E.* 2.1.244), but that may not be in point here, and, if it is, no opposite tradition is known concerning the Argives.

119 famam 'tradition'.
sibi conuenientia 'things which are consistent'.
finge: i.e. if you decide to innovate.

120 scriptor: probably voc., like *qui scribitis* (38). To take it as nom. in opposition to the subject ('as a writer') is less satisfactory, for what other capacity would be in point? As a voc., *scriptor* should come in the first sentence of the section; hence the punctuation in the text.

†**honoratum**† ... **Achillem:** if the text is right, *honoratum* is best taken as attributive: 'the admired Achilles', i.e. admired both in Homer (δῖος, ἀμύμων, θεοῖς ἐπιείκελος, etc.) and in the subsequent tradition. The variety in the words and phrases which follow (e.g. tireless, implacable, violently self-assertive) indicates that H. is not talking of a specific scene or episode but of general characteristics; this is confirmed by Medea, Ino, Ixion etc. in 123-4. Nevertheless, in view of the loss of face which he suffered by having to surrender Briseis (a slight which sets the *Iliad* in motion, and which receives much emphasis in Book 1), Achilles should not be described as *honoratus*. In fact the very opposite sense 'the slighted Achilles' would be expected. Unfortunately no convincing emendation has been proposed. (*Homereum, honore orbum, honorandum*, and a number of others have been tried.)

reponis: i.e. as others have before.

122   nihil non arroget armis 'let him claim everything by force of arms'; *sibi* is understood again. See *OLD arrogo* 3, not 4, where the meaning is 'assign' or 'bestow'. It may be going too far to think of deliberate irony, but if *honoratum* is right, the characteristics selected in 121-2 may reveal the reservations felt by a mature and civilised man about the heroic Achilles; cf. the vignette in *E.* 1.2.11-14.

123   inuictaque 'and indomitable'.

flebilis 'tearful'.

Ino: because she had cared for the infant Dionysus (son of her sister, Semele) Ino was driven mad by Hera. She fled from her husband Athamas with her two sons. He, however, seized one of the children and tore him to pieces. Ino and the second child dived into the sea and were changed into sea-deities; see Ov. *Met.* 4.499-542.

124   perfidus Ixion: Ixion, after promising marriage-gifts to his father-in-law, murdered him in a pit of hot coals; after being purified by Zeus, he repaid him by attempting to debauch Hera.

Io uaga: *quae in uaccam mutata, ad Egiptum peruenit factaque Isis, dea Egipti*, ps.-Acr. (cf. Ov. *Met.* 1.588-667, 724-46). But since H. is talking of ethos, her madness is doubtless included – madness which, as with Ino, was caused by Hera's jealousy.

tristis 'melancholic'. After murdering his mother (Clytemnestra) to avenge the death of his father (Agamemnon), Orestes was hounded by the Furies and lived in exile.

125   inexpertum: passive, 'untried'.

126   ad imum 'to the end'.

127   ab incepto: though logically it could go with *seruetur*, it is assigned to *processerit* for the sake of balance.

qualis ... processerit 'as it was ... when it made its entrance'. *processerit* is probably subjunctive by attraction.

128–30   difficile est proprie communia dicere 'it is hard to express general matters in a particular way'. In view of what has just been said, the general matters include characters. In their case, it is hard to express general qualities in particular characters. (The qualities of a hypocrite, *communia*, are expressed *proprie* in Tartuffe; see Dumarsais's formulation in B. II 439.) But the neuter pl. *communia* also includes themes and subjects. So, by the same token, it is hard to express, e.g., the clash between political and individual duty in particular terms (Creon vs. Antigone). In view of this difficulty, says H., it is wiser to follow tradition and to dramatise material from the Trojan epic (human and thematic) rather than to attempt something totally new. Having chosen characters and theme from the Trojan tradition, an author is still faced with the problem of treating and organising this material in a fresh and individual way. That problem is addressed in 131ff.

Because of the resemblance between *communia* (128) and *publica materies* (131) many commentators have assumed that they refer to the same thing. But, as we have just argued, 128 has to do with choice, 131 with treatment. The complexities of the controversy are set out in B. II, Appendix 1, 439.

128   tuque: *-que* here has the force of 'and so'.

129   rectius ... deducis = *rectius facis si deducis*. The subject of *deducis* is as general as the *scriptor* of 120; we are not justified in concluding that Piso was composing such a drama.

deducis in actus: the metaphor of composing as a kind of a spinning may be present, but the primary meaning here is that of transference or adaptation.

130   proferres: a pres. unreal subjunctive (Wo. 193.3), whereas *deducis* is imagined to be happening, and hence is indicative.

indictaque: as in *dicam insigne, recens, adhuc | indictum ore alio* (*C.* 3.25.7-8).

131   The language has a legal ring. *publica materies* is the body of mythological themes already handled by previous writers. H. is thinking of the Trojan cycle.

iuris: the gen. is possessive, like that of *sui iuris; OLD ius* 13c.

131-2   si | . . . orbem 'if you do not continue to circle the broad, common track'. The phrasing, which refers to the epic cycle as something trite and vulgar, recalls ἐχθαίρω τὸ ποίημα τὸ κυκλικόν, οὐδὲ κελεύθωι | χαίρω τίς πολλοὺς ὧδε καὶ ὧδε φέρει | . . . σικχαίνω πάντα τὰ δημόσια (Call. *Epig.* 30, Loeb edn, *A.P.* 12.43), 'I hate the cyclic poem, nor do I take pleasure in the road which carries many to and fro . . . I loathe all common things'. Cf. also τὰ μὴ πατέουσιν ἅμαξαι | τὰ στείβειν, ἑτέρων δ' ἴχνια μὴ καθ' ὁμά | δίφρον ἐλᾶν μηδ' οἶμον ἀνὰ πλατύν, ἀλλὰ κελεύθους | ἀτρίπτους, εἰ καὶ στεινοτέρην ἐλάσεις (Call. *Aetia* 1.1.25-8), 'Tread places which are not worn down by wagons; do not drive your chariot along the tracks of others, nor up the wide road, but on paths which have not been beaten down, even though your course be more narrow.'

133-4   fidus | interpres 'a faithful translator'; the fidelity has already been explained by *uerbo uerbum*.

134   imitator: H. means an imitator who follows his original slavishly; cf. *o imitatores, seruum pecus!* (*E.* 1.19.19).

desilies: the word suggests voluntary action ('jump' rather than 'fall'); so there may be a faint echo of the fable about the goat which jumped into a well at a fox's bidding (Phaedr. 4.9). But *artum* is not specific. We talk of 'painting oneself into a corner', or 'finding oneself in a straitjacket'.

135   The plosives do not appear to reinforce the sense, as they do in *S.* 1.6.57 *pudor prohibebat plura profari.* But perhaps they indicate fear.

pudor 'timidity', rather than shame at the thought of abandoning one's plan (ps.-Acr.). The imitator is afraid to add, subtract, or alter.

operis lex: to make a change which was inconsistent with the work's status as a tragedy would have infringed the law of the genre. Quite a lot about the law of tragedy can be inferred from the *AP*. A few hints about the law of satire are given in *S*. 2.1.1–4.

136 scriptor cyclicus: the epic cycle was a collection of post-Homeric epics artificially arranged by Alexandrian scholars so as to form a series running from the creation of the world to the end of the heroic age. Examples were the *Cypria* of Stasinus, the *Aethiopis* of Arctinus, and the *Little Iliad* of Lesches. The term 'cyclic poet' carried connotations of inferiority. For texts see *Hesiod, the Homeric Hymns and Homerica* (Loeb edn) 479–539.

olim: H. may have had a particular poem in mind.

137 This represents the start of an elaborate preamble which will lead to an anticlimax. So presumably we should regard the line as (i) pompous in itself, and (ii) the wrong sort of prelude to an epic. As for (i), there seems little wrong with *cantabo*. H. may perhaps object to *nobile*, because like a vulgar menu it seeks to secure approval in advance. In regard to (ii), the scope of the announcement is too wide; *fortunam Priami* could include everything that happened to Priam, and *bellum* would mean the whole of the war. The *Iliad* sets out to tell of a man's wrath, and the *Odyssey* of a man's return. The point had been made by Aristotle, *Poet.* 23.1459a30ff., and H. could have seen it in a passage of Theophrastus now lost.

138 promissor: probably coined by H. and applied satirically to the writer who promised more than he could achieve; cf. *promissi carminis auctor* (*AP* 45).

hiatu: 'a gaping mouth', hence 'bombastic utterance', used by Juvenal (6.636) of tragic diction; cf. Persius 5.3.

139 There was a Greek proverb ὤδινεν ὄρος, εἶτα μῦν ἀπέτεκεν (Diogenian. 8.75), 'A mountain laboured and then brought forth a mouse.' It is embodied in a fable (Phaedr. 4.24). Taking a hint from Virg. *Georg.* 1.181–2 (*tum uariae inludant pestes: saepe exiguus mus* | *sub terris posuitque domos atque horrea fecit*) H. has put *mus* at the end of the line, where it receives a comic emphasis from the separation of ictus and accent; he has substituted *ridiculus* for Virgil's more gentle *exiguus*; and he has taken *parturient montes* from the proverb to form an impressive prelude. The future tense is best explained as *fiet quod in pro-*

uerbio est. Nevertheless, though the line is justly famous, it is not well applied. The body equivalent to the *mus* ought, in order to provide sudden bathos, to be small and insignificant; but it is in fact the large and unwieldy body of an epic poem.

140   molitur: the idea of effort continues from 139.

141   Homer's lines are

> Ἄνδρα μοι ἔννεπε, μοῦσα, πολύτροπον, ὃς μάλα πολλὰ
> πλάγχθη, ἐπεὶ Τροίης ἱερὸν πτολίεθρον ἔπερσε·
> πολλῶν δ' ἀνθρώπων ἴδεν ἄστεα καὶ νόον ἔγνω

'Tell me, O Muse, of the man of many devices, who travelled right many a mile after sacking the holy citadel of Troy. And he came to know the cities and minds of many men.'

H. has not offered a translation, but an abridgement sufficient to make his point; for another version see *E.* 1.2.19–22.

captae post tempora Troiae: a grander and more poetic version of *post Troiam captam.*

142   Homer's νόον ('mind' or 'ways of thinking') is rendered by *mores* ('ways of doing things'). One tends to contrast intellectual Greek with practical Roman, but both words converge on the meaning of 'character'. Some have supposed that H.'s text had νόμον ('customs'), a reading known in antiquity.

143   What does the prelude lead to? Smoke, in the case of the inferior artist; light, in the case of Homer.

144   cogitat 'aims'.
speciosa . . . miracula 'spectacular marvels'.

145   Antiphaten: king of the Laestrygonians in *Od.* 10.100ff. He was a savage giant, with a wife the size of a mountain peak. The ending in *-n* is that of a Greek acc.
Scyllamque: a six-headed sea-monster described in *Od.* 12.85ff.
Cyclope: the one-eyed giant of *Od.* 9.182ff.
Charybdin: another monster, opposite to Scylla, on the other side of the straits. She sucked down the dark water and spewed it back again three times a day (*Od.* 12.104–5).

146 ˙ Meleager and Tydeus (Diomedes' father) were both sons of Oeneus. It is hard to see how the death of Meleager at Calydon in Aetolia (Ov. *Met.* 8.515–25) could have come into an account of Diomedes' return from Troy to Argos. But that may well be H.'s point. He has given this as an example of prolixity and irrelevance, typical of a cyclic poet. Perhaps he had an actual case in mind. Some scholars have thought that H. is referring to Diomedes' return to Aetolia from the war of the younger generation against Thebes, and indeed the scholiasts connect the line with Antimachus' *Thebaid*. But a return from Thebes would come oddly between the two references to Troy in 141 and 147.

147 gemino ... ab ouo: Helen, reputedly the cause of the Trojan war, was born from an egg produced by Leda, following her encounter with the swan (Zeus). The phrase could mean 'from the twin egg', i.e. one of two twin eggs (the other containing Castor and Pollux), 'from the two eggs', or 'from the egg containing twins' (the other being Clytemnestra). Since H. is thinking primarily of Helen, the first meaning is the most likely.

148 ad euentum festinat: i.e. he avoids needless digressions.

in medias res: i.e. he does not start from the beginning and work his way through to the end. Instead, he starts in the middle, and supplies what we need to know of the beginning in the course of the poem. Thus the *Iliad* begins in the tenth year of the war. (Virgil followed the same procedure.)

149–50 quae | ... relinquit: lit. 'things which he does not hope to be capable of being brilliant having been handled, he omits'.

151 mentitur 'uses fiction' (W.).

151–2 ita ... sic ... ne ... ne: for *ne* rather than *ut non* see G–L 552 R3: 'when the design or wish intrudes' or 'when a restriction or condition is intended'. Both apply here.

Is it chance that in talking of Homer's rapidity in 148–52 H. himself should give the impression of speed? One notes *festinat et ... rapit et ... relinquit atque ... mentitur.*

152 primo ... medio: dat. with *discrepet*; cf. *E.* 2.2.193–4 *nepoti* | *discrepet.* The abl. with this sense is preceded by *ab.*

154-5 The audience is thought of as remaining seated and silent until given the invitation *plaudite*.

eges: like our 'want', *egeo* + gen. can mean 'wish' or 'need'. Here it means 'wish'; cf. *S.* 1.1.59, where it cannot be the same as *est opus*: *at qui tantuli eget quanto est opus.*

aulaea: neut. pl. obj. of *manentis*. See on *E.* 2.1.189.

155   cantor 'singer', not 'actor' or 'piper'. *OLD* offers no instance of *cantor = histrio*, and the closing metres of comedies indicate that the piper would have been engaged in providing the accompaniment.

156   aetatis cuiusque ... mores: in modern parlance 'the behaviour-patterns of each age-group'. According to Diog. Laert. 8.10, Pythagoras divided man's life into four ages; see Ov. *Met.* 15. 199ff. and Bömer's notes, and Solon 27 (Edmonds I 140). Aristotle's treatment of the matter (to which H. was indebted) is to be found in *Rhet.* 2.12.1388b–2.14.1390b. For an excellent account of the whole topic, see Burrow.

157   mobilibus ... naturis ... et annis: lit. 'to changing natures and years', i.e. 'to characters as they change with the years'.

decor 'appropriateness'; *OLD decor* 3. In *Poet.* 15.1454a22 Aristotle uses ἁρμόττοντα (of ἤθη).

158   reddere ... uoces 'to reproduce speech', i.e. the speech which he hears going on around him, not necessarily in answer to a direct address. Aristotle says nothing of the child in *Rhet.* 2.12.1388b–2.14.1390b, because children were not speakers or listeners in court.

pede certo: i.e. without falling over.

159   signat humum 'treads the ground'.

colludere: only here in this literal sense with the dat.

159-60   iram | concipit ac ponit temere: lit. 'conceives and lays aside anger without thought'. The MSS have *colligit*, but this implies a slow accumulation of anger which conflicts with *temere* and is wrong for a child; cf. Lucr. *DRN.* 1.722–5 (Mt Etna working up to an eruption), Virg. *Aen.* 9.63–4. *concipit* first appeared in an edn of 1474. The two verbs are occasionally confused in the manuscript tradition. For *concipit* cf. Ov. *Met.* 1.166 *ingentes animo ... concipit iras*. Anger might have been added to fear, desire, hope, and love in *OLD concipio* 11.

161 imberbis: the evidence in *TLL* indicates that this, rather than *imberbus*, was the current form in H.'s day. Since the young man is over sixteen (*custode remoto*), one would expect his beard to be under way; but it looks as if *imberbis* was sometimes used rather loosely in the sense of 'young' or 'youngster'; cf. *E*. 2.1.85, where it is contrasted with *senes*. It does not mean 'clean-shaven'.

163 cereus ... flecti: the infin. explains the adj. – 'waxlike in his ability to be moulded'. See Wk. 1 (1896) Appendix 2.

asper 'rough' and 'stubborn' in contrast to *cereus*.

164 utilium 'practical advantages'.

aeris: for the gen. used with adjs. meaning full or empty, rich or poor, see G–L 374 n. 1.

165 sublimis 'with lofty ideas'. Was H. the first to use the word in this sense? Aristotle's word is μεγαλόψυχοι (*Rhet*. 2.12.11).

relinquere: for the infin. see on *flecti* above (163).

166 aetas animusque uirilis: in translating it may be convenient to alter the form: 'one who has reached manhood in age and attitude'.

167 amicitias: coming between *opes* and *honori*, the word is likely to mean 'useful connections' rather than 'friendships'.

honori 'status in public life'.

168 commisisse: the perf. infin. is metrically convenient and appropriate in sense, since it carries the idea of finality or completion. The aoristic infins. in 98, 435 and 455 are slightly different.

quod ... laboret 'what he would find difficult to alter later'.

170 quaerit: intransitive, as in *E*. 1.7.57 *et properare loco et cessare et quaerere et uti*. 'He is acquisitive' is not far from the meaning, but the connection with *inuentis* cannot be rendered by 'seek'/'find' in English.

et 'and [yet]'.

171 timide gelideque 'fearfully and without warmth'; cf. Arist. *Rhet*. 2.13.1389b31ff., especially ὁ φόβος κατάψυξίς τις ἐστίν, 'fear is a kind of chill'.

172 dilator: i.e. he puts things off. The word is not found elsewhere in classical Latin, and may be a Horatian coinage.

spe lentus: this is Ben.'s conjecture for *spe longus*, which cannot be made to yield satisfactory sense. (An old man is not 'far-reaching in hope' – not, at least, in a pagan, secular, context.) Modern editors have rejected *spe lentus* on the grounds that this would mean 'tenacious of hope'. But, like *tepidus*, *lentus* depends very much on its context. It can, admittedly, mean 'persistent' (e.g. in Ov. *Her.* 2.9 *spes quoque lenta fuit*); but more often it means 'sluggish'; and sandwiched, as it would be here, between *dilator* and *iners*, the word would be unambiguous. It would also answer to Aristotle's δυσέλπιδες in *Rhet.* 2.13.1390a4. The error in the MSS (for which Ben. quoted four parallels) may have been assisted by memories of *spem longam* in *C.* 1.4.15 and 1.11.7. The recent conjecture *mancus* (SB) is also worth considering.

pauidusque futuri: another conjecture of Ben.'s. The MSS have *auidusque*, which again is uncharacteristic of old men. It is uncomfortable to emend the text twice in the same line, but *auidus* may have been written in consequence of *longus*. *pauidus* is supported by Aristotle's καὶ δειλοὶ καὶ πάντα προφοβητικοί (*Rhet.* 2.13.1389b29–30). Moreover, in Aristotle the old man is contrasted with the young, who is full of hope and looks forward to the future (*Rhet.* 2.12.1389a18ff).

173 difficilis 'cantankerous'.

174 se puero: abl. abs. with *acti*.

175–6 We are not to think of the years advancing and receding over the same ground, like the tide. Tidal imagery is extremely rare in Latin poetry. Silius Italicus 14.348–9 says Archimedes knew the *pelagi lunaeque labores* and by what law Father Ocean made the tides to flow (*effunderet aestus*). Some alleged parallels in *OLD* and *TLL* seem to refer rather to the surf; e.g. Virg. *Aen.* 10.292 and Lucan, *BC* 4.428. Here the years move in a continuous stream. The human being is stationary. His years at first are in front of him, and as they come they bring many blessings. After the half-way point, his years (or rather an increasing majority of them) recede behind him, taking more and more of the blessings away. The second phase of the process is referred to in *E.* 2.2.55 *singula de nobis anni praedantur euntes*. There is an interesting variation in *C.* 2.5.13–15, where the young Lalage stands downstream (or down the road) from Horace's friend; the years which are taken from him are being brought to her: *currit enim ferox | aetas et illi quos tibi dempserit | apponet annos*.

176–7   seniles | … uiriles: the rhyme emphasises the balance of the two pairs. H. is talking about giving appropriate lines to each character, not about casting.

178   in adiunctis aeuoque … aptis: *aeuo* goes with both *adiunctis* and *aptis*; '[you will devote your attention to] the traits which are associated with, and suitable to, the character's age'.

moraberis: the MSS read *morabimur* or *morabitur*. H. never includes himself in precepts in the future tense (of the type 'we will fold in the cream and then put the mixture in the fridge'), and a subject for *morabitur* is not easy to find. Both readings interrupt the series of second person addresses: *tu … audi* (153), *si … eges* (154), *notandi … tibi* (156), *non … promes* (182–3), *multaque tolles* (183). The conjecture *moraberis* is therefore printed in the text. Ribbeck deleted the line, and B. regards it as suspect; without it, the *ne*-clause would recapitulate the foregoing ideas (starting with 156–7). A clearer case of this occurs in 406.

179   refertur 'reported', e.g. by a messenger.

180–1   There was a Greek saying that the eyes were more reliable than the ears: ὤτων πιστότεροι ὀφθαλμοί (*CPG* II 744; cf. Pfeiffer on Call. fr. 282). H. retains a hint of the idea in *fidelibus* but alters the emphasis from perception to emotion: what comes through the ear affects the emotions less vividly (*segnius*) than what is presented to the reliable eyes.

181–2   quae | ipse … tradit: *ipse mihi trado quae uideo, et alter mihi tradit quae narrat* (ps.-Acr.).

182–8   Moving quickly here, H. states that scenes of revolting violence (like Medea murdering her children) or sights which transgress the laws of nature (like Cadmus turning into a snake) should not be shown on the stage. The first principle is sharper than what we find in Aristotle: 'Fear and pity can be aroused by the spectacle, and also by the actual arrangement of the incidents. The second way is more essentially poetic and betokens a superior writer. The plot should be constructed in such a way that, even without seeing what is happening, the person who just hears it shudders and feels pity … To produce this effect by spectacle is less artistic and requires external aids' (*Poet.* 14.1453b1–6). The second principle is also more specific than

Aristotle's formulation 'Playwrights who employ spectacle to produce, not something terrible, but simply something monstrous have nothing to do with tragedy' (*Poet.* 14.1453b8–10). On the basis of what survives from the huge number of Greek tragedies, we cannot tell how often these (later) principles were ignored. Since H. makes no claim to be original, the greater particularity and dogmatism are presumably due to a post-Aristotelian source.

182–3   intus | digna geri: 'the infinitive with *dignus* is mostly poetical, not Ciceronian: more frequent with infin. passive than active'. So Palmer on *dignusque notari*, *S.* 1.3.24. H. is talking only of things going on in a tragedy. Hence *intus digna geri* means things which (given that they are going on in the plot) should only go on behind closed doors. *digna*, then, means '[only] fit', not 'worthy'.

184   mox 'in due course'.
   narret: subjunctive of purpose.
   facundia praesens: i.e. so that an actor (usually a messenger) may recount it in vivid terms on the stage. Since *praesens* is contrasted with *ex oculis*, it should not be taken in the sense of 'as an eyewitness'.

184–5 It gives a tighter structure if *ne . . . trucidet* etc. are understood as purpose-clauses explaining the foregoing precepts, rather than as independent prohibitions; hence the semicolon after *praesens* (184); see on 406. To take the purpose-clauses as introducing 188 spoils the self-contained *sententia quodcumque . . . odi.*

186 See on 91 above.

187   Procne murdered her son, Itys, and served him to her husband, Tereus, who had raped and mutilated her sister, Philomela. As Procne fled from Tereus, she was changed into a swallow (or a nightingale); see Ov. *Met.* 6.433–674. For the varied symbolism of the nightingale in later literature see Pfeffer.
   Cadmus, founder of Thebes, eventually went to Illyria with his wife, Harmonia, where they were both changed into large but harmless snakes; see Ov. *Met.* 4.576–603.

188 'I disbelieve such exhibitions and find them abhorrent.'

188–90 It seems clear that in 182–201, with its references to acts of violence, the *deus ex machina*, and the functions of the chorus, H. is talking of tragedy. So one assumes he was using a Hellenistic scholar who attempted to divide tragedy into five parts or acts. While such a division suits the tragedies of Seneca, we cannot tell how it was supposed to apply to Greek tragedy. The origin of such attempts may have been chap. 12 of Aristotle's *Poetics*, in which a tragedy is divided into prologue, episode(s), and exodus, punctuated by choral odes. But as, in classical Greek tragedy, the number of episodes varied, it is hard to see how the theory worked. The so-called 'Five-Act law' did not apply to Old Comedy; but there is evidence that it was employed by Menander. The Bodmer papyrus of the *Dyscolos*, e.g., has four marks of XOPOY, indicating five parts. There is no ancient evidence for any act-divisions in Plautus; Terence, too, employed a scheme of continuous action; see Duckworth 98–101.

productior 'more drawn out', hence 'longer'.

190 'A play which wants to be demanded and to be put on again for people to see.' Since *pono* is used by Asinius Pollio for putting on a play in Cic. *Fam.* 10.32.3 (*praetextam . . . posuit*), there seems to be no valid objection to *reponi*, and it is acknowledged by *OLD repono* 3. *spectanda* may be taken with *posci* as well as *reponi*; for the use of the word, cf. *nec redeant iterum atque iterum spectanda theatris* (*S.* 1.10.39). In both passages *spectanda* strengthens the idea of revival. The ancient variant *spectata*, adopted by many editors, seems by comparison somewhat otiose; for the play, by implication, has already been seen before it is demanded. The conjecture *reposci*, reported by Lambinus and accepted by B. and SB, makes good sense; and precedents for the confusion of *reponere* and *reposcere* can be cited (Prop. 1.17.11; Ov. *Met.* 13.235). If, in the present case, the two are thought to have more or less equal claims, the decision will go in favour of the manuscripts' reading.

191 intersit 'intervene', i.e. as a *deus ex machina*. The *machina* (μηχανή) was a kind of crane, for bringing gods down from the sky. For a playwright to introduce a god in this way, in order to rescue a plot from an impasse, was regarded as a dramaturgical failure: οἱ τραγῳδοποιοί, ἐπειδάν τι ἀπορῶσιν, ἐπὶ τὰς μηχανὰς καταφεύγουσι θεοὺς αἴροντες (Plato, *Crat.* 425D); φανερὸν οὖν ὅτι καὶ τὰς λύσεις τῶν μύθων ἐξ αὐτοῦ δεῖ τοῦ μύθου συμβαίνειν, καὶ μὴ ὥσπερ ἐν τῆι Μηδείαι ἀπὸ μηχανῆς . . . (Arist. *Poet.* 15.1454a37–b2). For other references see O.

191-2 nisi dignus ... | inciderit 'unless a knot has occurred which calls for a deliverer'. A *uindex* was someone who rescued another person from any kind of legal constraint. This exception means that the rule against the intervention of a god was not absolute. As justifiable examples, O. cites the appearance of Heracles in Sophocles' *Philoctetes* (which ensured that the hero would go to Troy), and that of Artemis in Euripides' *Hippolytus* (which made possible the reconciliation of Theseus and Hippolytus).

192 Tragedy began when a *hypocrites* (an actor, whether originally an 'expounder' or an 'answerer') emerged from the chorus; see Lesky (2) 29ff. Aeschylus introduced a second actor, and Sophocles a third (who was also employed by Aeschylus in his later plays). Here H. upholds this restriction, recommending that, if a fourth actor is brought on, he should not speak. The implications of this for Greek tragedy are discussed by P-C (2) 135-49. We are ill-informed about Roman tragedy; it is possible that by H.'s day the Greek restriction had come to be disregarded, and that he is reasserting it. Old Comedy occasionally allowed a fourth speaker; see P-C (2) 149-53. The practice in Greek New Comedy is disputed; see P-C (2) 154-6, and Sandbach 197-204. Plautus and Terence did not confine themselves to three actors (Duckworth 95-8). But, as remarked above, H. is thinking of tragedy.

193-4 'The chorus should staunchly perform the role of an actor and the duty of a man.' This is explained by what follows. The principle is enunciated by Aristotle: 'The chorus should be regarded as one of the actors; it should be an integral part of the play and share in the action – as in Sophocles rather than Euripides' (*Poet.* 18.1456a25-7); for the limitations of this in practice see Lucas's note.

194-5 'It should not sing anything between the acts which is not relevant to the plot and closely connected with it.' The *inter-* of *intercinat* (which is probably a coinage) governs *actūs*.

196 faueat 'take the side of', 'support', rather than merely 'be well disposed towards'.
 -que et 'both ... and'.

197 regat 'control'.
 amet †peccare timentes†: this comes close to repeating *bonis*

faueat (196); and it involves an unwanted use of *amo*, since H. is concerned with what the chorus should *do*, not with what it should feel. Ben. was attracted to *pacare tumentes*; but that would mean 'to subdue the arrogant', which is too imperious an idea; it also anticipates *superbis* (201). It seems a mistake to remove *timentes*, which goes well with *iratos* (cf. *E.* 1.4.12 *timores inter et iras*). If we keep *timentes* and abandon *peccare*, we need an infin. for *amet*. One possibility is *pacare* or *placare*, which occur in certain MSS. But while both verbs are common in the sense of 'soothe' or 'calm', the emotions concerned appear to be *hostile* emotions, like *ira, odium,* and *inuidia.* Campbell suggested *recreare* (*OLD recreo* 4a), but the succession of eight short *e*s seems unlikely. Instead of an obelus, which indicates total despair, the conjecture *firmare* might be considered. Virgil has *animum firmat*, followed by *deposita formidine* (*Aen.* 3.611–12); H. has *patres firmaret* (*C.* 3.5.46); other examples are given in *OLD firmo* 7a. The hypothesis would be that the beginning of *firm(are)* had been damaged at an early stage, and then restored as *pecc(are)* by someone who thought that the infin. went with *timentes.*

198   dapes ... mensae breuis: 'short' is transferred from the meal (cf. *cena breuis* in *E.* 1.14.35) to the table; but the effect is slight, since *mensa* itself could be used for a meal; *OLD mensa* 7a.

salubrem: continues the idea of 'healthy' from the meal. In *S.* 2.2.70–1 the first benefit of *uictus tenuis* is said to be good health – *ualeas bene.* Here the notion of 'sound', 'beneficial', is extended from *iustitiam* to *leges* and *otia.*

199   apertis ... portis: a sign of peace; cf. *C.* 3.5.23 *portasque non clausas.*

200   tegat commissa: i.e. preserve secrets entrusted to it.

202–15 Here we find, applied to music and the theatre, the very widespread view that the increase in Rome's wealth and power had led to moral decline – a view which recurred in writing of every period from the 2nd cent. B.C. on, and which drew for illustration on many areas, including school, family, business, and public life. The support given to Augustus in H.'s time represented the hope that he could do something to reverse the trend, while still retaining the gains of empire.

202   tibia 'pipe', or rather 'double pipe', for the pipes were played in pairs. Older authorities translate *tibia* as 'flute', but this is misleading because (i) the *tibia* (= the Greek *aulos*) was end-blown like a recorder, not side-blown like a flute; (ii) the *tibia* was a reed-blown instrument (in fact each pipe had a double reed); and so it did not sound like a flute (see on 202-3 below).

orichalco uincta 'bound with brass'. Some scholars think this refers to the 'sleeves' or 'collars' which opened and closed the holes, like the sleeve around the bottom of a bunsen burner (see on 203 below). But it seems rather more natural to take it as referring to the practice of encasing or wrapping the pipe in a thin sheet of metal.

202-3   tubaeque | aemula 'rivalling the trumpet'. Other ancient writers speak of the *aulos/tibia* as 'blaring' or 'booming', which again is wrong for the flute.

203   tenuis 'thin'.

foramine pauco 'with few holes'. For the rare use of *paucus* in the sing. B. quotes *Ad Herenn.* 4.45 (*uti pauco sermone*), Vitruv. 1.1.6 (*pauca manu*), and a few other instances from prose.

The earlier and simpler form of the pipe had four or five holes along the top (the fifth, or 'vent-hole' was not covered) and a thumb-hole underneath. The invention of 'sleeves' allowed a greater number of holes, which increased the range of the instrument. This keywork could not be operated in the course of an actual phrase. It would have been set beforehand and possibly adjusted during pauses. (For help with this and the preceding note, thanks are due to Dr J. G. Landels of Reading University, who is completing a book on ancient music.)

Those wishing to pursue this topic can start from the references in B. or else from *The New Oxford History of Music* I (1957) 380-1 and n. 6.

204   adspirare et adesse 'to accompany and assist'; the infinitives go with *utilis*.

utilis 'serviceable', hence 'sufficient'. In Greece, from an early stage, comes complaint about the increasing dominance of the pipe and music over voice and words. For the testimony of Pratinas (6th-5th cent.) as preserved in Athenaeus 14.617B-E, and of the ps.-Plutarch (*De mus.* 29-30, 1141C-D) see P-C (1) 14 (about Lasos),

17-18, and 291-3; and also Barker 273-4 and 235-6. For the combination of Greek and Roman in H.'s account, see above, pp. 32-3.

205 nondum spissa nimis go together. H. postulates an early theatre where there was plenty of room; contrast *E.* 1.19.41 (*spissis . . . theatris*) and 2.1.60 (*arto . . . theatro*).

206 quo: i.e. to the theatre.

sane: the sequence of thought is: the seats were not too crowded, for of course (*sane*) the community was easily counted, being small in numbers.

numerabilis: unlike *innumerabilis*, the word has no previous history and may be a coinage.

207 The simplicity of the pipe reflected the moral character of that early community.

frugi: an indeclinable adj., originally a predicative dat. of *frux* 'goodness'; hence 'honest'.

208 urbem: the best MSS have the pl. *urbis*, and this has been defended on the grounds that H. is speaking of Greece as well as Rome, e.g. *Delphis* (219). Nevertheless, *populus . . . uictor . . . murus* seem to indicate a single, though unspecified, community; and so *urbem* gives rather better sense.

209 uinoque diurno: daytime, as distinct from evening, drinking.

210 placari Genius: see on *E.* 2.1.144.

impune 'without any punishment being incurred', hence 'freely'.

211 numerisque modisque 'rhythms and tunes'.

212 saperet: here of aesthetic taste; the subjunctive is potential.

liberque laborum: for the gen. with adjs. involving separation, see G-L 374 n. 8.

213 turpis honesto: the terms are both social and moral; cf. our 'riff-raff' and 'the better sort'. If a writer intended to distinguish the moral from the social element, he had to make this clear, as in *S.* 1.6.63-4 *turpi secernis honestum | non patre praeclaro, sed uita et pectore puro.*

214 sic 'as a result of this process'.

priscae . . . arti: early musicians confined themselves to music, and to simple music at that.

motumque et luxuriem: lit. 'bodily movement and sumptuous decadence', an expression which is clarified in the next line.

215   traxitque: this suggests a long, heavily embroidered robe; cf. *et quibus aurata mos est fulgere lacerna* (Juv. 10.212).

uagus: describing the opposite of brisk, purposeful movement.

per pulpita: across the stage, not across the *orchestra*, which in the Roman theatre was filled with seats.

216   uoces creuere: the notes (i.e. the musical range) were increased by additional strings. Developments in the music of the lyre are attributed to Melanippides, Philoxenus, and Timotheus by the ps.-Plutarch, who says that Timotheus (*c.* 450–360 B.C.) increased the number of strings from the traditional seven (*De mus.* 29–30, 1141c–d); see P-C (1) 18 and 291; and Barker 235–6. The comic poet Pherecrates (fl. 430 B.C.) in his *Cheiron* makes Music complain about what Timotheus is doing with his twelve strings; see P-C (1) 39 and 48–9. Again H. draws on this Greek tradition for his brief, impressionistic summary.

seueris: the music of the lyre was thought of as graver and more austere than that of the pipe; it was the only music allowed in Plato's republic (*Rep.* 3.399c–d). Cicero, whether using a written source or repeating oral tradition, says that the lyre-music which accompanied the plays of Livius and Naevius (second part of 3rd cent. B.C.) had a *seueritas iucunda* (*De leg.* 2.39).

217   'And a headlong fluency brought with it a strange delivery.' H. may be echoing here the kind of complaint made about the language of the later Greek dithyramb, as represented by writers like Kinesias, Philoxenus, and Timotheus. These writers influenced tragedians like Agathon and Euripides. See P-C (1) 38–51.

218   utiliumque sagax rerum: i.e. possessing practical wisdom. The combination of *sagax* with a gen., and its conjunction with *sententia* (here = 'thought'), are probably original touches.

diuina futuri: cf. *imbrium diuina auis imminentum* (*C.* 3.27.10). For the gen. with adjs. of knowledge and ignorance see G–L 374 n. 4.

219   sortilegis ... Delphis: i.e. '[the thought of] lot-drawing Delphi'. 'Expressions like "that of" are avoided in Latin, either by such compression or by the repetition of the substantive' (W.). This is the only case quoted in *OLD* of the word used adjectivally. So, whether or not H. had heard reports of very early sortilege at Delphi, the expression has almost certainly a satirical colour in keeping with the preceding lines. H. did not admire pretentious obscurity.

Delphis: dat.; see on 152.

220 carmine ... tragico: this phrase renders the Greek word τραγωιδία, of which the second part is connected with ὠιδή = 'song'. The first part of the word comes from τράγος = 'goat', an etymology indicated by the Latin *hircus*.

uilem: this points to the antiquity of the competition; an animal which is now cheap was then a valuable prize. K–H prefer to see an amusing contrast between the insignificance of the goat and the high importance of the event.

certauit ob hircum: this gives the reason why tragedy was thought of as a 'goat song'. The same view is found in the Marmor Parium (*c.* 263 B.C.), which, recording the appearance of Thespis (*c.* 536 B.C.), speaks of a goat as a prize, ἆθλον ἐτέθη ὁ τράγος. (The evidence of Dioscorides, *A.P.* 7.4.10 χορὸν ὧι τράγος ἄθλων is more doubtful because of a textual problem; see Gow–Page II 252.) Other explanations of tragedy are 'the song sung around the sacrificial goat' and 'the song sung by a goat-like chorus'; see P-C (1) 112ff. (with Webster's additions), and Lesky (2) 12–16.

220–1 The writer who took part in those early tragic competitions subsequently also introduced wild satyrs without clothes. The writer in question is Pratinas of Phlius (SW of Corinth), who, according to the Suda, competed as a tragic poet with Aeschylus. 'He was the first to write *satyroi* ... and exhibited 50 plays of which 32 were satyric.' Dioscorides sees Phlius as the original home of the satyr-play (*A.P.* 7.37 and 707). Pausanias says Pratinas and his son wrote satyr-plays more celebrated than any, save those of Aeschylus (2.13.6). The ps.-Acr. on *AP* 216 says *is ... primus Athenis ... satyricam fabulam induxit.* (The *is* is probably Pratinas, not Cratinus.)

nudauit: *nudus* can mean 'without one's main garment'; *OLD nudus* 2. The illustrations of satyrs listed by Webster 6, 7, and 9 show loincloths or shaggy aprons.

asper 'in a rough manner'.

222   incolumi grauitate 'without sacrificing his dignity'. This is explained in 225–30. The dignity belongs equally to the dramatist and to his divine and heroic characters (who have already appeared in the serious plays).

eo quod 'for this reason, that . . .'

224   exlex 'freed from the constraints of the law'; i.e. enjoying the licence of the carnival.

225–6   'Nevertheless, it will be appropriate to make the satyrs, with their jokes and back-chat, attractive . . .'.

226   uertere seria ludo: lit. 'to turn [change] grave with gay', hence 'to pass from grave to gay'; *OLD uerto* 23b. *ludo* is abl.

227   ne: see on 151–2 above.

adhibebitur 'is brought on'.

228   nuper: i.e. in the tragedy preceding the satyr-play.

229   'Does not move, with a low style of talk, into a dim hovel'; i.e. does not move into a low style of talk, as if entering a dim hovel. It may be that *tabernas* is an allusion to the realistic *comoedia togata* of Afranius and others, sometimes called *fabula tabernaria*, because it was about the poor houses of common people. On these terms see Beare 264–6.

230   nubes . . . captet 'snatch at clouds and thin air'; the opposite extreme to the low style. *dum uitant stulti uitia, in contraria currunt* (*S.* 1.2.24).

231   effutire 'to spout', from *futis* (connected with *fundo*), a jar for pouring water.

leues 'frivolous'.

indigna: here with the infin. The sense = *quam non decet.*

232–3   moueri 'to dance'. The ps.-Acr. comments *sunt enim quaedam sacra, in quibus saltant matronae, sicut in sacrificiis Matris deum*; cf. the dances *sacro* | *Dianae celebris die* (*C.* 2.12.19–20). There is no reason to think that *matronae* were reluctant to dance at private celebrations. Dancing in public, however, might have been another matter. The word-order (*Satyris paulum pudibunda proteruis*) reflects the meaning –

tragedy is 'somewhat bashful among the ribald satyrs'. Some scholars prefer to take *paulum* with *intererit* 'will mingle only a little'.

234–5 dominantia nomina: *dominantia* is adapted by H. so as to translate the Greek κύρια (*dominus* being = κύριος). Τὸ κύριον ὄνομα was the authoritative, authorised, and hence proper word to denote any object. As such, it was distinguished from words which were meta- phorical, imported, obsolete, or otherwise unusual (cf. Cic. *De orat.* 3.149 *quae propria sunt et certa quasi uocabula rerum paene una nata cum rebus ipsis*). By using *dominantia* instead of the usual *propria*, H. has both enunciated and illustrated the principle of not confining oneself to plain words.

nomina ... | uerbaque: Plato used nouns and verbs (ὀνόματα and ῥήματα) to cover the whole of language; *Crat.* 431B; cf. Arist. *Rhet.* 3.2.1404b5.

Satyrorum scriptor: i.e. if ever I write satyr-plays. H. has no in- tention of doing so; he is merely using the first person for the sake of variety.

236–9 After refusing to confine himself to plain, literal, speech, H. now says 'I will also avoid adhering to the high manner – but I will not settle on so low a level as to confuse the linguistic style of comic figures (like Dauus, Pythias, and Simo) with that of the wise satyr Sil- enus, who was the teacher and guardian of the young Dionysus.' The resultant style is, in a sense, a 'middle' style, but it resists categorisa- tion, because (like the *sermo* as described in *S.* 1.10.11–15) it is always on the move.

236 colori: for the dat. cf. *differt sermoni* (*S.* 1.4.48).

237–9 Dauusne: Davus is a common name for comic slaves.

Pythias: ps.-Acr. comments *non dicit de Pythia Terentiana* [i.e. in the *Eunuchus*], *sed quae apud Lucilium tragoediographum inducitur ancilla per astutias accipere argentum a domino*. All this garbled note tells us is that the scholiast was thinking of a particular scene, in a play other than the *Eunuchus*. We could imagine a comic scene in Lucilius (or Caeci- lius), but *tragoediographum* cannot be right. Pythias is *audax*, 'brazen', a suitable adj. for a slave-girl.

emuncto ... Simone: *emungo* is used in the transferred sense 'I wipe someone's eye', i.e. 'I cheat him'; it is a low word, found in

Plaut. *Bacch.* 701 (*emungam ... hominem probe hodie*), Ter. *Phorm.* 682 (*emunxi argento senes*), and also, as it happens, in Lucilius, *ROL* III 903 (*quouis posse me emungi bolo*). Its lowness is appropriate to the present context. According to ps.-Acr. (above) Simo was Pythias' master. The name belongs to old men in Plaut. *Most.* and *Pseud.*, and Ter. *And.*

talentum: in the Greek world, as represented in Plautine comedy, a talent was a large sum of silver = 60 *minae*. An attractive girl cost about 30 *minae* (see, e.g. *Rud.* 45). A decent town house for 2 talents was absurdly cheap (*Most.* 639-44). Six talents was still on the low side (*Most.* 913).

239　Silenus: earth-born or the son of Pan, Silenus was the leader of the satyrs, as in Eur. *Cycl.* As such, he represented the wild forces of nature, and was inordinately fond of wine. At the same time, he was the tutor of the child Dionysus, and widely respected for his knowledge; thus in Pind. fr. 143 Bowra he preaches on the vanity of riches, in Ael. *Var. Hist.* 3.18 he tells of strange, remote places, and in Virg. *Ecl.* 6 he sings creation-myths. Socrates was compared to Silenus, because he concealed profound wisdom behind a snub-nosed, bearded face (Plat. *Symp.* 215B).

240　ex noto fictum carmen: by 'poetry newly fashioned from familiar elements' H. means style, not content, as is clear from *series iuncturaque* (242).

sequar 'I shall aim at'.

241 Some take *sudet* as parallel to *speret*, i.e. 'hope [and] sweat'. In that case the *-que* in *frustraque laboret* must be used adversatively in the sense of 'but'. Thus Wk. and the Loeb edn translate 'and yet'. It may be better, however, to imagine the contrast as beginning with *sudet multum*, in which case *-que* has its normal sense. The contrast is completed by *ausus idem* immediately beneath *speret idem*. For the thought cf. *E.* 2.2.124-5.

242　series iuncturaque 'linkage and combination'; cf. *in uerbis serendis* (46) and *callida iunctura* (47-8).

243 'So great is the distinction that accrues to words taken from the common stock'; *tantum* with *honoris*. Behind these ideas lies a passage of Aristotle's *Rhetoric*, in particular the following words: κλέπτεται δ' εὖ,

ἐάν τις ἐκ τῆς εἰωθυίας διαλέκτου ἐκλέγων συντιθῆι· ὅπερ Εὐριπίδης
ποιεῖ καὶ ὑπέδειξε πρῶτος (3.2.1404b18ff.). 'Artful concealment takes
place when one selects his words from ordinary language and puts
them together. That is what Euripides does; he was the first to point
the way.' In 240–3, then, H. takes over the idea of combining ordinary words in an original, but cleverly unobtrusive, way; but he adds
the important notion of effort, which is not in Aristotle's passage.

244 deducti 'brought on stage'.
   Fauni: i.e. satyrs, Faunus being identical with Pan.

245–7 Is *innati triuiis* continued and developed by *forenses* (vulgar
people of the market-place)? Or is there a chiasmus in which *innati
triuiis* (born at street corners) is taken up by *immunda . . . dicta* (dirty
talk), and *forenses* (boulevardiers) by *nimium teneris uersibus* (over-
sentimental verse)? The trouble with the first idea is that the rowdies
seem to be separated from their characteristic language by 246; while
the second idea prevents the natural progression from lower to lowest
implied by *ac paene* (*OLD paene* 1a). It seems preferable to adopt the
first interpretation and assume that the corner-boys go in for
sentimental–erotic songs. (Modern parallels are not lacking.)
   triuiis: probably dat.

246 nimium teneris 'over-soft', i.e. 'wanton'. For this nuance cf.
Cic. *Pis.* 89 *cum tuis teneris saltatoribus.*
   iuuenentur: probably another Horatian coinage, to parallel the
Greek νεανεύεσθαι and μειρακιεύεσθαι 'to act like a silly youth'.

247 crepent 'rattle off'.
   ignominiosaque: a deliberately unpoetic word; all the other examples in *OLD* are from prose.

248 quibus . . . res: the tone is lightly satirical, as not infrequently
when H. is talking of a class above that into which he was born. Thus
equus refers to the original order of knights, who could afford to provide their own horse; *pater* means the sort of father who could be mentioned in polite society (the lowest people in the community, i.e.
slaves and freedmen, had no legal fathers at all); *res* means not just
'possessions', but a fortune of 400,000 sesterces.

249 fricti ciceris . . . et nucis 'roasted chick-peas and [roasted] nuts'; roughly the equivalent of our fish and chips. The whole clause *si quid probat* is the object of *accipiunt* and *donant*.

250   aequis ... animis 'with approval'; cf. *audite o mentibus aequis | Aeneadae* (Virg. *Aen.* 9.234–5).

corona: 'The name of the victorious poet was proclaimed by the herald, and he was crowned in the theatre by the archon with a crown of ivy', P-C (2) 98, reff. in n. 6. That was the practice in Athens; what of republican Rome? (i) Crassus awarded *coronae* (bronze, gilt, or silvered) at his games (Plin. *NH* 21.5–6); (ii) a prize (*palma*) was available for actors (Plaut. *Amph.* 69; Cic. *Att.* 4.15.6; Varro, *LL* 5.178); and also (iii) for other kinds of *artifex* (Plaut. *Amph.* 70; *Poen.* 37); (iv) as for the playwright and his play, two passages come to mind: *uicit tua comoedia* (Plaut. *Trin.* 706), and *in medio omnibus | palmam esse positam qui artem tractent musicam* (Ter. *Phorm.* 16–17). Are these usages figurative, like *S.* 1.10.49, where H. denies any wish to take the crown from Lucilius' head? On *a priori* grounds, prizes for playwrights might seem likely. Yet the argument from silence has some force here; if such prizes *were* offered, we would expect to have several clear references to the practice.

251   subiecta 'immediately following'. Conversely, 'earlier' is often thought of as 'higher'; see *OLD superior* 3 and 4.

uocatur iambus 'is named Iambus'. This translation is suggested in view of the personification that follows.

252–3 The iambic line was regarded as quick, when not retarded by spondees; cf. *C.* 1.16.24 *celeres iambos*. H. may have at the back of his mind the derivation from ἰάπτω, 'I hurl'. If so, then *pes citus* offers an explanation for *uocatur iambus*, and *unde etiam* means 'for that same reason' (i.e. its speed). In paraphrase, 'Iambus ordered the name "trimeters" to be applied to his lines, even though he delivered six identical beats from beginning to end.' An iambic trimeter therefore had two feet to a metron, and so its feet were evidently working faster than the feet in a hexameter, which had only one foot per metron.

252   trimetris: attracted to the dat., like *tardo* in *illi | tardo cognomen damus* (*S.* 1.3.57–8) 'we give him the nickname "slowcoach"'.

accrescere: if right, the word is used, as *accedere* often is, like the pass. of *addo*.

253   iambeis: a Horatian coinage = the Greek ἰαμβεῖος.

senos: each line has six beats, hence the distributive; G–L 295.

254   primus ... sibi: lit. 'like himself first to last'; i.e. having iambic feet throughout.

†non ita pridem†: H. is apparently following a theory which held that spondees were admitted only at a later stage. Actually, as H. knew, Greek poets like Archilochus used spondees in the 7th cent. B.C. So *non ita pridem* poses a problem. Suggestions that H. is talking of what ideally ought to have happened (W.), or that he is indulging in playful exaggeration (Wk.), or that he is being intentionally vague (Russell) fail to convince; for the error is of too gross a kind. The conjecture *comiter idem* (Delz 146–8) seems unlikely, because (i) we do seem to need some indication of time, like 'soon afterwards', (ii) *comiter* would anticipate *commodus et patiens* (257). In charity to H. one resorts to daggers, as do B. and SB.

256   stabiles 'steady' or 'stately'.

in iura paterna recepit: lit. 'adopted into ancestral rights'.

257–8   non ut ... | cederet ... socialiter: a result clause limiting the scope of the previous statement 'not, however, taking the spirit of partnership so far as to withdraw ...'

sede secunda 'the second position', i.e. the second foot; so also with *quarta*.

258   hic: still Iambus.

Acci: see on *E*. 2.1.56.

259   nobilibus: the rarity of the iambus means that Accius' lines, like Ennius', lurch heavily along; therefore the word cannot convey straightforward praise. It is best to enclose it, as it were, in inverted commas: Accius' 'noble' trimeters. Some conservative critic may have used the phrase without irony.

259–60   Enni | ... uersus: the Latin order can be retained by saying 'As for the verses of Ennius, trundled onto the stage with their enormous weight ...' The heavily spondaic quality of the line, combined with the old-fashioned order of *cum magno pondere*, enacts H.'s criticism. Cicero, in his translation of Aratus (132), had *obuertunt nauem magno cum pondere nautae*; that was also Virgil's practice.

261 operae: the gen. defines *crimine* (262).

  nimium: with *celeris*.

262 premit 'pursues', *OLD premo* 6. The subject is Iambus. 'He
pursues them with the disgraceful charge of over-hasty and careless
workmanship and ignorance of the poet's craft.'

263 uidet 'notices'.

  immodulata 'unrhythmical' or 'unmusical'; probably another
coinage. The lack of a strong caesura in the 3rd and 4th feet suggests
that H. may be illustrating the fault in question.

264 indigna 'undeserved'. *Romanis poetis* is probably dat. after *data*.

265 uager 'am I to go on the loose?'; deliberative subjunct.

  licenter 'without any discipline'.

265–6 'Or am I to assume that *everyone* will notice my faults?'

266–7 tutus 'playing safe'.

  et intra | spem ueniae cautus: lit. 'remaining carefully within
the hope of pardon'; i.e. 'not straying carelessly beyond the hope of
pardon'.

267–8 uitaui ... merui: i.e. 'If I follow that course, all I've
achieved in the end (*denique*) is an escape from censure; I have not de-
served [real] praise.' By (real) praise H. means the praise of discerning
people like the Pisones (272–4), people who took their standards from
the *exemplaria Graeca* (268). If developed, this line of thought could
have led to something like Longinus' famous chapter (33) on the inferiority of the pure and blameless mediocrity to the flawed (but insig-
nificantly flawed) genius. But H. is writing about *ars*, not *ingenium*;
and anyhow he was never keen on the idea that a great artist's faults
should be indulged (see B. on 352). So he continues with a complaint
about the slipshod craftsmanship of Plautus.

268 uos: probably, as K–H say, the Pisones as representatives of the
present generation of poets.

269 nocturna ... diurna: an elegant form of emphasis: cf. the
more light-hearted example in *E.* 1.19.11 *nocturno certare mero, putere
diurno.*

uersate ... uersate: the verb means both 'to handle' and 'to ponder'.

270–4 Cf. the disapproving remarks on Plautus in *E.* 2.1.170–6.

270 uestri proaui 'your ancestors'. The word *numeros* suggests that H. is talking, not of Roman audiences in general, but of people who expressed literary opinions about comic writers.

271 nimium patienter: with *mirati* (272).

272 ne dicam stulte 'not to say stupidly'; *OLD ne* 13c.

272–3 si modo ... | scimus: the modification is only formal; H. has no doubt about *scimus*.

273 inurbanum: supply *dictum*. This takes up Plautus' *sales* (271). H. has a less favourable view of Plautus' wit than Cicero, who classes it with that of Old Comedy and the Socratic philosophers as *elegans, urbanum, ingeniosum, facetum* (*De off.* 1.104).

274 legitimumque sonum: this takes up Plautus' *numeros* (270).
callemus: transitive, 'have the skill to recognise'.

275 ignotum: i.e. the genre was unknown before.

276–7 plaustris uexisse: there is no other, independent, reference to Thespis' wagon (see the passages in P-C (1) 69–72). Jokes from wagons, however, *are* associated with the prehistory of comedy (e.g. Plat. *Laws* 1.637B, the Suda's note on τὰ ἐξ ἀμαξῶν, quoted by O., the schol. on Lucian, Ζεὺς Τραγωιδός VI 388, quoted by W.); we are told that at the festival of Dionysus in Athens a procession took place in the course of which people would hurl abusive jokes from wagons. If, then, H.'s source derived tragedy and comedy from a common origin, Thespis' wagon may have been thought of as a relic of those early days. But it would be unwise to place much reliance on the tradition.

poemata: verse-compositions, which in 277 are shown to have been dramatic (*agerent*).

Thespis: see on *E.* 2.1.163. For source material and discussion see P-C (1) 69–89; Lesky (2) 25–30.

277 peruncti faecibus ora: lit. 'thoroughly smeared with wine-lees in respect of their faces'; for the acc. see G–L 338, Wo. 19. Porph.

records *putant quidam tragoediam appellatam quasi trygadiam, quia faecem*
τρύγα *Graeci appellant.* H. may allude to this idea but he does not
sponsor it. The original status of *trygoedia* is not established; it might
be later than *tragoedia*. The matter is discussed by P-C (1) 741–6; see
also schol. on Ar. *Ach.* 398, 499, *Clouds* 296, and the treatise *De com.*
(Kaibel) 7.

278 H.'s truncated survey omits such intermediate figures as Choerilus and Phrynichus; see Lesky (2) chap. 3 and P-C (1) 63–9.

personae: the source on which H. depends here is of no historical
value. The same idea, but in fuller form, comes from the Suda, which
says that Thespis first covered his face with white lead, then hung
flowers over it, and finally wore a linen mask; then after some intermediate modifications by Choerilus and Phrynichus, Aeschylus first
used coloured and terrifying masks. (On the artificiality of this account, see Webster in P-C (1) 80.) The use of some form of mask was
immemorially old, and cannot be attributed to any historical figure.
If, however, H. and his source were thinking of the more elaborate
mask with high forehead and gaping mouth, that did not come in before *c.* 335 B.C. (see P-C (2) 189–90).

pallaeque ... honestae: the 'noble' or 'lordly' robe is a reference
to the Greek *syrma*, derived from σύρω, 'I trail'. This tradition is represented by Athenaeus 1.21D (τὴν τῆς στολῆς εὐπρέπειαν καὶ σεμνό-
τητα) and Philostratus, *Vit. Apoll.* 6.11 (46, Loeb edn) both about A.D.
200, and by a passage in the undated *Life of Aeschylus*. All three passages are quoted in P-C (2) 197–8. Mention must also be made of Ar.
Frogs 1060ff. (quoted in n. on 280 below), where Aeschylus claims to
have given heroes a more impressive costume. This rather unspecific
passage, written half a century after the death of Aeschylus, may have
given rise to the later tradition that Aeschylus had introduced the
syrma.

279 Aeschylus: see on *E.* 2.1.163.

modicis ... tignis 'laid a platform on lowish beams'; *tignis* is dat.
A low platform would allow movement to and from the *orchestra*; it
would be in line with various indications in our sources (whether
'table', 'wagon', or 'platform') that the actors were on a somewhat
higher level than the chorus; and being made of wood it would leave
no visible remains for archaeologists. Whether Aeschylus was actually
the first to introduce such a stage cannot be established.

280 magnumque loqui 'to use grandiloquent language'. Given the poet's auditory imagination, the idea of full, resonant delivery is not excluded; cf. *S.* 1.4.43–4 *os* | *magna sonaturum* (with the same use of an adverbial acc.). But style, not volume, is at the centre of H.'s meaning. The lines from Ar. *Frogs* mentioned above (on 278) are also relevant here:

κἄλλως εἰκὸς τοὺς ἡμιθέους τοῖς ῥήμασι μείζοσι χρῆσθαι·
καὶ γὰρ τοῖς ἱματίοις ἡμῶν χρῶνται πολὺ σεμνοτέροισι (1060–1)

Besides, it is proper that heroes should use larger expressions; they also wear clothing much more impressive than ours.

Nevertheless, although these lines may lie behind the tradition which H. is following, H. is not ridiculing Aeschylus.

nitique coturno 'to tread on the buskin'; another kind of elevation. For Roman misconceptions about the date of buskins see on 80–1 above.

281 successit uetus ... comoedia: 'comedy was later than tragedy in obtaining recognition by the state ... The first victory in a state-recognised contest was won by Chionides in 486 B.C. ... at the Dionysia', P-C (2) 82.

his: i.e. Thespis and Aeschylus.

282 libertas: the outspokenness of Old Comedy, as described in *S.* 1.4.1–5. Here it is said to have degenerated into licence.

282–3 H., or rather his source (Varro?), is drawing on a tradition represented by the scholia on Aristophanes (especially *Ach.* 67), the *Life of Aristophanes*, Euanthius, *De fab.* 2.4, and the Suda under Antimachus. These passages all speak of a law or laws curtailing the freedom of comedy. Modern scholars are inclined to discount these statements as being based on a misunderstanding. Even if, with Körte, *RE* XI 1233–6, we accept the statement made in the note on Ar. *Ach.* 67, the law in question lasted only 3 years, and it had nothing to do with the demise of Old Comedy. Nevertheless, H. adopts the tradition here; as we saw, he extended it to Rome's *Fescennina licentia* in *E.* 2.1.152–4.

284 turpiter: the examples in *OLD* show that the basic function of *turpiter* is to assert that the action or experience in question involved disgrace. Sometimes the phrase implies a contrast, as with *turpiter uiuere*, which implies a contrast with *honeste uiuere*. But with *turpiter fugere* there is no such contrast; *turpiter* simply emphasises that flight involves disgrace. Similarly when Ovid says *medicus turpiter aeger eram* (*Rem.* 314), he means that, to him as a physician, illness involved disgrace. So here *chorusque | turpiter obticuit* means 'the chorus fell silent – a thing which [in the context already explained] involved disgrace'. This is better than 'shamefacedly fell silent', for *turpis* does not mean 'ashamed'. It also seems preferable to taking *turpiter* with *nocendi*; for the rhythm of the line links it to *obticuit*; the phrase *sublato iure nocendi* is complete in itself, and would only be disturbed by the inclusion of *turpiter*.

286–7   uestigia Graeca | ausi deserere 'by daring to leave the paths of the Greeks'.

288   praetextas ... togatas: the name of the first type of play was derived from the *toga praetexta* worn by Roman magistrates. The *fabula praetext(at)a* was introduced by Naevius, who wrote *Lupus* and *Romulus* on the early history of Rome, and *Clastidium* on the defeat of the Gauls in 222 B.C.; see *ROL* II 136–8. Ennius (possibly) and Accius (certainly) also wrote in that genre; see *ROL* I 358–60; II 552–64. For the *comoedia togata* see on *E.* 2.1.57.

docuere 'have presented'; *OLD doceo* 5.

289–91 Latium's achievements have been less in literature than in valour and arms (i.e. war), because her writers have lacked care and patience.

290   lingua: i.e. in literature.

si non: the distinctions between *si non* and *nisi*, set out in G–L 591, are not always observed, at least in poetry. H. himself says *quo mihi fortunam si non conceditur uti?* (*E.* 1.5.12), where the positive *conceditur* does not precede and where the condition is not concessive. Other examples are to be found in Ovid and Juvenal.

291–2   o | Pompilius sanguis: 'in poetry, instead of the Voc. in apposition [in this case to *uos*], the Nom. is often found' G–L 321 n. 1. According to Plut. *Num.* 21, Numa Pompilius had four sons, of whom one, Calpus, was the ancestor of the *gens Calpurnia*. That was the *gens* to which the Pisones belonged. The phrase represents a ceremonious, but not here a solemn, address.

293 multa dies takes up *mora*, *multa litura* takes up *labor*. *dies* (f.) = 'lapse of time'; *OLD dies* 10. *litura*, from *lino* 'I smear', was used of an erasure on a wax tablet.

coercuit 'pruned'.

294 praesectum ... ad unguem 'to meet the test of the well-trimmed nail'. The sculptor or carpenter uses his nail to test the joints; so the nail must not be chipped or cracked. *praesectum* is the oldest reading; it goes naturally with *unguem* (see Plaut. *Aul.* 313, quoted on 297 below); and it would hardly have been corrupted into the commoner *perfectum*, which appears in many MSS. Granted, it may raise a question about the optimum *length* of the craftsman's nail; but most editors have not asked that question, and we are not obliged to believe that H. was any more expert or precise.

castigauit 'corrected', again with the notion of polishing or fining down.

295 misera ... arte 'poor, despised craftsmanship'. Such a dismissive view is attributed to Democritus (297); it is not, of course, H.'s own opinion.

fortunatius 'more blessed'.

296-7 excludit sanos ... poetas | Democritus: for Democritus see on *E.* 2.1.194. He wrote a book *On poetry* in which he said 'what the poet writes with inspiration (or possession; μετ' ἐνθουσιασμοῦ) and the divine spirit (καὶ ἱεροῦ πνεύματος) is very beautiful' (fr. B.18 Diels–Kranz). He might not, perhaps, have admitted to despising craftsmanship, for he also wrote 'Being endowed with a nature open to divine influence (θεαζούσης), Homer fashioned a fair structure of all kinds of words (ἐπέων κόσμον ἐτεκτήνατο παντοίων)'; see frag. B. 21 Diels–Kranz. Nevertheless, the heavy emphasis on irrational power was reproduced by Cicero *negat sine furore Democritus quemquam poetam magnum esse posse* (*De div.* 1.80; see Pease's note). Even more influential than Democritus was Plato, who in *Phaedr.* 245A made Socrates speak of a kind of possession and madness (κατοκωχή τε καὶ μανία) which comes from the Muses. Without such madness (ἄνευ μανίας), a poet cannot succeed, even though he may believe that he will be an adequate poet on the basis of art (ἐκ τέχνης); cf. *Ion, passim*. This idea of *furor poeticus* appears to be no older than the 5th cent. Earlier notions of inspiration were connected more closely with knowledge, memory and performance; see Murray. Here H. mischievously confuses *furor poeticus* with insanity; cf. *S.* 2.3.322 [*poemata*] *quae si quis sanus fecit sanus facis et tu*.

Helicone: see on *E.* 2.1.218.

ponere: i.e. to have them cut; *OLD ponere* 6b. This would be done by a barber. In Plaut. *Aul.* 312-13 we hear of a miser who cheated the barber by cutting his own nails: *quin ipsi pridem tonsor unguis dempserat, collegit, omnia abstulit praesegmina*; cf. Martial 3.74.3. The idea that uncut hair is a proof of poetic genius may be compared with *E.* 1.19.1-20, where the proof of Bacchic inspiration is the ceaseless consumption of wine.

298 balnea uitat: cleanliness and sociability are signs of a prosaic spirit.

299-301 The argument seems to run like this: 'Democritus says true poets are mad. As a result, a lot of people pretend to be mad by letting their hair grow. For such a man will acquire the esteem and name of a poet if he never entrusts to a barber a head which (he pretends) is quite incurably mad. I, however, blind and perverse fellow that I am, who could be *genuinely* mad, am doing the exact opposite and taking a cure.' The parenthesis '(he pretends)' is necessary to the sense; for such a man is actually an *un*-inspired, *would-be* poet; there is nothing wrong with his head. This interpretation, which is aided by the very exaggerated expression *tribus Anticyris ... insanabile*, is also necessary to the sense of what follows; for if H. had seriously meant that the man's *furor poeticus* was incurable he could hardly have said in the next line that he himself was taking a cure – a cure which would change him from an *insanus poeta* to a *sanus criticus*.

On the view offered here, the subject of *nanciscetur* is the type of man described in *bona pars*. This is slightly awkward, but there is something rather similar in *S.* 1.1.61-3, where the opinion of a *bona pars hominum* is quoted with *inquit* and then taken up by *quid facias illi*? 'What can you do with a man like that?' For *nomenque poetae* a parallel exists in *C.* 4.6.29-30 *Phoebus artem | carminis nomenque dedit poetae*. Peerlkamp's conjecture, *poeta*, in 299, which was proposed in order to obtain an easier subject for *nanciscetur*, is compatible with our general view of the passage, provided *poeta* is taken as referring to the third-rate, uninspired poet. In that case *nomen* (299) will mean 'reputation'. The change in the text is negligible, and the conjecture is accepted by B. and SB. Another possibility is to read *qui* for *si* (300) with Ribbeck. This preserves the preferable sequence *nomen poetae*, but involves a slightly less easy change. All in all, the case for emendation does not seem quite strong enough.

300   tribus Anticyris: with *insanabile*. Anticyra in Phocis on the gulf of Corinth produced hellebore, which was used in the treatment of madness (see on *E.* 2.2.137). 'Three Anticyras', therefore, meant something like 'three times the output of Anticyra', an intensification of *S.* 2.3.83 *nescio an Anticyram ratio illis destinet omnem*. This is more likely than 'all three Anticyras'; for while three places with that name are attested (in Phocis, Malis and Locris) there is no evidence that the third Anticyra grew hellebore.

301   tonsori Licino: unknown.

o ego laeuus: for the exclamation and hiatus cf. *o imitatores* (*E.* 1.19.19) and *o ego non felix* (*I.* 12.25).

laeuus: i.e. acting against my own interests and perhaps even the intention of heaven; hence 'perverse'. The rendering 'ill-starred' or 'unlucky', preferred by B. and *OLD laeuus* 4b, goes less well with *purgor* (302), which represents a conscious and voluntary decision.

302   purgor bilem: *purgor*, though pass. in form, is like a Greek middle in sense: 'I have my bile purged'; see Wo. 19. According to Greek medical theory, one's health depended on a correct mixture of the four humours: blood, phlegm, yellow bile, and black bile. Madness was thought to result from an excess of black bile (χολὴ μέλαινα – our 'melancholy'). So by taking hellebore, which was a laxative and an emetic, the patient would restore the proper balance; see Scarborough 117 and his references, and the note on *E.* 2.2.137.

sub uerni temporis horam 'as the season of springtime approaches'. According to the physician Celsus (2.13.3), this was the best time for the treatment.

303   faceret: potential subjunctive; understand 'if I stayed mad'.

304   nil tanti est: lit. 'nothing is of so great value', hence 'it's not worth it'. (So I'll be a critic instead.) This is supported by Seneca the Elder *tertio . . . cum abdicarer, aiebam: nil tanti est,* 'When I was disinherited the third time, I said "It's not worth it; [I may as well die]"' (*Contr.* 7.3.10); cf. Sen. *De ben.* 2.5.2.

   fungar uice cotis: the idea of the critic as a whetstone was contained in a saying of Isocrates, quoted by Plutarch, *Vit. Dec. Or. Mor.* x, Loeb edn 382. Asked how he made others capable of speaking when he could not speak himself, he said 'Whetstones can't cut, but they give an edge to iron.'

305   exsors 'having no share in'.

306   munus et officium: supply *scriptoris*.

307   opes: lit. 'resources,' hence 'subject-matter'.

307-8 We are probably not meant to distinguish between moral and literary values.

309   scribendi recte: together as in *S.* 1.4.13.
   sapere: the infin. is used as a noun: 'moral sense'.
   principium et fons: Cicero said *est eloquentiae sicut reliquarum rerum fundamentum sapientia* (*Orat.* 70).

310   Socraticae ... chartae: a vague phrase, including Plato, Xenophon, Panaetius, and others, and meaning, in general, 'works on moral philosophy'.

311 Cf. note on 40-1 above. Porph. quotes Asinius Pollio *male Hercule eueniat uerbis, nisi rem sequuntur.* In H.'s line *prouisam* carries some emphasis; 'once they see the matter set before them, the words will readily follow it'.

312   qui didicit: taken up by *ille* (315).

314   conscripti 'a senator'; the sing. is rare, the absence of *patris* unique.
   iudicis: the *iudices selecti* were the special jurymen empanelled annually by the praetor to try criminal cases; cf. *S.* 1.4.123, where a *iudex* is held up as a model to the young Horace by his father.

315   partes 'duties', 'task'; *OLD pars* 10a.
   profecto 'assuredly'.

315–16 H. is working with the idea that a person's character is shaped by his moral behaviour. So if you wish to portray, say, a general, you should have a clear picture in your mind of how a general is expected to behave; otherwise the character you present will lack credibility. As before, H. is talking of broad principles. He would doubtless have admitted that characters may deviate from the norm; but before you show them doing so, you must first know what the norm is.

318 doctum 'trained'.

319 speciosa locis 'attractive in virtue of its moral observations'. so Quint. *IO* 7.1.41 writes of misguided speakers who are content with *locis speciosis* which contribute nothing towards proving their particular case.

morataque recte: i.e. with properly drawn characters; *morata* from *mos*.

Though these two virtues are not sufficient to make a play first-rate, they are more fundamental than certain qualities of style.

320 In this line *uenus*, *pondus*, and *ars* all refer to style, especially diction. For *pondus* as a desirable quality in words, see *E.* 2.2.112, where words *sine pondere* are supposed to be removed. The word can also refer to an undesirable quality, as in 260 above. So the context is all-important. Here the complimentary force is established by the position of *pondus* between *uenus* and *ars*.

323 Since *Grais* is repeated for emphasis, one assumes that the same syllable was stressed on each occasion. This supports the view that, when the Latin hexameter was read, accent took precedence over ictus; cf. Wilkinson 94–5. *Graius* is more dignified than *Graecus*.

ore rotundo 'a well-rounded utterance', i.e. not delivery, but 'a smooth and easily moving style', with well-formed periods, as opposed to choppy and irregular sense-units; cf. Cic. *Orat.* 40, where in Isocrates' view Theodorus is *praefractior* [rather too rough or broken up] *nec satis rotundus*.

324 praeter laudem nullius auaris 'greedy for nothing except glory'.

325 Romani pueri: adversative asyndeton; i.e. instead of a connection, 'on the other hand' is understood.

longis rationibus 'by lengthy calculations'.

325–30 One *libra* (pound) or *as* contained 12 *unciae*. The commonest fractions of the *as* were *semis* ($\frac{1}{2}$ = 6 *unciae*), *triens* ($\frac{1}{3}$ = 4 *unciae*), *quadrans* ($\frac{1}{4}$ = 3 *unciae*), *sextans* ($\frac{1}{6}$ = 2 *unciae*). H.'s *centum* is not intended to be arithmetically exact; it just represents a very large number. The schoolmaster questions the son of Albinus. Ps.-Acr. says Albinus was a usurer, but H. probably picked the name out of a hat – 'Jones minor'. The lesson is intended to convey the praise of thrift.

327 quincunce: a sum of 5 *unciae*.

328 quid superat? 'what's left?'

poteras dixisse: mild impatience, 'you could have answered by now'.

eu: a Greek exclamation; cf. our imported 'bravo!'.

329 redit uncia 'an *uncia* is added', i.e. to the *quincunx*.

quid fit 'what is the total?', 'what does *that* make?'

330 aerugo 'verdigris', hence greed as a canker of the mind; in *S.* 1.4.101 it = 'malice'.

cura peculi: *peculium* was money managed by one incapable of legal ownership, e.g. a child or a slave; so such *cura* would not befit a gentleman.

331 imbuerit: properly of liquid, 'has stained'.

332 linenda cedro: lit. 'deserving to be smeared with cedar-oil', which was used as a preservative.

cupresso: a chest of cypress, which was a long-lasting type of wood; ps.-Acr. says its smell keeps away moths.

334 iucunda takes up *delectare*, **idonea uitae** takes up *prodesse*. See further on 343–4 below.

335 esto: the second (or future) imperative; see G–L 268.2.

cito: with *percipiant* rather than with *dicta*.

336 dociles . . . fideles 'receptively' . . . 'firmly'.

337 The hearer's mind is thought of as a vessel. H. is here talking of a particular type of usefulness (*prodesse*), viz. the didactic passages in a play.

338 This is a particular aspect of 'pleasure' (*delectare*), viz. the fictitious nature of the plot. Such fiction should be close enough to reality to be credible. Behind this idea lies the threefold classification of narrative found in *Ad Herenn.* 1.13: (i) *historia*, a true account of past events (*uerum*); (ii) *argumentum*, a fictitious but credible account, like the plot of a (new) comedy (*uerisimile*); (iii) *fabula*, an account containing things neither true nor credible, e.g. things recorded in tragedies (*falsum*); cf. Cic. *De inv.* 1.27. As one would expect, the classification is Greek (ἱστορία, πλάσμα, μῦθος); the earliest known mention of it is in Asclepiades of Myrlea (in Sext. Emp. *Math.* 1.12.252), which puts it back to the 2nd cent. B.C. at least.

338-40 As the precept *esto breuis* is followed by a final *ut* + two verbs (335-6), so the precept in 338 is followed by a final *ne* and *neu*. If this is right, it points to a light punctuation after *ueris* (338); cf. on 184-5. The alternative is to put a strong stop after *ueris* and to take *ne* and *neu* as prohibitions.

339 'So that a play should not ask for itself that whatever it chooses should be believed.' Either *uelit* or *uolet* is possible; *uelit* is printed here, because it has rather stronger support in the MSS, including B.'s a, B,C(?), and K. For the subjunct. cf. Cic. *De orat.* 2.66 *si enim est oratoris, quaecumque res infinite posita sit, de ea posse dicere.* The indic., however, is commoner before the time of Livy.

340 pransae: the perf. participle of *prandeo* is act. in sense.

Lamiae: Lamia was a Libyan queen whose children were all killed by Hera out of jealousy. She then became a typical ogress, devouring the children of others; so the schol. on Ar. *Peace* 758; Diod. 20.41.

extrahat: the subj. is *fabula*; a shorter and more vivid way of saying 'a play should not show a child being pulled out'; cf. *Satyros nudauit* 'presented unclothed Satyrs' (221). The line provides a touch of ghoulish humour.

341 centuriae seniorum: in the *comitia centuriata*, as organised by Servius Tullius, there were 18 centuries of *equites* and 5 classes of *pedites*, graded according to wealth. The 1st class had 40 centuries (later 35) of *seniores* and of *iuniores*; the 2nd, 3rd, and 4th classes had 10 centuries of each; and the 5th had 15 of each. Members of the *centuriae* *seniorum* (units which survived down to H.'s day) were all over 45. Here these middle-aged men, interested only in *prodesse*, banish from the stage any works which are *expertia frugis*, i.e. not sober and edifying.

342   celsi ... Ramnes: the Ramnes were the first of three centuries of knights organised by Romulus (therefore preceding the centuries of *equites* mentioned in the last note), the other two being the Tities and the Luceres (Liv. 1.13.8). They are *celsi*, because they are of high birth, have a high opinion of themselves, and belong to the cavalry; they are therefore under 30. This last point is implied by the fact that they are contrasted with the *seniores* (341). In literary matters they are interested only in *delectare*, and so they pass by with disdain any poetic drama which is dry, i.e. lacking in sweetness and charm.

So the older men are contrasted with the suppressed adjective (*iuniores*) appropriate to the other group, while the mounted Ramnes are contrasted with the suppressed *pedites*, a pattern remarked on in the note on 115–16 above. Both groups voted in the *comitia centuriata*; see next note.

343   omne tulit punctum: this completes the metaphor of voting.

tulit: for assertions which always have been and always will be true, the Romans sometimes used the so-called gnomic perfect; cf. Juv. 10.7–8 *euertere domos totas optantibus ipsis | di faciles*; 2.83 *nemo repente fuit turpissimus*.

punctum: see on *E.* 2.2.99.

dulci: abl. cf. *S.* 2.4.55–6 *Surrentina uafer qui miscet faece Falerna | uina*.

The combination of *dulce* and *utile* is by no means a bland, superficial formula. If *dulce* is taken as including every delight, and *utile* as embracing everything that helps us to understand and cope with our human condition, then the terms are capable of illuminating the whole of art. See pp. 231–2 below.

345   Porph. on *E.* 1.20.2 says *Sosii illo tempore fratres erant bibliopolae celeberrimi*. Here H. says they will make money from a successful book; the author (346) will win fame.

346   Lit. 'and extends his life for a well-known writer so that it becomes long'. *longum* is thus proleptic.

347 sunt ... quibus ... uelimus: for *sunt qui* see G–L 631.2.

ignouisse: the aoristic infin. is common after verbs of wish and ability, and also after impersonal verbs like *decet* and *licet*. Nevertheless, a passage like Virg. *Georg.* 3.435–6, where there is no apparent difference in meaning between the present and the aorist infin., shows that metrical convenience was often the decisive factor:

> ne mihi tum mollis sub diuo carpere somnos
> neu dorso nemoris libeat iacuisse per herbas.

349 The fault described is not just a minor slip, but one showing gross incompetence; *persaepe* makes the fault a very frequent one; and the separation of *semper* (350) from 348, where it is also needed, is extremely awkward. So the line has been bracketed as a gloss (an explanatory comment) on 348.

350 quodcumque is governed by the infin. *ferire* understood; cf. Lucr. *DRN* 4.402–3 *uix ut iam credere possint | non supra sese ruere omnia tecta minari,* and Bailey's note. The lyre and the bow were cognate symbols, requiring the correct tension of strings. Together they represented the peaceful and violent aspects of Apollo; cf. e.g. *C.* 1.21.11–12 *insignemque pharetra | fraternaque umerum lyra, C.* 2.10.18–20 *quondam cithara tacentem | suscitat Musam neque semper arcum | tendit Apollo.*

351–3 These lines recall the humane tolerance of *S.* 1.3, e.g. *cum mea compenset uitiis bona* (70). But there H. is talking of ordinary people; here he has in mind the better kind of poet. To tolerate the average poet would be inconsistent with 372–3. Again, the occasional blots which are forgiven here are condemned in *E.* 2.1.235–7, because there they are the sign of overall incompetence.

352 quas ... fudit: the metaphor is drawn from the hazards of ancient pen and ink; cf. Pers. 3.11–14:

> inque manus chartae nodosaque uenit harundo.
> tum querimur crassus calamo quod pendeat umor.
> nigra sed infusa uanescit sepia lympha,
> dilutas querimur geminet quod fistula guttas.

352–3 The alternatives do not exclude each other; rather *incuria* is taken up and included in a larger explanation; even the accomplished poet, being human, makes an occasional mistake.

353 quid ergo est? implies that H. is about to state his conclusion.

354–7 The construction is 'As a copyist who continually makes the same mistake is censured; as a musician who always gets the same note wrong is mocked; so a poet who is continually negligent is in my view a second Choerilus.' Actually the idea of the *same* mistake is not necessary to H.'s argument, and is omitted in the main clause.

354 peccat idem: for the internal acc., which is common with *pecco*, see G–L 332–3.

355 quamuis est monitus 'however much he is warned'. The indic. with *quamuis* appears first in poetry with Lucretius; then it becomes more frequent, so that in the post-Augustan period it is used just like *quamquam* with the indic., though the subjunct. is also common; so G–L 606 n. 1.

ut citharoedus: the main manuscript tradition has *et*; but *ut* (supported by Ben.) represents a sufficient gain in sharpness to warrant its inclusion in the text.

356 ridetur: since *rideo* is often transitive, it can be used with a personal subject in the passive.

chorda ... eadem: on the lyre one string sounded one note.

oberrat: lit. 'strays with the same string'. This, it seems, is the first appearance of the verb.

357 Choerilus ille: see on *E.* 2.1.233 and 237–8; *ille* suggests notoriety.

358–60 The sense runs as follows: 'I am astonished and amused on the few occasions when Choerilus is first-rate; by the same token I take it amiss when Homer, who is *normally* first-rate, lapses; but one must make allowances for the length of his work.'

358 bis terue 'twice, or even thrice' = *raro*; *bis terque* 'twice, ay and thrice' = *saepe*. The phrase goes closely with *bonum*.

359 quandoque = *quando*, as in *C.* 4.1.17 and 4.2.34.

360 The writer now blends into his work: 'it is permissible that sleep should [occasionally] creep up on a work of long duration'.

361–5 There are three pairs of pictures. In the third pair (365) the second picture is clearly meant to be superior. In the second pair *amat obscurum* does not sound like praise, and 364 tips the balance decisively in favour of the second picture. It is not certain, however, that in the first pair the two pictures (*a*) and (*b*) are compared with one another in the same judgemental way. After what he has said about Homer, H. may mean that in a large picture one should be willing to overlook occasional blemishes – blemishes which become insignificant when one stands back and surveys the work as a whole. If that is so, then the first picture (*a*) is being compared with itself at different distances; and the same will apply to the second (*b*). It is possible that H. preferred the first type of picture, but he does not say so. When he moves on to the second and third pairs, however, he does make his preferences clear. This kind of variation in his reasoning is quite characteristic. As for the general topic of *ut pictura, poesis*, its ramifications are endless; see the studies of Howard and Lee, and, for more recent references, B. II 371 and III 593. Mention should also be made of the almost equally famous saying of Simonides τὴν μὲν ζωιγραφίαν ποίησιν σιωπῶσαν προσαγορεύει, τὴν δὲ ποίησιν ζωιγραφίαν λαλοῦσαν, 'he calls painting silent poetry, and poetry speaking painting' (Plut. *Mor.* 346F, Loeb IV 500). Simonides, however, was talking about the art, H. about artefacts. It should perhaps be added that although impressionist techniques of painting were known in Rome, they are not relevant to this passage.

361–2 erit quae ... capiat: on *est qui* + subjunct. see G–L 631.2.

stes | ... abstes: placed over each other in this position for emphasis; the subjunctives are those of the ideal, or generalising, second person singular; Wo. 195, G–L 567.

367 tibi: certainly with *dictum*, probably also with *tolle*.

368 tolle: the idea of picking up is very subordinate to that of taking away, as it is in most of the examples in *OLD tollo* 10a and b.

368–9 certis ... concedi 'only some activities are, by rights, allowed to be moderate and tolerable'.

369–71 In view of the singular verbs, *et* is most conveniently translated as 'or'.

369   consultus iuris 'an expert on points of law'; for the gen. with adjs. of knowledge see G–L 374 n. 4.

370   mediocris: goes with both *consultus* and *actor*.

370–1   The eloquent Messalla and the knowledgeable Cascellius form a chiasmus with *consultus iuris* and *actor causarum*.

   Messallae: M. Valerius Messalla Coruinus (64 B.C. – A.D. 8) fought for Brutus and Cassius at Philippi, then went over to Antony, and finally joined Octavian, for whom he fought at Actium (31 B.C.). He was given a triumph in 27 B.C. for his campaigns in Aquitania. Messalla also enjoyed distinction as a patron (Tibullus was one of his clients), as a man of letters (he wrote poetry, history, and a work on grammar), and as an orator (he is praised in Tac. *Dial.* 18.2 and Quint *IO* 10.1.113).

   Cascellius Aulus: born *c.* 104 B.C., he was admired for his independent spirit when (presumably as *praetor urbanus*) he refused to assist the Triumvirs in the proscriptions of 41 B.C. (Val. Max. 6.2.12). As well as being a distinguished jurist, he was a lively and amusing talker. He is said to have declined the offer of a consulship.

   When two characters are mentioned closely together, and one is certainly alive, we would expect the other to be alive too. But we cannot insist on it here; for if the *AP* belongs to 10 B.C., Aulus Cascellius must have been over 94. It is wiser to assume that his reputation was still fresh.

372   in pretio est 'has his value'.

373   columnae: one thinks naturally of *S.* 1.4.71 *nulla taberna meos habeat neque pila libellos*, but there books are tied on the pillars in such a way as to permit browsing; this is clear from 72 *quis manus insudet uulgi Hermogenisque Tigelli*. Here H. is talking of pillars containing not only books (which are not in point), but advertisements; every poet on display is 'a major new talent'. Martial speaks of a *taberna | scriptis postibus hinc et inde totis* (1.117.10–11). This written material is unlikely to have consisted only of book-rolls, for the next line reads *omnis ut cito perlegas poetas,* 'in such a way that you can read quickly through all the poets'. That sounds much more like lists or sheets with names, titles, and publicity 'blurb'. If this idea is right, H.'s words could be translated 'that poets should be middling is not allowed by men, gods, or bill-boards'. *concessere* is a gnomic perf.; see on 343.

374 symphonia discors: an oxymoron, like *concordia discors* (*E.* 1.12.19). Dinner-parties were often accompanied by music, though not usually with musical effects like those described by Petron. *Sat.* 32–4 and 36.

375 crassum unguentum: the host would provide perfume, which could be used like hair-oil: cf. *C.* 2.7.7–8 *nitentis* | *malobathro Syrio capillos.* That same ode implies that the scent was thin enough to be poured out: *funde capacibus* | *unguenta de conchis* (22–3). One might therefore infer (especially in view of the out-of-tune music) that thick, scented ointment was universally disliked. Pliny, however, tells us that some people preferred it: *quosdam crassitudo maxime delectat, spissum appellantes, linique iam, non solum perfundi unguentis gaudent* (*NH* 13.4.21). Perhaps in polite circles their taste was regarded as coarse; there may even have been some who enjoyed Sardinian honey (next note).

Sardo cum melle papauer: Pliny, *NH* 19.168 tells us that white poppy-seeds, roasted, and coated with honey, were served as dessert. Sardinian honey, however, like that of Corsica, is said to have tasted horrible (*pessimi saporis est*, according to Porph.); one recalls the words of Thyrsis in Virg. *Ecl.* 7.41 *ego Sardiniis uidear tibi amarior herbis*; that explains the flavour of the honey.

376 duci 'be conducted'; *OLD duco* 11b. This rather sophistical argument is based on the premise that no pleasure is to be gained from second-rate poetry. As these elements (music, scented ointment, and poppy-seeds in honey) are not necessary to a meal, but are included purely for pleasure, it follows that if they do not give (any) pleasure they have no *raison d'être*. So, if a poem fails to give (any) pleasure it ought not to be offered to an audience.

377 The line has no strong caesura in the third or fourth foot, but no special effect appears to be intended.

378 'If it misses the top level even by a little, it sinks to the bottom.' For perf. + pres. in iterative action see G–L 567.

379 If a man has no interest or ability in field events, he keeps away from the equipment. The idea is made more specific in 380–2.

380 Ball, discus, and hoop were associated with Greek-style games. *C.* 3.24, a censorious ode, complains about the well-born lad who can't ride and is afraid to hunt; he's better at bowling a Greek hoop:

ludere doctior | *seu Graeco iubeas trocho* (56–7); in *S.* 2.2.10–13 ball and discus are recommended for those with Greek tastes, who find Roman exercises too strenuous. Here, however, there is no disapproval; H. is talking only of the skill which such games require. For the gen. with *indoctus* see G–L 374 n. 4.

   quiescit: lit. 'remains inactive', i.e. does not compete.

381   spissae 'densely packed'.

   impune: properly 'without punishment'; here 'without constraint', hence 'uninhibitedly'. Cf. Quint. *IO* 6.1.43 *omnia libere fingimus et impune.* The sense *merito* (W.) is not supported by *TLL*.

   coronae: a *corona* was circular in shape; hence a ring of spectators, as in *E.* 1.18.53. The plural here is the poetic equivalent of a singular; but we may be encouraged to think of the constituent elements, as in *niues* 'snow[-flakes]'; see G–L 204 n. 6.

382   uersus: governed by *fingere*.

   quidni?: ironical, 'and why not?'

383   liber: a free man as opposed to a slave.

   ingenuus: a free man by birth, as distinct from a freedman.

   praesertim: the terms are arranged in a rising scale.

   census: perf. participle pass.; *censeor* with the retained acc. of the sum of property assessed is previously recorded only in Cic. *Pro Flacc.* 80; the abl. is more common; see *OLD censeo* 6a.

383–4   equestrem | **summam nummorum** 'the equestrian sum of money', i.e. 400,000 sesterces. An unskilled labourer might earn about 1,000 a year.

384   uitioque ... omni: i.e. 'entirely respectable'. Any crime or misdemeanour was supposed to be noted by the censor.

   The combination of legal status, free birth, a large fortune, and a good character qualified a Roman to do *almost* everything; but writing good poetry called for a different combination, viz. *ingenium* + *ars*, see below, 385 and 408–11.

385   inuita ... Minerua: *id est, aduersante et repugnante natura* (Cic. *De off.* 1.110). Minerva (i.e. Athene) was the goddess of wisdom, learning, and the arts.

386   id ... iudicium ... ea mens 'such is your judgement, such your good sense'. This turns what looked like a precept (385) into a statement of fact. A dextrous touch. Young Piso, then, will not write poetry merely because it is the thing to do; he will be guided by his natural, creative, impulse.

386–7 si ... olim | scripseris: possibly H. is gently restraining Piso, but the natural inference is that the young man was not engaged in writing a satyr-play or anything else.

387 Maeci: Sp. Maecius Tarpa, many years before (in 55 B.C.), had the task of selecting the plays to be performed in Pompey's theatre (Cic. *Fam.* 7.1.1); his reputation as a critic is confirmed by *S.* 1.10.38 (*iudice Tarpa*), written about 35 B.C. Here his name is coupled closely with Piso senior and H. (*et patris et nostras*); so it is natural to infer that he is still alive. It seems very forced to take the name as generic ('a Maecius').

388 nonumque ... in annum: the figure was probably suggested by Catullus 95, which welcomed Cinna's *Zmyrna*: *nonam post denique messem | quam coepta est.* As Quintilian saw (*IO* ep. to Tryph. 2 *suadet ne praecipitetur editio*), H. is cautioning Piso not to 'rush into print'. But the nine-year rule is a light-hearted exaggeration; certainly H. did not obey it himself.

389 membranis intus positis 'keeping your sheets of parchment inside the house'. Does this mean the rough copy (B.) or the final version (W.)? An earlier passage runs as follows: *sic raro scribis, ut toto non quater anno | membranam poscas, scriptorum quaeque retexens* (*S.* 2.3.1–2). This seems to imply two stages: (i) lines or phrases (*scripta*) are jotted down (possibly on a wax tablet); (ii) a draft of the completed poem is prepared on *membrana* (parchment). Instead of producing such a draft, Horace (says Damasippus) keeps deleting the preparatory work done in stage (i). Here in the *AP* a third stage seems to be envisaged (iii), in which a final version is prepared for publication (*edideris*). This final version may well have omitted some of the material contained in the *membranae* of stage (ii). This omitted work can be destroyed (*delere licebit*). Such an interpretation lies between those of B. and W.

390 nescit uox missa reuerti: in *E.* 1.18.71 H. had written *et semel* *emissum uolat irreuocabile uerbum*, and in *E.* 1.20.6 *non erit emisso reditus tibi.* These passages support the belief that the present expression, though briefer and more epigrammatic, retains its metaphorical force 'a word, once let out, does not know how to return'; the creature implied in the metaphor is not specified, but a bird seems most likely.

391   sacer interpresque deorum: in view of the two following words, *sacer* must be a noun = 'priest'; ps.-Acr. comments *id est sacerdos*, and then quotes Virg. *Aen.* 6.645 . . . *Threicius longa cum ueste sacerdos.*

392   caedibus et uictu foedo: *caedibus* on its own would point to the killing of animals; but the addition of the very strong phrase *uictu foedo* 'revolting diet' suggests that H. is also thinking of cannibalism. For a collection of passages on cannibalism and vegetarianism see Mayor on Juv. 15.78–107 and 173–4; see also the article by Rankin (2).

Orpheus: son of the Thracian king Oeagrus and the Muse Calliope, Orpheus was presented with a lyre by Apollo and taught to play it by the Muses. His playing and singing had a magical effect on nature, and even prevailed on Pluto to allow the return of Eurydice. This aspect of Orpheus is not elaborated here; it is even stated that his power over brute nature was just an allegory of his teachings about vegetarianism and the sacredness of life. Nevertheless, the persuasiveness of Orpheus as a teacher clearly came from his gifts as a musician. He is coupled with the singer and player Amphion (394) and must surely be included amongst the *diuini uates* in 400.

393   rabidosque: to be taken with both *tigris* and *leones.*

394   Amphion: Amphion and his twin brother Zethus were sons of Antiope and Zeus. Amphion, who was a musician, was despised by his warrior brother; but when they combined to build the walls of Thebes, Zethus had to use his physical strength to move the stones, whereas Amphion, whose magic lyre had been given him by Hermes, simply played and sang, and the stones moved obediently into place.

Thebanae conditor urbis: a corresponding allegory; it was because of his (political) role in the foundation of Thebes that Amphion was reputed to be able to move stones.

396   uellet: subjunctive because the *quo*-clause is virtually in indirect speech.

sapientia: predicate; 'this, once, was wisdom'.

398 concubitu prohibere uago 'to bar [people] from promiscuous intercourse'.

dare iura maritis 'to lay down laws for married couples'.

399 oppida moliri 'to build towns', by promoting harmony and co-operation. The mythical example of Amphion has been given. Solon is an example of a historical poet-statesman; see Edmonds 1 104–14 (testimonia), 114–54 (poems). A more nebulous figure is the Cretan poet Thales, mentioned by Plut. *Lycurg.* 4.

ligno: either dat., as in *nomina tabulae aereae incisa sunt* (*CIL* VIII 21825), or abl., as in *iuuat arbore sacra | . . . incidere carmina* (Calp. Sic. 1.34–5).

400 nomen 'renown'.

diuinis uatibus: the idea of holy bards goes back to Homer's θεῖοι ἀοιδοί; cf. *C.* 4.9.28 *uate sacro. diuinis* also includes the idea of 'prophetic'; cf. *interpresque deorum* (391).

401 post hos insignis 'gaining distinction after these'.

402 Tyrtaeusque: a 7th-cent. Athenian elegist, who gave courage to the Spartans in their struggle against the Messenians. See Edmonds 1 50–78. One may note especially the couplet

τεθνάμεναι γὰρ καλὸν ἐνὶ προμάχοισι πεσόντα
ἄνδρ' ἀγαθὸν περὶ ἧι πατρίδι μαρνάμενον

(10.1–2)

For it is a fine thing for a good man to fall and die fighting in the front line for his native land. (Cf. Hom. *Il.* 22.71–3.)

H. might have attracted less admiration, and less odium, by his *dulce et decorum est pro patria mori* (*C.* 3.2.13) had it been more widely realised that the sentiment was Greek. (Nisbet (4) has proposed *dulci decorum est.*)

402–3 mares . . . in Martia bella: Varro wrote *Mars . . . quod maribus in bello praeest* (*LL* 5.73). So by the otherwise superfluous *Martia* H. is glancing at the proposed etymology as well as obtaining alliteration.

animos . . . uersibus exacuit: according to Plutarch (*Mor.* Loeb edn III 416; XII 318; and *Vit.* Loeb edn X 52) Leonidas called Tyrtaeus 'a good poet for whetting [?] the spirits of young men', ἀγαθὸν ποιητὴν νέων ψυχὰς κακκανῆν. Granted, κακκανῆν is a restoration, but it is accepted by modern editors as a Doric infin. and rendered by LSJ as 'stir up, incite'. A derivation from ἀκόνη 'whetstone' is far from clear, but such an idea could still have prompted H.'s *exacuit*.

403 sortes: from very ancient times, oracles, like those delivered at Delphi, were cast in the form of hexameters.

404 uitae monstrata uia est: H. is thinking of didactic poets, like Solon, Phocylides, and Theognis (see Edmonds I), and no doubt also of Hesiod.

404–5 gratia regum | ... temptata: Greek tyrants of the 6th and 5th centuries, like Hiero (Syracuse), Hipparchus (Athens), and Polycrates (Samos), promoted literature for the same reasons as Augustus, and offered similar rewards. Hence their 'favour was courted'.

405 Pieriis ... modis: i.e. lyric poetry, like that of Pindar, Bacchylides, Simonides, and Anacreon. Pieria, a district in Macedonia in the region of Mt Olympus, was associated with the Muses.
ludusque 'entertainment' or 'performance'; H. is thinking of drama.

406 et: explanatory, as if to say 'I mean the entertainment which marked the end of a long season of work'. For these country festivals see *E.* 2.1.139ff.
ne forte '[I say this] in case ...' Here the *ne*-clause cannot introduce what follows; it must be added to what goes before.
pudori: predicative dat.; Wo. 68. There is no need to be ashamed of poetry; for it has contributed in many ways to the benefit of mankind.

407 Musa ... Apollo: since this sentence sums up the section beginning in 391, it must include all the genres mentioned; it cannot be confined to lyric.
lyrae sollers: for the gen. with an adj. of knowledge see G–L 374 n. 4. Here, and in other places, H. seems to have extended the usage.

408–9 natura ... an arte | quaesitum est: the claims of nature and art had often been discussed. Aristotle, in *Poet.* 8.1451a24, allowed the possibility of both to Homer (ἤτοι διὰ τέχνην ἢ διὰ φύσιν); Neoptolemus talked of a combination of τέχνη and δύναμις (B. 1 55). Ovid, too, saw that it was not really a question of one or the other, but a matter of balance – a balance which was not to be found in Ennius: *Ennius ingenio maximus, arte rudis* (*Tr.* 2.424), or in Callimachus: *quamuis ingenio non ualet, arte ualet* (*Am.* 1.15.14). Cicero found both qualities in Lucretius' poetry: *multis luminibus ingeni, multae tamen artis* (*QF* 2.9.3). In another passage (*Pro Arch.* 15) he seems to concede that natural ability and art can appear separately: *etiam illud adiungo, saepius ad laudem atque uirtutem naturam sine doctrina quam sine natura ualuisse doctrinam*. But he concludes that the really great achievements require both: *atque idem ego hoc contendo, cum ad naturam eximiam et illustrem accesserit ratio quaedam conformatioque doctrinae, tum illud nescio quid praeclarum ac singulare solere existere*. H. accepted this last contention, as we see from 409–11; but in a work of the present kind the emphasis naturally fell on *ars*.

409   diuite uena 'a rich vein of talent'; cf. *C.* 2.18.9–10 *ingeni* | *benigna uena*.

410   rude: unshaped and undeveloped by art and training.

   quid possit: the older MSS have *prosit*, and many editors adopt it. More recent MSS, and John of Salisbury (12th cent.) in *Metalogicus* 1.8, read *possit*, which Ben. accepts (but on rather unconvincing grounds). Let us consider the following statements: (i) 'x cannot accomplish anything by itself, so it asks the assistance of y.' The thought here is neat and unexceptionable. (ii) 'x is of no service (to the poet) by itself, so it asks the assistance of y.' Here 'service' and 'assistance' are very close together in meaning, but the service is service to the poet, whereas the assistance is assistance to x. This slight awkwardness, which is absent from the passage of Quintilian usually quoted in support (*IO Praef.* 26–7), tips the balance in favour of *possit*.

411   coniurat amice 'makes a friendly pact'.

412   metam: here the finishing- rather than the turning-post; *OLD meta* 2b.

414   uenere et uino: an auditory effect like our 'wine and women'.

414–15   qui Pythia cantat | tibicen 'the piper who plays the Pythian piece', i.e. the hymn in honour of Apollo's victory over the Python, which was a competition-piece at the Pythian games, held at Delphi every four years. *cantat* alone, of course, does not necessarily imply competition; but the whole context does. This interpretation, which is that of ps.-Acr., is preferable to that which understands *Pythia cantat* as meaning 'plays at the Pythian games' and defends it by *coronari Olympia* (*E.* 1.1.50). For *coronari Olympia* is an extension of *uincere Olympia*, a Graecism = νικᾶν ᾽Ολύμπια, which becomes ordinary enough to appear in Vitruvius and Pliny. The same cannot be said of *cantare Pythia*.

415   didicit: to supply *Pythia* as an object limits the verb unduly. For the absolute use cf. Juv. 6.66 *Thymele tunc rustica discit*, and the other examples in *OLD disco* 1d.

416   nec satis est: the older MSS read *nunc*, but the contrast is not between 'then' and 'now', but between athletes and musicians who have learnt their trade and would-be poets who have not. This difficulty is avoided by *nec*, which occurs in some more recent MSS. The sequence of thought is 'nor [in the case of poetry] is it enough'.

pango: an archaic word, which here is meant to sound pretentious. Perhaps 'I fashion'.

417   occupet ... scabies: probably a saying like our 'the Devil take the hindmost'. According to the scholiasts, the expression comes from a children's game; cf. *rex eris si recte facies* (*E.* 1.1.59–60).

417–18   mihi ... fateri: these are not really the would-be poet's words, but H.'s; cf. Juv. 1.103ff., which again say what the satirist wants to say, but are not convincing in his character's mouth.

418   The construction is *mihi turpe est fateri [me] nescire quod non didici*.

sane: in the sense of 'simply', the word could go either with *nescire* ('that I am simply ignorant of what I never learnt') or with *fateri* ('simply to admit that I am ignorant etc.'). For *sane* giving that kind of emphasis cf. *E.* 1.7.61 *non sane credere Mena*. To join *sane* with *didici* produces a less natural word-order (we would have expected *non sane didici*). If *sane* meant 'at least', *aut* would have given a better sequence than *et* at the beginning of 418.

419–21 The parallel runs thus: the auctioneer lures the crowd with his patter; they hope to pay little and to gain by the bargains on offer. The rich poet lures the audience with his invitation; they hope to pay little (a few meaningless compliments) and to gain substantially (by a free dinner).

420 adsentatores 'yes-men'; nowhere else in Latin poetry.

421 This verse also occurs in *S.* 1.2.13, where it is less needed; but that does not mean that the earlier occurrence is spurious, especially as there may be a common (archaic?) source for these two verses and *S.* 2.3.184 *nudus agris, nudus nummis . . . paternis.*

422–5 These lines go further than *iubet ad lucrum ire*; if he's the sort who can supply a delicious dinner and provide other services too, then he will find it hard to tell a true friend from a false one. Plutarch wrote an essay on this very problem; see *Mor.* (Loeb edn) 1 261ff.

423 leui pro paupere 'for a feckless and penniless client'. Many editors take the phrase as neutral, but *adsentatores* has already engendered misgivings. Moreover, the host is not motivated by pure charity any more than the auctioneer. What he wants is applause. Persius brought this out very forcefully in his adaptation:

> calidum scis ponere sumen,
> scis comitem horridulum trita donare lacerna,
> et 'uerum' inquis 'amo, uerum mihi dicite de me'. (1.53–5)

423–4 artis | litibus: the best MSS have *atris litibus*, which is feeble in itself and not well supported by *atrae curae* (*C.* 4.11.35–6). In view of *eripere* and *implicitum* (*pauperem*), the reading *artis*, 'tight' (approved by Ben. and found in some later MSS), is much superior.

424–5 inter- | noscere: is the tmesis supposed to depict the separation of true from false? It is reasonable to see an intentional effect in *circum-spectemus* (*E.* 2.2.93–4), but not in the other cases in the *sermones* (*S.* 1.2.62–3 and 2.3.117–18).

425 beatus 'the lucky fellow', ironical.

426 quid: with both *dona*[*ue*]*ris* and *donare.*
  cui = *alicui*, as usual after *si, nisi, num* and *ne*; G–L 107.1 R.

427   tibi: for dat. of agent with the perf. pass. see G–L 215.

429   super his 'over these bits', *super* being used as in *C.* 4.2.42–3 *publicum ludum super impetrato | fortis Augusti reditu*, and in *E.* 2.1.151–2 *fuit . . . cura | condicione super communi*.

etiam: *etiam* is usually second word in its clause; in the three other Horatian cases where it is first (*S.* 1.7.5, *E.* 1.18.107, and *C.* 4.6.19) there is no additional verb; so there is a slight irregularity here. Perhaps it is connected with the fact that another *super his* has been suppressed.

429–30   pallescet ... stillabit ... saliet, tundet: perhaps deliberately, H. has not explicitly mentioned the emotions which accompany these physical manifestations; for in the flatterer's case they are not real. But what emotions are assumed? Fear for *pallescet*, pity for *stillabit*, but what for *saliet* and *tundet*? It would avoid repetition if *saliet* could mean 'jump to his feet'. *OLD* gives no instances; but compounds could have this sense, e.g. Cat. 65.22 *aduentu matris prosilit*, and Varro, *Men.* 451 Astbury *subsilio et hostias . . . relinquo. tundet pede terram* immediately suggests extravagant joy, as in *C.* 1.37 *pede libero | pulsanda tellus*. But it is worth asking if dancers at funerals ever stamped on the ground in this way. If so, this would lead smoothly to the next line.

431   *OLD* lists half a dozen references to *female* mourners (*praeficae*). According to Porph., *male* mourners used to be employed in Alexandria. For all we know, male mourners may on occasion have appeared in Rome in H.'s time. If they did not, then it would be better to amend H.'s text to *quae conductae* rather than believe that the reference is purely literary, without any basis in Roman life. Lucilius, after all, had spoken of women in a passage which H. had in mind: *mercede quae conductae flent alieno in funere | praeficae, multo et capillos scindunt et clamant magis* (*ROL* III 995–6). So why should H. have altered the gender, unless there were some topical explanation?

432   prope plura: a modification of Lucilius' *multi magis* (above). Other changes can be observed by comparing the texts.

ex animo: with *dolentibus*; cf. Cat. 109. 3–4 *facite ut . . . id sincere dicat et ex animo*.

433   derisor: the man cannot be, in the simple sense, a mocker; for he is the insincere counterpart of one who gives genuine praise (*uero* *laudatore*). Doubtless because of this difficulty, Nisbet (3) 229 conjectured *adrisor*. The main problem about accepting this is the fact that in *E.* 1.18.10–14 the *derisor* is explicitly one who *flatters* his host, echoing everything he says. It is not quite satisfactory to explain this earlier passage by saying that the *derisor* is so called because, although he flatters his host, he mocks everyone else (cf. *S.* 1.4.87–8 *amet quauis aspergere cunctos,* | *praeter eum qui praebet aquam; post hunc quoque potus*). Could it be that the term came to be used in an attenuated sense as 'a hired entertainer', who could behave in either way? Seneca implies that there was only a very thin line between an *adrisor* and a *derisor*; in fact Satellius Quadratus was both (*Ep.* 27.7) *stultorum diuitum adrosor, et, quod sequitur, adrisor, et quod duobus his adiunctum est, derisor.*

434   reges 'kings' or 'princes', rather than 'wealthy men'. H. had probably heard stories about eastern kings from a Greek source, cf. Diodorus 20.63.1, where Agathocles (the Sicilian tyrant of the late 4th, early 3rd cent. B.C.) is said to have used wine in this way. With *S.* 1.2.86 *regibus hic mos est* etc. cf. Xen. *Cyr.* 3.3.26 ὅπερ ... ποιοῦσιν οἱ βάρβαροι βασιλεῖς.

urgere 'ply'.

culillis: from *culillus*, or possibly *culilla*, 'cup' or 'goblet'.

435   torquere mero: i.e. subject them to the ordeal of wine, on the principle *in uino ueritas*; cf. *E.* 1.18.38 *commissumque teges et uino tortus et ira.*

laborent: subjunct. in a subordinate clause in virtually indirect speech.

436   an ... dignus: indirect question. There seems no reason to supply a negative, as K–H and B. do.

437   fallent: the fut. indic., as often, gives advice.

animi sub uulpe latentes: 'What creature, desiring to conceal his guile, would try to do so with a fox's skin of all things in the world? What possible disguise would excite livelier suspicion than the coat of this proverbial trickster?' (Housman 1 160–1). But there is no mention of skin or disguise. The fox is not masquerading as any other animal, or vice versa. H. is referring to the fable of the crafty fox who persuaded the crow to sing and then made off with the cheese (Phaedrus 1.13). The moral therefore is: would-be poets (*si carmina condes*) should beware of flatterers; i.e. 'the [malicious] intent that lies hidden within the [flattering] fox'. With this passage in mind, Persius (5.116–17) speaks of the real fox on the inside, whereas H. speaks of the insincere fox on the outside. But really Persius is only marginally relevant, for he *does* bring in skins and disguises: *pelliculam ueterem retines*.

B. and SB obelise, sharing the misgivings expressed by Housman and others, but not accepting any of the various conjectures proposed.

438 Quintilio: Porph. gives his name as Quintilius Varus of Cremona, but there is some possibility of confusion here with P. Alfenus Varus of Cremona. See Nisbet (2) intr. to *C.* 1.18 and 1.24. But there is no need to doubt the identity of this Quintilius with the man mourned in *C.* 1.24, where the expression *nudaque Veritas* (7) chimes well with the critic's candour.

438–9 si quid recitares ... aiebat 'whenever one recited ... he used to say'. For the subjunctive in generalising conditions see Wo. 195–6.

sodes 'please', from *si* + *audes*.

439 negares: supply *si*; the mood is parallel to that of *recitares*.

440 bis terque: see on *bis terue* (358).

441 male tornatos 'badly turned'; the metaphor is taken from metal turned on a lathe (*tornus*).

incudi: dat. of *incus* 'anvil'. The workman must start again.

442 uertere: supply *delictum*: 'to alter the fault'; cf. *E.* 2.1.154 *uertere modum*, where again the idea is to change something for the better. The phrase *stilum uertere* (*S.* 1.10.72) is rather different; it means 'to invert one's pen' for the purpose of erasure.

malles: cf. *recitares* and *negares* above.

443 insumebat 'he would not expend [i.e. waste]'.

444 quin 'to stop you'; *nullum uerbum insumebat* is the equivalent of *non impediebat*, so *quin* is quite regular.

445 uir bonus et prudens: in *E.* 2.2.109ff. the poet, in criticising his own work, is urged to take on the spirit of a *censor honestus*; here the same perceptiveness and the same candour are attributed to the good critic, but he is seen, in a complex and unusual double metaphor, both as a figure of legal authority and as one who tends vines and fruit trees (see on 449).

inertes 'without energy', 'useless'; cf. *uirtute carentia* (*E.* 2.2.123).

446 duros: harshness was primarily a matter of sound and rhythm; e.g. a line might have an unpleasant sequence of consonants or too many spondees.

446–7 incomptis … signum: lit. 'he will smear a black sign opposite the untidy with a horizontal stroke of the pen'. The mark in question was an obelus in the margin, like that employed by Zenodotus and Aristarchus (see on 450), when they were indicating what they judged to be spurious lines.

atrum: the word carries force; for although in H. the lines are not spurious, they are nevertheless to be condemned. Another kind of mark, not described here, was the letter theta, standing for θάνατος ('death'). This was prefixed to the names of the condemned or the dead – a custom alluded to in Pers. 4.13 *nigrum uitio praefigere theta*.

447 ambitiosa: as a term in literary criticism, it means 'overelaborate', 'pretentious'.

448 parum claris: lit. 'bits that are not sufficiently clear'.

449 From 445 on, we have a series of words linking the authority of the critic with the authority of a legal figure, whether a prosecutor (*reprehendet, culpabit, arguet*), a censor (*reprehendet, culpabit, coget, notabit*), or a judge (*allinet atrum signum, coget*). Intertwined with this we have another, more imaginative, series, in which the critic is seen as a grower of fruit trees or vines. This metaphor has a share in *reprehendet inertes*; for *iners* could be applied to useless growth, as in Lucan, *BC* 5.403–4 *Apulus arua* | … *inerti tradidit herbae*. In 446 *duros* would suit 'hard woody growth' (West 60). The next sentence is dominated by the legal figure, but it is not unreasonable to imagine a tree being marked for winter pruning (West 60); and there was a potential metaphor available in *incomptis*; Fronto, admittedly 2nd cent. A.D., uses *como* for trimming bushes (Loeb edn I 48). In 447 *recidet* is right for pruning; cf. *S.* 1.10.69–70 *recideret omne quod ultra* | *perfectum traheretur*. For *ambitiosa*, 'spreading' or 'sprawling', cf. *C.* 1.36.20 *hederis ambitiosior*. It is possible that *parum claris lucem dare* still exploits the pruning metaphor; in that case, what is the object of *coget*? The most likely object seems to be

the plant or tree as a whole. This can be sustained if the critic is supposed to compel the *poem* to admit light to dark places. And that, indeed, may be the best interpretation; for up to now we have been
dealing with the critic and the poem, and the same is true again in
449. The *poet* would be something of an intrusion in 448, even though
he would be the most natural object of *coget* if the expression were
taken on its own.

arguet 'show up'.

ambigue dictum: H. is talking of ambiguity as a source of confusion or irritation (cf. *Ad Herenn.* 2.16; Quint. *IO* 7.9), not as a source of
poetic richness. For the latter see Empson's influential study.

450 Aristarchus: the great scholar Aristarchus of Samothrace (*c.*
216–145 B.C.), who was Head of the library at Alexandria from *c.* 153
on, established a school, and wrote numerous editions, commentaries,
and critical treatises. For an account of his huge achievement, see
Pfeiffer (2), chap. 6.

451-2 As a result of his trifling errors, which cumulatively are not so
trifling, the poet is given an unfavourable reception. We are meant, of
course, to think of a recital.

452-3 in mala ... | ut mala: anyone who thinks the jingle inten-
tional ought to say what the intention may be. Otherwise one will
assume it is inadvertent.

derisum semel 'when once he has been mocked'; *semel* emphasises
the irrevocable nature of the main action; cf. *C.* 4.7.21.

453 mala ... scabies 'the accursed scab'. The term *scabies* could
include several different conditions, of which the worst was leprosy;
see Celsus 5.28.16.

morbus regius: i.e. jaundice. No one knows why it was called 'the
king's ailment'. One unconvincing proposal was that it called for an
enjoyable treatment which only kings could afford (Celsus 3.24.5). It
is not clear whether H. thought jaundice or 'the scab' infectious.

urget 'afflicts'.

454 fanaticus error: as a noun, *fanaticus* was a temple-servant
(*fanum*), hence a devotee. The adj. was commonly applied to devotees
of orgiastic religions like those of Bellona and Cybele; see the notes of
Mayor and Courtney on Juv. 4.123. K–H make the interesting

suggestion that the *error* refers to the begging priests of Diana, who wandered around the streets, and who, like other priests of a similar kind, could be highly menacing. But the natural sense of *error* with *fanaticus* is 'madness' (cf. *fanatico furore* in Florus 2.7.4); 'madness' also goes better with *urget*.

et iracunda Diana: Diana was often connected with the moon; hence ps.-Acr. says *sicut lunaticum aut morbosum, ita insanum poetam fugiunt sapientes.* The *et* describes the *fanaticus error* further by designating its source.

456   qui sapiunt 'sensible people'.

agitant: 'tease' seems better than 'chase' here, in view of *sequuntur*. The word *incauti* goes with both verbs.

457   sublimis: nom. 'head in air'. Not only is this more graphic than the acc. pl. with *uersus*, it also leads naturally to the next line and then to the well or pit.

ructatur: lit. 'belches'; the word may have lost some of its coarseness by H.'s time (so W. and B.); but this is not reflected in the entry in *OLD*.

458   ueluti merulis intentus . . . auceps is a unit.

decidit: since the falling precedes the shouting, this is probably perf. tense; G–L 567.

auceps 'fowler', from *auis* + *capio*.

459   In *Theaet.* 174A Plato tells how the sage Thales fell into a well while looking at the stars; cf. H. *E.* 2.2.135.

longum: the Greek parallel μακρὸν ἄυσεν (Hom. *Il.* 3.81) might suggest loudness, but the Latin parallels favour length of time, e.g. Plaut. *Epid.* 376 *nimis longum loquor*; *Pseud.* 687 *nimis diu et longum loquor*, and the examples in *OLD longus* 13. Had H. meant 'loud', he would probably have said *magnum*; cf. Plaut. *Mil.* 823 *magnum clamat.*

460   non sit 'there would not be', a 'future ideal' apodosis; Wo. 193 no. 7.

curet: for *est qui* + subjunctive see G–L 631.2.

461   si curet: a 'future ideal' protasis; see on 460. The apodosis here is *dicam* (463).

462   qui 'how?'.

qui scis an ... proiecerit: we have to translate 'how do you
know he didn't throw himself in?' *OLD scio* 4c offers three parallels
from comedy: Plaut. *Most.* 58; Ter. *Eun.* 790, *Hec.* 235. The formula is
the equivalent of 'perhaps' or 'probably'; so we do not have a negative with *nolit*. This idiom is distinct from a case like *C.* 4.7.17 *quis scit
an adiciant* 'who knows whether [the gods] are adding?' – an ordinary
indirect question.

prudens 'deliberately'.

se proiecerit: several good MSS have *se deiecerit*, but *proiecerit* is to
be preferred (i) because of the superior sound-sequence *prudens ...
proiecerit*; (ii) because a scribe with the idea of 'down' in his mind
might well have altered *pro-* to *de-*, especially in view of *demittere*
immediately above. Alternatively *de-* might have been a conscious
'correction' by someone unaware of the fact that *pro-* sometimes denotes downward motion, as in *protero*. Ben. cites *E.* 1.20.15 *in rupes pro-
trusit asellum*, where early editors substituted *detrusit*. He also recalls
the action of Somnus, who threw Palinurus into the sea: *proiecit in undas*
(*Aen.* 5.859). B. cites *S* 1.3.91, where both *deiecit* and *proiecit* appear in
the tradition. (There *deiecit* is better, because knocking the dish off the
table was accidental; *proiecit* might have implied a deliberate action.)

463 Siculique poetae: i.e. Empedocles; see next note.

465 Empedocles: a Sicilian aristocrat (*c.* 493–*c.* 433 B.C.) who
wrote on philosophy, science, and religion. His poem *On nature* (Περὶ
φύσεως) described a world cycle in which the four elements came
together and then separated under the contrary influences of Love
(Φιλία) and Strife (Νεῖκος). His *Purifications* (Καθαρμοί) explained
how, by observing certain rules of purity, the soul could escape the
cycle of rebirth and become divine; see Guthrie II 122–265. In one of
his fragments (112 Diels–Kranz) he addresses the citizens of Acragas,
saying 'I move among you as an immortal god, no longer mortal,
honoured amongst all, as is fitting ...'. Perhaps that is the passage to
which H. is alluding in *immortalis haberi | dum cupit*.

frigidus: deliberately placed in the middle of *ardentem Aetnam*. The
opposites were important in Empedocles' system. In fr. 21 the sun
(hot, bright, dry) is juxtaposed with rain (cold, dark, wet). More immediately relevant is fr. 105, where he says that 'in human beings the
blood around the heart is thought' αἷμα γὰρ ἀνθρώποις περικάρδιόν ἐστι

νόημα. This can be fairly supplemented by Virg. *Georg.* 2.483–4 *sin,
has ne possim naturae accedere partes,* | *frigidus obstiterit circum praecordia
sanguis,* i.e. if the lack of inspired wisdom prevents me from writing
about nature (like Empedocles and Lucretius), I shall write about the
countryside. Servius' note explains *secundum physicos qui dicunt stultos
esse homines frigidioris sanguinis, prudentes calidi*; and a more specific assertion is made by ps.-Acr. in his comment on the present passage *Empedocles enim dicebat tarda ingenia frigido circa praecordia sanguine inpediri.*
If, then, Empedocles associated coldness with intellectual dullness,
that would add point to H.'s expression. Finally, the idea of 'dull' or
'lacking in liveliness' is found in *frigidus* when applied to attempts at
cleverness which do not come off; cf. the Greek ψυχρός, and see Cic.
De orat. 2.256 and 260, and *Orat.* 89; Longinus 4–5.

466   insiluit: Empedocles' followers seem to have claimed that the
great man vanished mysteriously from their midst (cf. the case of
Romulus); his more sceptical opponents alleged that he had counter-
feited an ascent into heaven by diving into Etna; but the trick was revealed when the volcano erupted and returned one of his sandals; see
Diog. Laert. 8.69. For versions of the death of Empedocles, see Wright
15–17.

H. may well have admired Empedocles, who was a man of outstanding distinction; but he treats him, as he treats other philosophers, with a degree of irreverence. Thus Epicurus presides over a
herd of pigs (*E.* 1.4.16); Polemo caught philosophy on his way home
from a party (*S.* 2.3.254); Democritus' animals ate his crops while the
sage was rapt in contemplation (*E.* 1.12.12); and Pythagoras is related to a plate of beans (*S.* 2.6.63).

sit ius liceatque: a solemn doublet, like our 'right and proper'. H.
closes by appealing to a rather special form of poetic licence; for a
more conventional form see 9–10 *pictoribus atque poetis* | *quidlibet audendi
semper fuit aequa potestas.*

467   idem facit occidenti 'is doing the same as a murderer'; cf.
Lucr. *DRN* 4.1174 *eadem facit . . . omnia turpi.* The construction is mod-
elled on the Greek τὸ αὐτό plus the dat. The spondaic ending is the
only one in H.'s *sermones.* Its purpose here has not been explained.

468   nec semel hoc fecit: i.e. it's not the first time he (the crazy poet) has done this; cf. *E.* 1.17.55–62. One thinks of the boy who cried 'wolf'.

iam 'thereupon', with *fiet*; *OLD iam* 6.

469   homo: i.e. an ordinary human being as opposed to a quasi-divinity.

ponet 'lay aside', like *deponet*.

famosae 'famous', not 'notorious' (W.). The death will be famous, he hopes, and will lead to deification by his admirers.

470   factitet: frequentative of *facio*, 'persists in composing'.

471–2   Is he accursed as a result of some profanity?

471   minxerit: from *meio*, a low word appropriate to the act described. Tombs and monuments were liable to such desecration; cf. the oath of Priapus *in me ueniat mictum atque cacatum* (*S.* 1.8.38), and the provision of Trimalchio *ne in monumentum meum populus cacatum currat* (Petron. *Sat.* 71). Notices were put up to prevent such defilement, e.g. *pueri, sacer est locus, extra* | *meiite* (Pers. 1.113–14; see Jahn's note *ad loc.*, which quotes inscriptions with the same warning).

triste: not just 'gloomy', but also suggesting an atmosphere of supernatural menace – something like 'sinister'.

bidental: a place struck by lightning was fenced off and consecrated. The ritual involved the slaughter of sheep, and the word *bidens* 'a creature with two teeth' was used for a sheep. That is the explanation offered by Nigidius Figulus (Nonius 53.23), who was a friend of Cicero's. He wrote on grammar, theology, and natural science, and was said to dabble in magic. Porph., who rejected this idea, thought the name came from the two-pronged *fulmen* of Jupiter. Cf. Pers. 2.27.

472   mouerit 'disturbed'.

incestus: *in* + *castus*, hence 'unholy'. It refers back over two clauses; so, keeping the present order, one might translate 'thus committing sacrilege'.

certe furit: '[whatever the explanation] certainly he is mad'.

473   obiectos caueae ... clatros 'the bars set across its cage'; *caueae* is probably dat.

474   acerbus: in view of the bear on the rampage, and of the phrase *occiditque legendo* (475), it seems better to take *acerbus* as 'pitiless' (*OLD* 3a), rather than in the more diluted sense of 'unwelcome' or 'disagreeable' (*OLD* 7).

475   tenet: the fatal hug explains the choice of the bear-image.

occiditque legendo: cf. 'If Foes, they write, if Friends, they read me dead' Pope, *Epist. to Dr Arbuthnot* 32.

476 The leech (*hirudo*) is in apposition to the subject of *arripuit, tenet* and *occidit*, viz. the bear-like poet. For the disconcerting change of image, cf. *I.* 6, where the hound suddenly becomes a bull (12).

APPENDIX

The status of the private odes

A good deal of what is said in *E.* 2.1 and the *AP* about the social functions of poetry can be related to 'public' odes, like *C.* 3.1–6, *C.* 4.4–5, and *C.* 4.14–15. But no specific comment is made about the private, less formal, pieces, many of which are just as famous. No doubt the plea for freshness and alertness in *E.* 2.1 is meant to create a mental climate in which these odes (like other recent work) can be given a fair hearing. No doubt, too, the precepts for producing a *legitimum poema* in *E.* 2.2.109–25 apply to the writing of an ode about love or friendship; and not all that is said about craftsmanship in the *AP* is confined to epic, drama, and choral lyric. Nevertheless, the point still stands. The *Odes* themselves are more illuminating, but even they do not provide any comprehensive or systematic discussion about their purpose and function. Horace is devoted, he tells us, to lyric poetry as a way of life (1.1); he aspires to be admitted to the company of the Greek lyric poets (1.1); later, he rejoices at obtaining admission (3.30; 4.3); in particular he glories in being the first *Roman* to obtain admission (3.30; 4.3; cf. *E.* 1.19). So poetry brings fame to the writer, both in his lifetime and after death. The same point is illustrated from Greek literature: fame is not restricted to great figures like Homer and Pindar; it is also shared by love-poets like Anacreon and Sappho (4.9). The latter gives delight in the world of the dead, even though Alcaeus, with his war poems, may attract a larger audience (2.13). As well as achieving lasting fame for himself, the poet can also confer it on others – *dignum laude uirum Musa uetat mori* (4.8.28). That lies behind the promise which Horace makes to Lollius (4.9.30–4); and that is why, so far from dancing attendance on the rich and powerful, *he* is courted by *them* (2.18.10–11).

But a poet's fame is not an achievement in itself. It comes as the *result* of an achievement, namely impressing the reader in various ways, often over many centuries. In the case of Horace (unlike Catullus), love poetry is seen as a kind of game (*lusimus* in 1.32.2; *ioci* in 2.1.37), a game which was played long ago by Anacreon (*lusit* in 4.9.9) and continues to give delight. We cannot, of course, know what reality lies be-

230

hind the addresses to Chloe (1.23), Glycera (3.19), Phyllis (4.11), and
the rest; but that does not prevent us from catching the poet's tone,
whether coaxing, teasing, bitter, or nostalgic. In other poems we
warm to his good humour as he issues invitations to pleasure (1.20;
1.26; 3.8); or we admire how he conveys sensible advice in a dis-
tinctively Horatian way (1.11; 2.2; 2.10). At other times, again, what
impresses us is the poet's sensitivity, as he offers comfort to friends
under strain (2.7; 3.29), encouragement in the face of morbid fears
(2.17), or consolation on the death of a friend (1.24). Some of the
verses are haunted by a deep melancholy:

> omnes eodem cogimur, omnium
> uersatur urna serius ocius
>   sors exitura et nos in aeternum
>   exsilium impositura cumbae. (2.3.24–8)

But great art can say that men are weak, futile, and insignificant crea-
tures, and yet, by saying it in that manner, assure us of the opposite. If
we ask the secret of poetry – how it is that certain words with certain
sounds and associations, arranged in certain rhythmical patterns, can
affect us in these ways – Horace will tell us that it is all the work of the
Muses (1.26; 3.4.21–36) or Mercury (3.11), or Apollo (4.6.29–30);
which is a time-honoured device for frustrating further inquiries.

These notes (no more than an outline) are assembled from various
observations scattered through the *Odes*. There is no passage, or collection of passages, corresponding to Horace's vindication of his *Satires* (*S.* 1.4; 1.10; 2.1). So on what general theory, one wonders, would
Horace have expounded the function of, say, *Diffugere niues* (*C.* 4.7)? It
could only have been done, it seems, in terms of *utile* and *dulce*. In one
sense this is unsatisfactory; yet one ought not to forget how inclusive
those terms actually are. A poem is *utilis* in the public sense if it promotes the welfare of the community (military, political, social, or
religious); it is *utilis* to the individual if it helps him to understand,
order, and cope with his experience of the world. The idea of *utilitas*
is not confined to technical utility, as in some passages of Virgil's
Georgics, or even to everyday ethical wisdom, as in the aphorisms of
Publilius Syrus. Similarly, the meaning of *dulcis* is not limited to the
sweet and pretty. Anger, terror, and grief may be included, as Horace
makes clear when he elaborates *dulcia sunto* by adding *et quocumque uo-*

lent animum auditoris agunto (*AP* 100). This quality of attractiveness, which the Greeks called ψυχαγωγία, had already been mentioned in *E.* 2.1.211–13, where the poet was described as one

> meum qui pectus inaniter angit,
> irritat, mulcet, falsis terroribus implet,
> ut magus, et modo me Thebis, modo ponit Athenis.

Here, in the *AP*, the poet's attractiveness is seen in his ability to make the audience laugh or cry (101–11).

Yet Horace insists that, on its own, each of these qualities is inadequate. Thus the elders assail works which aren't wholesome, while the young knights despise poems that are dry; every vote, however, is won by the man who mixes beneficial with sweet:

> omne tulit punctum qui miscuit utile dulci (*AP* 343).

The mixture, evidently, is a kind of drink – a blend of dry (and morally beneficial) with sweet (and emotionally attractive). The beneficial and the attractive operate together (343; cf. 334). It is clear, then, that in the writing most highly esteemed by Horace 'the poetry' (sound, metre, imagery, texture, and so on) is not superimposed on 'the thought', like icing sugar sprinkled on a cake. All the ingredients are mixed together and then baked, as it were, in the poet's imagination. The same point is made by Lucretius in *DRN* 4.11–25, where the atoms of bitter medicine mingle with the atoms of honey, and by Horace himself in *S.* 1.1. 24–6, where the letters of the children's alphabet are actually biscuits.

When Horace talks about the powers of poetry, he has in mind its effects on other people, whether individually or collectively. He never makes the narcissistic claim that he writes only for himself. Yet there is in his work a private element which is easily forgotten, just as one tends to forget that the tubby, sociable character who was fond of parties and good talk also had periods (perhaps increasingly long periods) when he wished to be alone (*E.* 1.7.1–13; 10.6–10; 11.7–10; 14.19–21). Seclusion, particularly rural seclusion, is regularly presented as the setting in which his poetry is written (e.g. *C.* 1.17.13–14; 22.9–12; 3.13; 4.3.10–12); and the significance of that idea is enhanced rather than impaired by the fact that it is as old as Hesiod (*Theog.* 1.35).

In *S.* 2.1.24–9 Horace tells us that, while other people have different pursuits, he takes pleasure in enclosing words in feet, in the manner of Lucilius:

> me pedibus delectat claudere uerba
> Lucili ritu

A purely private experience. There is nothing so explicit about the composition of the lyrics. The precepts in *E.* 2.2.109ff. and *AP* 438ff. could apply to any genre, and anyhow have to do with the later phase of correction and polishing. For the initial, creative, phase we receive only hints, as in the opening of *C.* 3.4 and 3.25 – poems which relate to his more official odes. Still, when he talks of that half-legendary incident from his childhood (*C.* 3.4.9–20), or thrills at the presence of Bacchus in *C.* 3.25 or 2.19, or affirms his devotion to pipe and lyre in *C.*1.1, Horace shows an awareness of unusual powers; and that carries with it a sense of privilege. So when he expresses gratitude to the Parca (*C.* 2.16.37–40) or Faunus (*C.* 2.17.27–30), Melpomene (*C.* 3.30.16; 4.3.1) or Apollo (*C.* 4.6.29–30), or to the gods in general (*C.* 1.17.13–14), he is thanking them not just for making him a celebrity but also for giving him that peculiar delight which is known only to the Muses' favourites.

BIBLIOGRAPHY

Allen, W., 'O fortunatam . . .', *T.A.P.A.* 87 (1956) 130–46

Barker, A., *Greek musical writings* 1 *The musician and his art* (Cambridge 1984)

Barwick, K., 'Die Gliederung der rhetorischen τέχνη und die horazische Epistola ad Pisones', *Hermes* 57 (1922) 1–62

Beare, W., *The Roman stage* (3rd edn, London 1964)

Becker, C., *Das Spätwerk des Horaz* (Göttingen 1963)

Bo, D., *Q. Horati Flacci Opera* III (Paravia 1960)

Bowra, C. M., *Greek lyric poetry* (Oxford 1961)

Brink, C. O., *Horace on poetry* 1 *Prolegomena to the literary epistles* (Cambridge 1963); II *The Ars Poetica* (Cambridge 1971); III *Epistles Book II: the letters to Augustus and Florus* (Cambridge 1982)

Burrow, J. A., *The ages of man* (Oxford 1986)

Cody, J. V., *Horace and Callimachean aesthetics* (Brussels 1976)

Coffey, M., 'Notes on the history of Augustan and early imperial tragedy', in *Studies in honour of T. B. L. Webster* (Bristol 1986) 1 46–52

Conington, J. and Nettleship, H., *The works of Virgil* (5th edn London 1898) II

Courtney, E., *A commentary on the Satires of Juvenal* (London 1980)

Crook, J., *Law and life of Rome* (London 1967)

Crowther, N. B., 'Nudity and morality: athletics in Italy', *C.J.* 76 (1981) 119–23

Dahlmann, H., 'Varros Schrift De poematis und die hellenistisch-römische Poetik', *A.A.M.* 3 (1953)

Daremberg, C. and Saglio, E., *Dictionnaire des antiquités grecques et romaines*, 5 vols. (Paris 1877)

Daviault, A., *Comoedia togata* (Paris 1981)

Delz, J., 'Textkritische Versuche an der Ars poetica des Horaz', *M.H.* 36 (1979) 142–52

Dilke, O. A. W., 'When was the *Ars poetica* written?' *B.I.C.S. 5* (London 1958) 49–57

Doblhofer, E., *Die Augustuspanegyrik des Horaz in formalhistorischer Sicht* (Heidelberg 1966)

Duckworth, G. E., (1) *The nature of Roman comedy* (Princeton 1952)

(2) 'Horace's hexameters and the date of the *Ars poetica*', *T.A.P.A.* 96 (1965) 73–95

Duncan-Jones, R., *The economy of the Roman empire* (Cambridge 1974)

Earl, D., *The age of Augustus* (London 1968)

Edmonds, J. M., *Elegy and iambus*, 2 vols. (Loeb Classical Library, repr. 1961)

Empson, W., *Seven types of ambiguity* (3rd edn London 1953)

Erskine-Hill, H., *The Augustan idea in English literature* (London 1983)

Fraenkel, E., *Horace* (Oxford 1957)

Fraser, P. M., *Ptolemaic Alexandria*, 3 vols. (Oxford 1972)

Frederiksen, M., *Campania* (British School at Rome 1984)

Friedländer, L., *Roman life and manners under the early empire*, 4 vols., Eng. trans. (London 1909–13)

Garton, C., *Personal aspects of the Roman theatre* (Toronto 1972)

Gildersleeve, B. L. and Lodge, G., *Latin grammar* (repr. London 1948)

Glucker, J., *Antiochus and the late Academy* (Göttingen 1978)

Goldhill, S., 'The great Dionysia and civic ideology', *J.H.S.* 107 (1987) 58–76

Gow, A. S. F. and Page, D. L., *The Greek Anthology. Hellenistic epigrams*, 2 vols. (Cambridge 1965)

Grant, M., *Gladiators* (Harmondsworth 1971)

Greenberg, N., 'The use of *poiema* and *poiesis*', *H.S.C.P.* 65 (1961) 263–89

Griffin, J., 'Augustus and the poets: *Caesar qui cogere posset*', in *Caesar Augustus: seven aspects* (edd. F. Millar and E. Segal, Oxford 1984)

Grube, G. M. A., (1) *A Greek critic: Demetrius on style* (Toronto 1961)
(2) *The Greek and Roman critics* (Toronto 1965)

Guthrie, W. K. C., *A history of Greek philosophy*, 6 vols (Cambridge 1962–81)

Handford, S. A., *The Latin subjunctive* (London 1947)

Halliwell, S., 'Ancient interpretations of ὀνομαστὶ κωμῳδεῖν in Aristophanes', *C.Q.* n.s. 34 (1984) 83–8

Harvey, A. E., 'The classification of Greek lyric poetry', *C.Q.* n.s. 5 (1955) 157–75

Harvey, R. A., *A commentary on Persius* (Leiden 1981)

Herrick, M. T., *The fusion of Horatian and Aristotelian literary criticism, 1531–1555* (New York 1946)

Hilgers, W., *Lateinische Gefässnamen* (Düsseldorf 1969)

Hopkinson, N., *A Hellenistic anthology* (Cambridge 1988)

Housman, A. E., *The classical papers of A. E. Housman*, 3 vols. (edd. J. Diggle and F. R. D. Goodyear, Cambridge 1972)

Howard, A. A., 'The αὐλός or *tibia*', *H.S.C.P.* 4 (1893) 1–60

Humphreys, A. R., 'The social setting' and 'The literary scene', in *The Pelican guide to English literature* IV (Harmondsworth 1968)

Immisch, O., 'Horazens Epistel über die Dichtkunst', *Phil. Suppl.* 24 (1932)

Jenkins, G. K., *Ancient Greek coins* (London 1972)

Jensen, C., *Philodemus über die Gedichte, fünftes Buch* (Berlin 1923)

Jocelyn, H. D., (1) *The tragedies of Ennius* (Cambridge 1967)

(2) 'The fate of Varius' *Thyestes*', *C.Q.* n.s. 30 (1980) 387–400

Jones, A. H. M., *Augustus* (London 1970)

Kenney, E. J., *Lucretius, De rerum natura Book III* (Cambridge 1971)

Kiessling, A. and Heinze, R., *Q. Horatius Flaccus, Briefe* (5th edn, repr. Berlin 1957)

Kilpatrick, R., (1) *The poetry of friendship: Horace, Epistles I* (Edmonton 1986)

(2) *The poetry of criticism: Horace, Epistles II* (Edmonton 1989)

Kindstrand, J. F., *Bion of Borysthenes* (Uppsala 1976)

Kraay, C. M., *Greek coins* (London 1966)

Latte, K., 'Reste frühhellenistischer Poetik im Pisonenbrief des Horaz', *Hermes* 60 (1925) 1–13

Lee, R. W., '*Ut pictura poesis*: the humanistic theory of painting', *The Art Bulletin* 22 (1940) 197–269

Lesky, A., (1) *A history of Greek literature*, Eng. trans. (London 1966)

(2) *Greek tragic poetry*, Eng. trans. (New Haven 1983)

McGann, M. J., (1) 'Horace's Epistle to Florus', *Rh. M.* 97 (1954) 343–58

(2) *Studies in Horace's first book of Epistles* (Brussels 1969)

McLeod, C., (1) 'The poetry of ethics', in *The collected essays of Colin McLeod* (ed. O. Taplin, Oxford 1983) 280–91

(2) *Horace, the Epistles* (Rome 1986)

Maidment, K. J., 'The later comic chorus', *C.Q.* 29 (1935) 1–24

Mattingly, H., *Coins of the Roman empire in the British Museum* I (London 1923)

Maxfield, V. A., *The military decorations of the Roman army* (London 1981)

Mayor, J. E. B., *Thirteen satires of Juvenal*, 2 vols. (London 1893 and 1888)

Morel, W., *Fragmenta poetarum Latinorum* (Stuttgart 1963)

Moritz, L. A., *Grain-mills and flour in classical antiquity* (Oxford 1958)

Murray, P., 'Poetic inspiration in early Greece', *J.H.S.* 101 (1981) 88–100

Nettleship, H., 'Horace (2), the *De arte poetica*', *Lectures and essays*, 1st series (1885) 168–87

Nisbet, R. G. M., (1) *Cicero, In Pisonem* (Oxford 1961)

   (2) with Margaret Hubbard, *A commentary on Horace: Odes Book I* (Oxford 1970), *Book II* (Oxford 1978)

   (3) Review of Shackleton Bailey, *C.R.* n.s. 36 (1986) 227–34

   (4) 'The old lie: *dulce et decorum est*', *Omnibus* 15 (1988) 16–17

Norden, E., 'Die Composition und Litteraturgattung der Horazischen Epistula ad Pisones', *Hermes* 40 (1905) 481–528

O'Brien-Moore, A., *Madness in ancient literature* (Weimar 1924)

Page, D. L., 'The elegiacs in Euripides' *Andromache*', in *Greek poetry and life* (edd. C. Bailey *et al.*, Oxford 1936) 206–30

Pfeffer, W., *The change of Philomel* (New York 1985)

Pfeiffer, R., (1) *Callimachus*, 2 vols. (Oxford 1953, 1965)

   (2) *History of classical scholarship* (Oxford 1968)

Pickard-Cambridge, A. W., (1) *Dithyramb, tragedy, and comedy* (2nd edn repr. Oxford 1970)

   (2) *The dramatic festivals of Athens* (2nd edn Oxford 1968)

Platner, S. B. and Ashby, T., *A topographical dictionary of ancient Rome* (Oxford 1929)

Podlecki, A. J., 'The Peripatetics as literary critics', *Phoenix* 23 (1969) 114–37

Pollitt, J. J., *The art of Greece, 1400–31 B.C.* (Englewood Cliffs, N.J. 1965)

Quincey, J. H., 'The metaphorical sense of λήκυθος and *ampulla*', *C.Q.* 42 (1948) 32–44

Rankin, H. D., (1) *Archilochus of Paros* (Park Ridge, N.J. 1977)

   (2) 'Eating people is right: Petronius 141 and a τόπος', *Hermes* 97 (1969) 381–4

Rawson, E., '*Discrimina ordinum*: the *lex Iulia theatralis*', *P.B.S.R.* 55 (1987) 83–114

Richter, G., *A handbook of Greek art* (8th edn London 1983)

Rose, H. J., *A handbook of Greek mythology* (repr. London 1965)

Rudd, N., 'Pope and Horace on not writing poetry: a study of *Epistles* II.2', in *English satire and the satiric tradition* (ed. C. Rawson, Oxford 1984) 167–82

Russell, D. A., and Winterbottom, M., *Ancient literary criticism* (Oxford 1972)

Saller, R. P., *Personal patronage under the early empire* (Cambridge 1982)

Sandbach, F. H., 'Menander and the three-actor rule', in *Hommages à Claire Préaux* (edd. J. Bingen *et al.* Brussels 1975) 197–204

Sandys, J. E., *A history of classical scholarship*, 3 vols. (Cambridge 1903)

Scarborough, J., *Roman medicine* (London 1969)

Schenkeveld, D. M., *Studies in Demetrius on Style* (Amsterdam 1964)

Scullard, H. H., *Festivals and ceremonies of the Roman republic* (London 1981)

Seaford, R., *Euripides: Cyclops* (Oxford 1984)

Shackleton Bailey, D. R., *Profile of Horace* (London 1982)

Shorey, P., 'Φύσις, μελέτη, ἐπιστήμη', *T.A.P.A.* 40 (1909) 185–201

Sifakis, G., *Studies in the history of Hellenistic drama* (London 1967)

Skutsch, O., *The Annals of Q. Ennius* (Oxford 1985)

Steidle, W., *Studien zur Ars Poetica des Horaz* (repr. Hildesheim 1967)

Sutherland, C. H. V., *Roman coins* (London 1974)

Syme, R., (1) *The Roman revolution* (repr. Oxford 1960)

(2) *Tacitus*, 2 vols. (Oxford 1958)

(3) *History in Ovid* (Oxford 1978)

(4) 'The sons of Piso the Pontifex', *A.J.P.* 101 (1980) 333–41

(5) *The Augustan aristocracy* (Oxford 1982)

Tarrant, R. J., 'Horace' in *Texts and transmission* (ed. L. D. Reynolds, Oxford 1983) 182–6

Taylor, L. R., *The divinity of the Roman emperor* (Middletown, Conn. 1931)

Ussher, R. G., (1) *Euripides: Cyclops* (Rome 1978)

(2) 'Letter writing', in *Civilization of the ancient Mediterranean*, edd. M. Grant and R. Kitzinger (New York 1988) III 1573–82

Warde Fowler, W., *Roman festivals* (London 1899)

Warmington, E. H., *Remains of old Latin*, 4 vols. (repr. Loeb Classical Library 1979)

Webster, T. B. L., 'Monuments illustrating tragedy and satyr play', *B.I.C.S. Suppl.* 14 (1962)

Weinberg, B., *A history of literary criticism in the Italian renaissance*, 2 vols. (Chicago 1961)

Weinbrot, H., *Augustus Caesar in 'Augustan' England* (Princeton 1978)

West, D. A., *Reading Horace* (Edinburgh 1966)

White, P., 'Horace, *Epistles* 2.1.50–54', *T.A.P.A.* 117 (1987) 227–34

Wickham, E. C., *Horace* II: *The Satires, Epistles, and De arte poetica* (Oxford 1903)

Wilkins, A. S., *The Epistles of Horace* (London 1896)

Wilkinson, L. P., *Golden Latin artistry* (Cambridge 1963)

Williams, G. (1) Review of C. O. Brink, *Horace on Poetry* I, *J.R.S.* 54 (1964) 186–96

    (2) *Tradition and originality in Roman poetry* (Oxford 1968)

Wimmel, W., *Kallimachos in Rom* (Wiesbaden 1960)

Wiseman, T. P., 'Satyrs in Rome? The background to Horace's *Ars Poetica*', *J.R.S.* 78 (1988) 1–13

Woodcock, E. C., *A new Latin syntax* (London 1959)

INDEXES

1 Proper names

Discussion in the Commentary will be found under the relevant line numbers.

241

2 Literary topics